Surrogate Motherhood

INSTITUTIONAL STRUCTURES OF FEELING

George Marcus, Sharon Traweek,
Richard Handler, and Vera Zolberg, *Series Editors*

SURROGATE
MOTHERHOOD

*Conception
in the Heart*

Helena Ragoné

Westview
PRESS

A Member of the Perseus Books Group

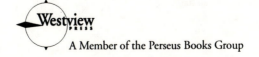

Institutional Structures of Feeling

Copyright © 1994 Published by Westview Press, A Member of the Perseus Books Group

Published in 1994 in the United States of America by Westview Press, Inc., 5500 Central Avenue, Boulder, Colorado 80301-2877, and in the United Kingdom by Westview Press, 36 Lonsdale Road, Summertown, Oxford OX2 7EW

Library of Congress Cataloging-in-Publication Data
Ragoné, Helena
    Surrogate motherhood : conception in the heart / Helena Ragoné.
        p.   cm. — (Institutional structures of feeling)
    Includes bibliographical references (p.   ) and index.
    ISBN 0-8133-1978-1 — ISBN 0-8133-1979-X (pbk.)
    1. Surrogate motherhood.   2. Surrogate mothers—Attitudes.
I. Title.   II. Series.
HQ759.5.R34   1994
306.874'3—dc20   93-44717
                                                                              CIP

Printed and bound in the United States of America

10 9

To Gail, with love

Contents

Tables and Figures

Acknowledgments

As I COMPLETE THIS BOOK I realize how greatly indebted I am to many individuals for their contributions. I would like to thank the following people for their continuing support of my work on surrogate motherhood: Lina Fruzzetti for her encouragement, unwavering support, and belief in this project; Louise Lamphere for her incisive comments; Lucile Newman for her earnest commitment to this project and for keeping me in good cheer; and Bill Beeman for many insightful comments and continued support. Thanks are owed to all my anonymous reviewers. A special thanks to David Schneider for his encouragement and for reading and commenting on this book; like so many others, I am greatly indebted to him for his pioneering work on American kinship. I would like to thank Marilyn Strathern for her encouraging comments on this book and for her many thought-provoking analyses of reproductive technologies. Particular thanks to Sarah Franklin for her warm support and encouragement and to Jane Raese, my production editor, for her patience and conscientiousness. A sincere thanks to my editor, Gordon Lester-Massman, for his continuing encouragement.

For assistance with the early formulation of this project, I would like to extend my thanks to Dwight Heath, Marida Hollos, and Barbara Babcock. I would also like to thank those who supported me early in my studies and continue to provide support: Judith Wishnia, June Starr, Sally Sears, Alan Harwood, Jane Martin, Naomi Bishop, Lucille Kaplan, and Barbara Luedtke. A very special thanks to my friends Patricia and Alan Symonds, to my uncle, Ernest DeLuca, and to my brother, J. R. Ragoné, for their unwavering support. Thanks also to Bernard Bruce and Tom Franklin.

This book has been made possible first and foremost by the support of the directors, psychologists, assistants, and other staff members of the surrogate mother programs. My only regret is that I am unable to thank them by their proper names since pseudonyms have been used throughout the project. A very special thanks to the director of the Brookside program and to his wife, for their belief in this project and for their generosity and friendship. Thanks also to the entire staff of the Brookside; their cooperation in this project and continued support have greatly contributed to the making of this book. My thanks to the director of the Wick program and her family, for her generous support of this project. Special thanks are also due to the director of the Allen program, for her cooperation. I want also to thank the director of the Catlin program, the director of the Harper program, and the administrative assistant of the Drake program. Above all, I want to thank my life partner, Gail Hanlon, for her innumerable contributions. From the early days of formulating this project, her insightful comments on and editing of the manuscript have had a profound effect on the resulting book.

A simple thank-you cannot possibly convey my indebtedness to the surrogate mothers and commissioning couples who have participated in this study; without them this ethnography would have never been possible. It is my sincerest hope that I have been able to provide an illuminating account of their motivations, experiences, feelings, and understanding of surrogate motherhood in such a way as to reveal some of the nuances of the process.

Helena Ragoné

Introduction

For ethnography serves at once to make the familiar strange and
the strange familiar, all the better to understand them both.

— Jean Comaroff and John Comaroff,
Ethnography and the Historical Imagination

*I*N THE WAKE OF the publicity created by the Baby M case, it seems unlikely that anyone in the United States remains unfamiliar with or has
yet to form an opinion about surrogate motherhood. The Baby M case,[1]
in particular, raised and ultimately left unanswered many questions
about what constitutes motherhood, fatherhood, family, and kinship. A
great deal of the currently available material on surrogate motherhood is
speculative or polemical in nature; it ranges from the view that surrogate
motherhood is symptomatic of the dissolution of the American family[2]
and is a threat to the sanctity of motherhood to charges that it reduces or
assigns women to a new breeder class, one structurally akin to prostitu-
tion (Dworkin 1978), or that it constitutes a form of commercial baby
selling (Neuhaus 1988). Most of these theories were formed on the basis
of few actual cases of surrogate motherhood, and it is the aim of this
book to provide an ethnography in which the actual participants are
heard and their experiences revealed.

My interests in gender, reproduction, and women's work first co-
alesced into a whole when I began to conduct research on surrogate
motherhood. Although surrogate motherhood is but one of the currently available reproductive strategies for remedying childlessness, it
holds a particular fascination for scholars and laypersons alike; this fascination seems to result from the fact that surrogate motherhood runs
counter to, yet is in some ways consistent with, American cultural assumptions and ideologies about the importance of family, motherhood,

1

fatherhood, and kinship. Whereas some theorists view assisted reproduction as representative of a profound departure from traditional reproduction, I have, over the course of my research, come to view the
new reproductive technologies less as a departure from than as a reaffir-
mation of the importance of the family, parenthood, and biogenetic relatedness. Therefore, it seems to me that even though the means of
achieving a family may have changed, the motivation or end result has
not.

When I first began to consider the idea of studying the subject of surrogate motherhood in 1987, the Baby M case had created a great deal of
controversy in the United States. The decision of the lower court to
award custody to the biological father and to permit his wife, Elizabeth
Stern, to adopt the child was overturned by the New Jersey Supreme
Court, which then awarded custody to William Stern but prohibited
Elizabeth Stern from adopting the child and granted Mary Beth
Whitehead visitation rights. The decisions of the two courts reflect public opinion (Hull 1990b:154).

Some of the individuals with whom I originally discussed the subject
were concerned that commercial surrogate motherhood might, as a result of such decisions, soon become illegal. Their predictions forced me
to consider carefully the efficacy of undertaking a study that might possibly be rendered obsolete in midstream, but it was a risk I was willing to
take because the subject intrigued me and because no ethnographic
study on the subject had yet been undertaken. Fortunately for the sake
of this research project, their predictions did not materialize: Although
most state legislatures have "considered laws to ban or regulate surrogate motherhood" (Andrews 1992:50), at present only four have banned
it.

It is beyond the scope of this book to present, in any comprehensive
way, the contentious legal debate that continues to surround surrogate
motherhood. A great deal has been written on the subject of surrogate
motherhood by ethicists and theologians in the United States and Britain; that too is an area I have elected to omit because numerous articles
and position papers now provide a comprehensive review of the literature. Moreover, feminists' concerns about potential abuses of reproductive technologies are also beyond the scope of this book; it should, however, be noted that although assisted reproductive technologies offer the
infertile more options and choices, the long history of medical abuses
perpetuated against women (Davis 1986, Dreifus 1977, Barker-Benfield
1977) and the increasing medicalization of childbirth (Michaelson 1988)
should not be ignored.

My primary objective, which I hope I have in some small way attained, is to present to the reader the ways in which surrogate mother–

program directors, surrogates, and commissioning couples understand and view surrogate motherhood. When directors questioned me about my personal feelings about surrogate motherhood—and they all did so before agreeing to participate in this study—I was able to tell them honestly that I did not have any strong personal feelings on the subject or any hidden agenda.[3] I did, however, tell them that I was of the opinion that if American society accorded women equal access to education, employment, and other related opportunities, fewer women would elect to participate in surrogacy as a means by which to attain satisfaction and fulfillment.[4]

The daunting first step was to establish contact with the directors of the established surrogate mother programs; afterward, I reasoned, I would attempt to gain access to their client base, not just their surrogates, but also their couples. To my knowledge no researcher had until that time been accorded access to that particular population. My research goal was to collect as much data as possible about surrogate motherhood, factoring in considerations such as time constraints and funding limitations.[5] One of my primary interests was to ascertain whether surrogates and couples were experiencing shifts in their perceptions as to what constitutes family, motherhood, and fatherhood, in other words, to determine what factors were or are involved in a couple's willingness to enlist the services of a third party to assist them in their quest to have a child; I also wanted to discover why surrogates were willing to conceive, gestate, and part with a child and to identify the specific strategies programs and individuals were employing during the surrogate process. To this end, I designed an interview schedule for eliciting information from couples and surrogates.

In 1988, when I began my research, surrogate mother programs and directors had been the subject of considerable media attention, a great deal of it sensationalized and negative in character. Directors of surrogate mother programs were, as a group, distrustful, not only of the media, but also of anyone who they believed might draw negative conclusions about surrogate motherhood. Their distrust developed, in part, in response to the media's penchant for highlighting the negative outcomes of surrogate motherhood while ignoring the success of thousands of surrogate arrangements; the great number of successful outcomes pale in comparison to the publicity generated by those cases that have gone awry.

To date, legislation has been overwhelmingly restrictive of commercial surrogacy; as a consequence, program directors tend to view negative portrayals of surrogacy as potentially dangerous propaganda for anti-surrogacy organizations. Surrogate mother programs, depending upon their size, reputation, and longevity, gross between $100,000 and

$1 million per year and consequently have a great deal at stake. Granting access to a researcher such as myself constitutes a calculated risk since the program has little or no power to censor data compiled during the course of the research project, and many of the directors have been disappointed in the media portrayals produced on the basis of information provided by their programs.

My introduction to the world of surrogate motherhood was not unlike that of other anthropologists who have entered the field to begin their research. I began by writing letters to the various program directors, introducing myself, outlining my research interests, and providing references, which I then followed up with telephone calls. The fact that I was an anthropologist and interested in kinship boded well, since most directors seemed genuinely curious about an anthropological approach to the topic. After I had established initial contact with the directors, I scheduled research trips to visit their programs, and the process of developing working relationships with various directors began in earnest. Because directors were the first point of contact with surrogate motherhood, I decided to explore how they came to direct such programs and their concerns and perspectives; I was also interested in observing the daily workings of the programs, the interactions between staff and couples and staff and surrogates, because I felt that although surrogates had been studied, the influence of programs had not. Over time, I was able to further articulate my research goals and objectives to program directors, in particular, my interest in understanding the strategies that surrogates and couples employed, specifically how they viewed their behavior in the context of American kinship ideology.

Throughout this book, I have changed the names of the participating surrogate mother programs[6] and their personnel, surrogates, and couples to protect their confidentiality, and I have also disguised other identifying characteristics of couples and surrogates as needed whenever I believed them to be traceable to particular individuals.

The research for this book was conducted between fall 1988 and fall 1990, with additional follow-up trips in winter 1992 and winter 1994. There are, in the United States, eight established surrogate mother programs, and in addition, there are a number of small, part-time businesses in which lawyers, doctors, adoption agents, and others arrange surrogate mother contracts. None of the latter have been included in this study. In order to provide as stable and representative a sample as possible, I chose to include only established programs. The oldest of them, the Frick, was founded around 1980, and none of the programs in this study has been in business for less than ten years as of 1994. The Frick program was the only one that refused to participate; although I had spoken with the director personally, he did not offer an explanation for his decision, notifying me through a member of his staff. In spite of the Frick program's decision not to participate formally in this study, I have included it because of its prominence in the surrogate industry, the wealth of published information already available on it, and the fact that I was able to speak with several ex-surrogates from the Frick program and with others in the industry who had knowledge of it.[7]

There are two discernible kinds of surrogate mother programs, which I refer to as "open" and "closed." In the open programs, surrogates and couples are introduced; they meet in person and select each other, interacting closely throughout the entire surrogacy process, that is, the period of insemination, pregnancy, and delivery. In the closed programs, couples are given a sheet of biographical information and an accompanying photograph in order to select surrogates; the couples and surrogates usually meet only to finalize the stepparent adoption and again when they appear in court for the pro forma suit for paternity brought by the father after the birth of the child.[8]

Three open programs, the Brookside, the Allen, and the Wick, participated in earnest; the bulk of the research has been derived from them. Two others, the Harper and the Drake, participated in a more limited fashion by providing information about their programs, objectives, goals, and structure, but because of funding constraints, I was unable to visit these programs or to speak with any of their current surrogates or couples; I did, however, speak with surrogates who had at one time been employed by the Drake program. The director of the Catlin program was also the attorney who wrote for the Drake program the first surrogate mother contract in the United States (a contract that all surrogate mother centers use as model). At first she agreed to participate fully, extending me a generous offer to visit her program and to stay as a guest in her home. However, scheduling problems of a personal nature prevented her from participating at the time my initial fieldwork was being conducted.[9]

Between 1987 and 1989 two surrogate mother programs discontinued their operations. The Grey program permanently closed its doors and the Smith program filed for bankruptcy; however, data from the Smith program have been included because I was able to contact and conduct interviews with three ex-surrogates who had been associated with it. The Smith program's demise also provided me with an invaluable opportunity to observe the importance of program structure in shaping and facilitating the surrogacy experience for surrogates, something that might not have come to my attention without this example. At the time of this writing (1994), the Harper program's future is uncertain because legislation banning commercial surrogacy recently went into effect in the state in which it is located. It was suggested, by a Brookside staff member with whom I spoke, that the director of the Harper program might continue to arrange surrogate contracts in order to test the constitutionality of the recently passed legislation banning commercial surrogacy in her state.

Because of legislative developments such as these and, as mentioned earlier, in the interest of developing a stable sample, I elected to study only those programs that have been responsible for shaping the surrogate industry in the United States today. Over time, it became increasingly clear to me that the industry is in a constant state of flux, greatly subject to the vicissitudes of state legislatures, anti-surrogacy strategies, and financial mismanagement. Many of the changes are also the result of advances in the rapidly developing world of reproductive medicine. For example, in 1987 the first gestational surrogate child (produced through in vitro fertilization) was born in the United States, in 1989 the first frozen embryo gestational surrogate child was born, and in 1991 the first frozen embryo was shipped from England and implanted into the womb of an American surrogate.

Twenty-eight surrogates and seventeen individual members of couples were formally interviewed. Every individual was administered the same interview schedule, and each interview was approximately two and one-half hours in length. The study involved hundreds of hours of formal interviews (both by telephone and face to face) with surrogates, couples, program directors, and program staff and thousands of hours of participant observation. In the interest of collecting as varied a sample as possible, I took great care to locate surrogates and couples in every possible stage of the surrogate process. I hoped, for example, to discover whether there were any discernible differences between the experiences of a surrogate who had just parted with a child and those of a surrogate who had given birth several months or years earlier. I had a similar goal for couples; I felt that it was important to learn how couples felt about being new parents as compared to how they felt about raising a child two, three, or even six years later. I selected couples and surrogates from as many regions of the United States as possible (as well as two couples from Europe) and from both rural and urban areas in order to broaden the geographic sample size. Aside from these formal interviews, I also engaged in innumerable conversations with surrogates, observing them as they interacted with their families, testified before legislative committees, and socialized at program gatherings with directors and others. Since ex-surrogates are often employed by surrogate programs, I frequently became acquainted with such women on the staff, and although these conversations are not formally included, they provided me with invaluable information on surrogates.

At the Brookside program, I was given access to what are known as the "master lists," lists that contained the ages, kind of employment, and so on, of every couple and surrogate enrolled in the program. On the basis of that information, I would select a surrogate or couple; in the case of couples, a member of the staff would telephone them in advance (while I was present in the room), asking them if they would be willing to participate in the study; none of the couples so contacted refused. The center would also on occasion telephone their surrogates in advance, but for the most part I was permitted to establish initial contact with them, and this procedure eventually became the norm as the staff came to know me better. At the Allen program, the director herself agreed to be interviewed by me on several occasions and discussed her program at length, but she would not grant me access to her couples because she felt that they should be protected from all such inquiries. She did, however, allow me to contact her surrogates (a subject that will be discussed in greater detail in Chapter 1) and did not telephone them in advance, allowing me to establish the initial contact with them. The director of the Wick program permitted me limited access: I would ask her if she had a surrogate and couple yet to be matched and a couple and surrogate recently matched, and she would select them and then allow me to telephone both parties directly.

After initial contact with couples or surrogates had been established, I would then telephone or visit the couple or surrogate at a prearranged time to conduct an interview with them. Because couples and surrogates are located throughout the United States and the world, it was not financially feasible to conduct only face-to-face interviews; for that reason, most of the interviews included in this work were conducted over the telephone. In addition to telephone interviews, I conducted face-to-face interviews with surrogates and couples whenever possible. Quite often, I stayed as a guest at the homes of program directors, a situation that provided me a unique opportunity to observe directors interacting with their own spouses and children, with couples and surrogates, and with staff. The opportunity to observe the daily workings of the surrogate mother programs was invaluable. After-hours problems that sometimes resulted in phone calls to directors' homes, as well as one program's organized response to the threat of a potential ban by its state legislature (an effort that failed), provided unexpected and invaluable contributions to my understanding of surrogacy. I was, for example, able to spend an evening with an English couple who had flown into the United States from England to pick up their infant son; because we were both staying as guests in the home of the director of the Brookside program, I was able to observe and share in their first few hours of parenthood. At the Brookside program, I attended staff meetings and observed intake interviews, from beginning to end, for example, a meeting of the Brookside director, psychologist, medical coordinator, and administrative coordinator with a prospective surrogate and her husband, and one with a prospective couple.

A comparison of telephone interviews with face-to-face interviews showed, perhaps not surprisingly, that the telephone interviews tended to be more personal and revealing, a factor that I attribute to the highly personal, delicate, and emotionally charged nature of the subject matter. Surrogate motherhood touches upon the pain brought about by infertility and childlessness, feelings of inadequacy, guilt, and self-blame; consequently, it may have been somewhat easier for respondents to be candid with a researcher over the telephone than in person. As in all but the most structured interview situations, personal digressions often provided some of the most interesting data. *Surrogate Motherhood: Conception in the Heart* documents the journey undertaken by the participants, the inner workings of the surrogate mother programs, the feelings, motivations, expectations, and experiences of surrogate mothers, fathers, and adoptive mothers as they participate in and help to create and define surrogate motherhood.

After careful consideration, I have elected to use the following terms to identify the participants: "surrogate," "father," and "adoptive mother." When surrogates were asked whether they would prefer to be referred to as "surrogate" or "birth mother" (because "birth mother" is considered by some to be a more accurate term than surrogate, at least in the case of traditional surrogacy), all the participants said that they would prefer to be called "surrogate mother."[10] As for the couples, they are generally referred to by the programs and their surrogates as "the father" (or "dad") and "the adoptive mother" (or "mom") or, in the case of gestational surrogacy, simply as the "mother." The term "father" is, in the case of surrogate motherhood, an accurate appellation in American kinship terms since he is both the biological and the social father. "Adoptive mother" is also an accurate term in that she will become the child's legal adoptive mother. And in the case of gestational surrogacy, the woman who contributes the ovum is also understood by the participants to be the biological mother and hence the "mother."

During my very first meeting with a surrogate mother program director, I noticed a poster hanging over the director's desk. In it a stork was depicted flying over the rooftops of a city and carrying a baby. The caption read, "We Know Where Babies Really Come From." The juxtaposition of the stork of childhood fairy tales and the cryptic double entendre connoting the advent of assisted conception came to serve in my mind as a metaphor for surrogate motherhood. The stork is traditionally used as a euphemism to hide the biologicality of conception and birth, particularly from children. This buffer against the explicit rendering of "traditional" reproduction was now joined with the poster's slogan, blending what was once considered the "traditional," or "natural," with the new forms of assisted reproduction and providing the participants a familiar backdrop with which to identify.[11]

Looking through my early notes I can see that I felt a sense of excitement, first at having successfully made contact with the directors and then with having been permitted to conduct research in their programs. But I also felt somewhat unsettled, as nothing can really prepare someone for the world of surrogate motherhood, where surrogates and couples are being interviewed and matched with each other; surrogates are being timed for peak ovulation and scheduled for inseminations; and still other surrogates are awaiting confirmation of pregnancies, in labor, or delivering children. As I sat in the office of the director of the Wick program that first day, I listened to her talking on the telephone to surrogates and couples, and in between telephone calls she would tell me what the call was about: that a conception had been confirmed or that a couple were still waiting to be matched with a surrogate, letting me know about their painful history of infertility. I hope that this work conveys some of this early sense of curiosity and excitement along with providing the more fully developed synthesis afforded by the perspective I have gained over time.

Chapter 1 provides the reader an introduction to surrogate mother programs: the differences between the "open" and "closed" programs, the goals and objectives of the industry, the various points of contention among directors, as well as some of the discrepancies between the real and the ideal outlined in the inter- and intra-program guidelines. This chapter also explores the strategies by which programs determine the effectiveness of their advertising campaigns in their efforts to attract more surrogates and couples. In addition, Chapter 1 underscores the importance of the program itself and the ways in which programs attempt to provide a structure that participants can depend upon to assist them through the process. It reveals the ways in which the program director and/or psychologist attempts to superimpose some of the traditional ideas and values associated with reproduction onto this nontraditional reproductive strategy.

The aim of Chapter 2 is to move beyond the surrogates' stated motivations to a more complete and complex rendering of their motivations. During the early days of my research, I began to realize that the stated motivations of surrogates were frequently contradicted during the course of their interviews. These inconsistencies, in conjunction with the oftentimes memorized quality of their reasons for choosing to become surrogate mothers, led me to turn to these instances of contrary evidence and to begin to focus upon their unstated motivations. The surrogate's emphasis on the joy and ease of pregnancy clearly was not consistent with the presence of ectopic pregnancies and miscarriages. Her emphasis on "traditional values" appeared to be at odds with her decision to become a surrogate—all of this led me to explore this conflict, this shadowy, or unexplained, area that seemed to loom between the two views, and here I found what the surrogate was deemphasizing. I soon began to recognize that surrogacy serves as a bridge between a woman's domestic roles as wife, mother, and homemaker and her newfound public persona as a surrogate mother. By exploring the contradictions surrogate motherhood creates in the lives of the women who choose it, in particular, how it provides these predominantly working-class women an opportunity to transcend the limitations of their domestic roles while leaving intact the constellation of meanings associated with "traditional" motherhood, I came to view surrogate motherhood in terms akin to the stork metaphor, as both consistent with and transformative of traditional reproduction.[12]

Until now, there has been a dearth of empirical data on the motivations of fathers and adoptive mothers. Most studies have tended to assume that the fathers' and adoptive mothers' motivations are a logical extension of Euro-American kinship ideology, that is, to have a child that is biologically related to at least one member of the couple, in this case, the father, and with donor insemination (DI), the mother. The couples' inaccessibility as a research population may have contributed to much of the lack of empirical information on the nuances of their motivations. And whereas biogenetic relatedness is a primary motivational factor for couples, the decision to pursue a surrogate remedy to their childlessness is a decision that is often considered a last resort, only after years of pursuing other biological and nonbiological solutions such as adoption. Years of agonizing over their infertility and having to come to terms with their options precede this final decision. Once the decision has been made, the couple then has to develop strategies to protect their marriage from the stress produced by the surrogacy arrangement, and they must make numerous practical, emotional, and symbolic decisions about how best to approach surrogacy together. In Chapter 3, I develop the idea of the fertility continuum and theorize that the life experiences of infertile couples, with respect to that continuum, have far-reaching predictive value for their decisions to pursue reproductive technologies.

Chapter 4 explores the ways in which couples, surrogates, and programs interact, providing an analysis of why certain aspects of the folk and scientific models of procreation tend to be highlighted by the participants and other aspects are deemphasized or even ignored. The various ways in which participants tacitly accept or manipulate notions of

American kinship ideology and definitions of motherhood are also detailed. As will be shown in the body of the text, all the participants attempt to re-create the conventional social norms that surround "traditional" motherhood, fatherhood, and reproduction and to erase any suggestion of illegitimacy, adultery, or anomaly. Surrogate mother programs, as a general rule, employ psychologists or other staff members whose purpose it is to redefine and then reinforce the importance of family. For example, although programs discourage the formation of affectional bonds between the surrogate and the child, open programs encourage the formation of bonds between the surrogate and couple, in particular, those between the surrogate and the adoptive mother, celebrating the concept of motherhood and family; through this union the programs attempt to deemphasize the nontraditional elements of surrogate motherhood. Borrowing from the attendant ceremonies and rituals so often taken for granted, participants attempt to link themselves to tradition or, failing that, create new rituals to commemorate their relationship and the child's birth. In this way, they highlight those values and aspects of surrogate motherhood that they can safely emphasize, providing us with an opportunity to see American cultural values about parenthood, family, and important life events such as birth in a new light.

Surrogate Mother Programs

*I*N THE UNITED STATES there are currently eight established commercial surrogate mother programs;[1] there are also a number of individuals who arrange surrogate contracts on a free-lance or occasional basis but who cannot be said to direct a program per se. Across the United States couples are now able to contract the services of surrogate mother programs in order to have a child that is biologically related to at least one member of the couple (the father) or, with gestational (in vitro fertilization, IVF) surrogacy, biologically related to both members of the couple. As little as fifteen years ago a couple in which the wife was infertile was presented with only two choices, to adopt a child or to accept their childlessness. Surrogate motherhood has created a third option for those who are financially able to avail themselves of this choice, the option to have a genetically related child from the moment of her or his birth.[2] Although some programs have considerably lower operating costs and lower overhead than others, most couples in surrogate mother contracts pay fees that fall within the $28,000 to $45,000 range.

The demand for surrogate motherhood is created largely by a diagnosis of female infertility, although a woman need not be infertile in order to employ a surrogate. Factors contributing to the popularization of surrogate motherhood and other reproductive technologies are both medical and social. In the United States there are reportedly 2 to 3 million infertile couples (OTA 1988:3). A diagnosis of infertility is defined as the "inability of a heterosexual couple to produce a pregnancy after one year of regular intercourse," that is, unprotected intercourse (Stangel 1979:4). The social factors that have contributed to this rise in the rates of infertility and that have resulted in an increase in the demand for reproductive technologies are the trend toward later marriages and the tendency for growing numbers of women to delay having children until later in their reproductive lives.

The programs under consideration in this chapter were selected because they were well established and representative of surrogate mother programs in the United States; included are the Drake, Frick, Harper, Smith, Brookside, Allen, and Wick programs.[3] The manner in which a program approaches the surrogacy arrangement is related to several factors: the director's professional background, the director's personal experiences with surrogacy, the program's size, and whether it is an "open" or a "closed" program.

The open programs provide participants with a biographical sketch outlining the motivations of the potential surrogate or couple for pursuing surrogate motherhood (see Appendix A for couple's biographical sketch and Appendix E for surrogate's biographical sketch), and if on the basis of this statement (and a photograph), the parties find themselves compatible with each other, the program formally "matches" them or introduces them to one another, and the director and/or psychologist informs the couple and the surrogate about the tentative match. After an initial meeting (in some programs, the introduction occurs at the program offices; in others, participants meet in a restaurant or another neutral location), the surrogate and the couple then decide if they wish to proceed with the relationship and become formally paired. In the open programs, once paired, they continue to interact throughout the process, that is, insemination, pregnancy, and delivery. In the closed programs, although couples select surrogates from a sheet of biographical data and a photograph provided by the programs; the surrogate does not have the same degree of choice about her couple, and the two parties do not interact with each other, meeting only to finalize the paternity suit and the stepparent adoption once the child is born.

In the older and more established programs (those in operation a minimum of ten years as of 1994), none of the program directors had initially set out to develop a surrogate mother program (then a relatively new concept), and the routes that eventually led them to surrogacy were often circuitous. For example, the director of the Wick program was at one time a surrogate in the Drake program and her dissatisfaction with her experiences there eventually inspired her to open her own program; the director of the Harper program was herself the adoptive mother of a child conceived by a surrogate; and the Brookside director first became involved with surrogacy indirectly through drafting legal contracts for an infertility specialist. Unlike these older and more established programs, many of the newer programs were established by individuals whose backgrounds were in related fields, such as adoption.

The one salient feature that unites all program directors is their publicly stated and personally held conviction that they are performing a much needed and valued service for society, an exuberant attitude that has also been observed among physicians and staff at IVF clinics (Bonnicksen 1989:27). The Brookside director's response to seeing a couple pick up their child for the first time is very typical: "Isn't this great? Such wonderful people. ... I love what I do." Directors as a whole tend to be charismatic and enthusiastic about their work, considering it almost a mission or calling rather than a profession. When I initially began my research, I could not help but note the persuasiveness and dedication of directors and staff and their sense of commitment to the task of alleviating the pain and despair couples experience as a result of their infertility.

What follows are what I have loosely referred to as the industry's guidelines. These guidelines can be understood as at times tacitly agreed upon and at other times expressly agreed upon criteria to which the programs subscribe and to which they theoretically adhere. The guidelines are the product of the industry as a whole, developed and refined over the past several years in response to negative publicity such as that generated by the coverage of the Baby M case; other guidelines have been formulated for in-house use by individual directors over time, through trial and error.

Although there is a national organization of surrogate mother programs, which has annual meetings attended by some program directors (other directors attend infrequently, if at all), the surrogate industry as a whole tends to be somewhat rivalrous and factionalized. All the established program directors are acquainted, and quite often they have been formerly in one another's employ. Competition permeates the industry; there are numerous examples of animosity between directors, which makes it extremely unlikely that all the program directors will appear at the same event at a given time. One of the greatest sources of discord among the directors appears to be the belief that she or he is running the superior program. In confidence, some directors are more willing than others to discuss the shortcomings of other programs and their directors, but in public a concerted effort is made by all to maintain a united front. This is especially true when a politically charged issue such as the Baby M case arises or when there is a legal challenge to surrogacy such as the legislative effort to ban surrogacy in California in 1989.

Surrogate Program Guidelines

The guidelines created by the industry are of two types, which can best be understood as being either extra- or inter-program. Extra-program guidelines were primarily designed as a public relations strategy, to protect the industry from potential negative publicity by averting situations that might be perceived as immoral, exploitative, or transgressive, with certain of these guidelines serving both an extra- and an inter-program function. An example of the dual function of a guideline is the purported refusal of programs to accept a surrogate who is currently receiving public assistance. As the director of the Wick framed the issue, "It's a shame I can't accept them; I lose a lot of really great gals," a sentiment shared by most program directors. Here the extra-program strategy for not accepting women on public assistance stems from the fear that doing so would create the impression that these women are being exploited by upper-middle-class couples and that their reasons for wanting to become surrogates are solely financial, that they are essentially selling a child. However, the inter-program guideline, which is designed to provide programs and directors with baseline criteria in the selection of candidates for surrogacy and which seeks to develop a protocol that will result in increased efficiency, recommends rejecting a woman on public assistance because of the possibility that she may, because of financial need, deny her feelings about parting with the child, a potentially disastrous situation.

Lists of extra-program and inter-program guidelines follow; it should, however, be noted that these guidelines are unwritten and unenforceable and that a program's stated public policy may differ, at times radically, from its actual practice. It was during the course of conducting research that I recognized that program directors consistently referred to several procedures used for selecting surrogates and operating a program, for example, physiological and psychological screening of surrogates, the sponsoring of surrogate support groups, and post-birth program directives. I began to compile a list of these guidelines as they were presented to me informally during the course of this project.

Extra-Program Guidelines

1. Couples should be asked to provide medical proof of their infertility.
2. Only heterosexual, married couples should be permitted the option of participating in the surrogate mother program.
3. Unmarried heterosexual women or men should not be permitted to engage the services of a surrogate.
4. Lesbians, lesbian couples, gay men, or gay male couples should not be permitted to engage the services of a surrogate.
5. Women who are receiving public assistance should not be permitted to become surrogate mothers.
6. [In the open programs], surrogates should be paid a monthly fee once pregnant rather than a single sum after the child has been born.

Guidelines 1 through 5 are primarily designed to avert potentially controversial situations that may cast a negative light on surrogacy. A concerted effort is made by programs to create the image and ultimately foster the belief that surrogate motherhood is not socially deviant and that it need not have negative or deleterious consequences for any of the parties involved or for society as a whole, that is, if surrogates are properly screened and guidelines for both surrogates' and couples' behavior are made explicit. One of the principal means by which to accomplish this objective is to permit only those individuals who have historically been regarded as the "traditional family" to participate; thus lesbians, gay men, and unmarried heterosexual women or men are, in theory, barred from participation. Several directors informed me in private that their decision to permit only married heterosexual couples has less to do with their own personal convictions than it does with the belief that the industry must reject policies that anti-surrogacy groups could potentially use to turn public and legislative opinion against them.

Guideline 6, concerning the use of monthly payments at the open programs, is designed to avert the perception that surrogates are being paid for a product, a baby, rather than for a service, namely, pregnancy. This strategy is not unlike that employed with adoption whereby the birth mother's living expenses may be paid for by the adopting couple although the couple is forbidden by law to pay for the baby. However, this and other guidelines are not followed by all the programs: The Drake and Harper programs continue to pay their surrogates the full sum after the child has been born in spite of the open programs' recommendations.

As previously mentioned, in the Brookside, Allen, and Wick programs, these guidelines are primarily designed for the purpose of creating good public relations, and they are sometimes ignored. Certain programs have long-term goals for the industry as a whole, whereas other, more shortsighted, programs often ignore the effects of their practices on the industry as a whole and, in particular, on its future, in the interest of making an immediate profit. That practice causes a degree of dissension among programs. I learned, for example, of an instance in which a woman on public assistance was accepted as a surrogate and of the somewhat dubious practice of accepting a couple in which the wife was not infertile. Programs will, however, go to extraordinary lengths to guard against the possibility that information such as this will be made public, because of the very real fear that anti-surrogacy organizations might make use of it in their efforts to ban the practice of surrogacy.

Inter-Program Guidelines

1. All potential surrogates should undergo a series of psychological tests, for example, the Minnesota Multiphasic Personality Inventory, as well as medical screening, including HIV testing and hormonal tests.

2. Surrogates should have had and kept at least one child in order to ensure that they are both biologically and emotionally "proven."
3. Surrogates in open programs should attend semi-monthly or monthly support-group meetings; in some programs, attendance is mandatory.
4. Life and medical insurance should be provided to the surrogate if she is not covered by either her own policy or her husband's policy.
5. The surrogate should not be given information as to the financial status of her couple in order to avoid a situation in which the surrogate withholds the child in an effort to receive additional financial reimbursement.
6. Adoptive couples are not screened, that is, they are not subject to any psychological testing in any of the programs since programs maintain that it is the couple's right, as it is the right of all adults, to become parents.
7. No formal counseling services are offered to the couples, but they are afforded twenty-four-hour access to either the program director or the psychologist.
8. All programs advise couples and surrogates to terminate their relationship once the child is born, although photographs and cards for the holidays are considered appropriate in both open and closed programs.
9. [In the open programs], couples are encouraged to tell their child about its birth origins.

There are further differences in the application of the above criteria between open and closed programs; for example, the closed programs do not usually offer their surrogates counseling services since closed programs generally draw surrogates from all over the United States and it is therefore impossible for the surrogates to meet as a group. For example, a closed program such as the Drake program has an administrative assistant phone its surrogates monthly to assess their progress rather than seeing them in person. It appears that closed programs are less concerned with providing surrogates psychological support and reinforcement than open programs are, and in general closed programs tend to view the process as more a business contract than a social and business contract.

One of the few unchallenged beliefs shared by all programs is that these couples have as much right to be parents as anyone else; because of this assumption, none of the programs undertakes any extensive screening of its couples. Like the extra-program guidelines, inter-program guidelines are subject to an individual director's whim, interpretation, or judgment call. I discovered several instances in which programs did not adhere to stated inter-program guidelines; for example, one program accepted a surrogate who had not kept her first and only child (she had put the child up for adoption). Although all programs screen their surrogates to some degree, most of the serious problems that have occurred can be traced to an inadequate screening process. For example, in the Baby M case, the psychologist contracted by the Frick program to assess the psychological health of applicant Mary Beth Whitehead concluded that she might not have resolved her need to have another child of her own, adding that "it would be important to explore with her in somewhat more depth whether she will be able to relinquish the child at the end" (as quoted in Chesler 1988:177). In spite of this proviso, the psychologist and program approved Mary Beth Whitehead's application. Thus, the actual implementation and/or interpretation of these guidelines is greatly dependent upon the individual program director.

Besides the difference among the surrogate mother programs determined by whether the program is open or closed, there are other variables, such as the professional background of the director, that affect the way in which a program is structured. The Harper and Allen programs, for example, are administered by women who are clinical psychologists by profession; both of these directors exhibit an extraordinary degree of sympathy toward the adoptive couple's situation. The Harper director is infertile and, as we have seen, is herself the adoptive mother of a child conceived by a surrogate, and the Allen director specializes in counseling infertile couples, who may or may not wish to pursue a surrogate remedy. In both cases, the directors' sympathy lies primarily with their couples and they make strikingly similar pronouncements about them. The following are typical comments made by the Allen director when discussing her couples: "They have already been put through the wringer of infertility; it is my job to help them in whatever way I can," or "I have experienced their pain, their guilt, their feelings of inadequacy and failure" (*San Diego Union* 1982:D-1). The sympathy of both of these directors for, and desire to be of assistance to, their couples manifests itself in the structure of their programs. For example, the Allen director refused to provide me with access to her couples because of her desire to protect their privacy; when asked if she would at least offer her couples the option of participating in this study, she replied, "What's in it for them? They have been through enough. They are private people." Clearly, the protection of her couples' confidentiality and privacy was of paramount importance to her, but she did not hesitate to give me access to her surrogates, even allowing me to make the initial contact, stating that "surrogates love to talk about their experiences. They will talk to anyone."

When I suggested that perhaps I could interview her couples without having any knowledge of their names or their addresses, she insisted that even offering them the option of participating in the study would constitute a violation of their privacy. Her protective attitude toward her couples was emphatic (and may have been in response to other factors of which I was unaware, perhaps uncertainty as to their opinion of her program) and unusual: Every couple contacted through other programs willingly agreed to be interviewed. Though exaggerated, the Allen director's deference to the couple is reflected throughout the industry.

In keeping with this emphasis on protecting couples' privacy, the Harper director, for her part, refused to allow me to visit one of her offices where two staffers field all incoming phone calls from prospective surrogates and couples, insisting that my presence would constitute "a breach of their confidentiality." This emphasis on and sympathy for the couple is further manifested in the Harper program's controversial practice of permitting couples to decide whether they want their surrogate to undergo amniocentesis. Amniocentesis is, as a rule, reserved for and recommended for women who are considered to be in high-risk groups, owing to their age, medical condition, or family history, and when one considers that the average age for surrogates (in this study) was twenty-seven,[4] the risks posed by the amniocentesis procedure far outweigh any possible benefits. When questioned directly about this practice, the director of the Harper program informed me that she outlines to her couples the risks posed by the amniocentesis procedure, for example, miscarriage, and then allows them to make the decision. However, a policy of allowing couples to override the medical criteria that, above all, seek to avoid unnecessary risk to the pregnant woman and fetus when there is no medical need for amniocentesis seems misguided. In an instance such as this, the surrogate's control over her reproduction is compromised. Unfortunately, surrogates may not be aware of their right to refuse this procedure. The Harper program is also willing to arrange either open or closed contracts, depending again upon the couple's preference.[5]

The ways in which the personal background of the director influences a program's approach can also be seen in the case of the Wick program. In contrast to the Allen or Harper program, the Wick is administered by a woman who considers the surrogate's satisfaction the central focus of her program. She herself was once a surrogate in the Drake program, a closed program, and her dissatisfaction with the treatment she received there provided her with the incentive to found her own program later. Her approach could not be more different from that of the Harper and Allen programs. The Wick director's focus on the surrogate is exemplified in the following quote: "If it wasn't for surrogates none of this is possible. They do all the work." Most of her surrogates spoke of her in positive, affectionate terms, for example, "Sue is the greatest, she is so wonderful." Her couples, however, frequently expressed annoyance with her.

Minor complaints, including difficulty contacting her and not having their phone calls returned promptly, were common.

Even so slight a degree of couple dissatisfaction indicates that the director's approach stands in stark contrast to that of the other programs with their courteous deference toward the needs and desires of couples. Additional testimony to the Wick program's success with its surrogate-centered focus is the fact that this is the only program that does not advertise for surrogates. The Wick director is able to rely on informal networking among surrogates, and she has also developed a professional network through her presentations at infertility conferences, such as those held by RESOLVE (an infertility organization), through which she establishes contact with potential clients.[6]

Of the seven programs considered in this chapter, the three administered by women differed from the three administered by men in several ways. First, men direct the three largest programs. Women directors claimed to feel more comfortable working alone or with few assistants and exhibit reluctance to delegate responsibility to their staff, when they have staff, which may explain their smaller size.

When the administrative program styles of women and men are compared, the differences between the programs become fairly distinct. The women who direct the Allen and Wick programs work alone, without staff (physicians, psychologists, and lawyers are contracted as outside consultants), and the Harper director employs two women whose tasks include screening incoming calls. One of the staffers at the Harper program was herself a surrogate (as we have seen, that is not unusual in this industry). Her duties included establishing and maintaining contact with surrogates, greeting them at the airport, transporting them to doctor's appointments, and entertaining them as guests in her home. One would expect that such an employee would be allowed to field questions, but when I asked the director if I could speak with her assistant about the daily workings of the program, she replied, "I would rather you heard it from me; that way I know it is accurate." This reluctance to delegate responsibility was expressed by the Wick director as well. When I asked her why she had not considered hiring someone to answer her calls while she is out of her office (rather than using a telephone answering machine), she said she did not believe it would be possible for her to find someone with whom she would be happy.[7]

The men directors tend to delegate much more responsibility than the women directors to members of their staff and exhibit complete confidence in their staff's ability to field questions accurately and appropriately. For example, I was not able to speak with the director of the Drake program since he could not spare the time, but he permitted his assistant to speak with me. At the Brookside program, I engaged in many conversations with the director, but I also interviewed (numerous times) all his staff members, sat in on staff meetings, and was able to observe the staff answering calls and meeting with prospective surrogates and couples. The Brookside is one of the two largest programs, the Frick being the other one; both are administered by attorneys and have large staffs, in excess of eight at the Brookside, including resident psychologists. The Drake program, the third largest program, is run by a physician; he handles examinations, inseminations, and deliveries, leaving him little time to deal with other administrative aspects of the program.

It might be argued that the directors who operate the three larger programs have little choice but to delegate responsibility to other personnel, but by hiring additional staff to handle various functions, these directors have been able to expand their programs and consequently arrange more contracts. The Wick director claimed to be satisfied with nine to ten contracts per year, in the 1988–1990 period; however, she now arranges approximately twenty a year.[8] In contrast, the Allen director expressed a desire to expand her number of contracts from between five and eight to fifteen but felt unable to do so because she did not have the necessary staff. The Harper director, with three or four contracts per year, has two staff members, but her obvious reluctance to allow them to answer questions about her program reflects the general pattern displayed by women administrators of programs, namely, a reluctance to either hire staff or entrust their existing staff with greater responsibilities.

Open Versus Closed Programs

The differences between open and closed programs and the effect those differences have upon the overall approach of a program could be the most profound distinction between programs. A comparison of the Drake program (closed) and the Brookside program (open) illustrates the striking contrasts between the two types. The high degree of cooperation and willingness to participate in this project exhibited by the Brookside and the two other open programs reflects their attitude toward surrogacy, specifically, the belief that surrogacy provides a positive solution to childlessness and that the dissemination of accurate, factual information concerning surrogate motherhood will counteract the negative accounts that have until now tended to shape public opinion as well as some scientific or scholarly opinions. The Drake program's approach to surrogacy and that of other closed programs can best be summarized as the belief that surrogacy is a business transaction, a legal contract between an infertile couple and a surrogate, not a meaningful social contract (or one with an affectional dimension).

In the Drake program, as in all closed programs, surrogates and couples do not interact with each other since any kind of personal interaction is viewed as unnecessary, and no meetings except those that are unavoidable take place (for example, the finalization of the social mother's stepparent adoption). Couples select their surrogates from the photographs and brief biographical sketches provided by the programs, which indicate the surrogate's age and her personal and family health history. All correspondence between the surrogate and her couple is monitored or screened by the program. As one Drake surrogate related:

I would get letters from my couple and half of it was blocked out. I can't imagine what my letters to them must have looked like!

Addresses, phone numbers, and anything else that might inadvertently provide a clue as to the identity or location of the couple are deleted from the correspondence between them. All telephone conversations are arranged through the program, with a staff person closely monitoring the call, ready to end the conversation if the need should arise.

Couples who sign a contract with a closed program have little responsibility for their surrogate, which is quite likely one of the primary reasons they choose closed programs. The fact that the needs and desires of couples are given precedence over those of surrogates can be seen in the Drake program's policy with respect to the actual delivery: Nurses are instructed to remove the child from the surrogate at the moment of birth; thus the surrogate is not offered an option to spend any time at all with the child. Once the child has been delivered to the couple, the surrogate is given the agreed-upon sum and the relationship is thereby formally terminated.

Complaints from surrogates who had been employed by the Drake program were numerous. One surrogate told me that she was informed by the director that he would be inducing her labor early so as not to have to alter his vacation plans, a plan she successfully resisted. Another surrogate complained about the adoptive mother's curtness to her. Although a post-birth call from the surrogate to the couple to inquire about the child's health is considered acceptable by closed programs, when this surrogate placed a call through the program to inquire about the baby's health four days after the birth, she reported that the adoptive mother scolded her (see Chapter 2). This same surrogate later discovered that the adoptive mother had never in fact been diagnosed as infertile but simply had not wanted to become pregnant. The issue of fertility is of great importance to surrogates and is often one of their primary motivations for choosing to become a surrogate (Parker 1983); the discovery that the adoptive mother was not infertile left this surrogate feeling betrayed.

Unlike open programs, where couples are advised and sometimes even admonished to treat their surrogates well, insensitivity on the part of the couples in the Drake program and presumably in other closed programs does not appear to be unusual, since the relationship is viewed as a business arrangement with little or no social component. In open programs, couples are expected to maintain a warm relationship with their surrogates and always act with consideration for their surrogate's feelings, but closed programs do not place any of these responsibilities on their couples.

In the Drake program, couples are quickly matched with a surrogate, the only significant or determining factor in a closed program being phenotype. Timely provision of a surrogate is, of course, considered an advantageous factor by couples, who have often waited for years to have a child. By contrast, most open programs have waiting periods of from three to four months to one year for couples waiting to be matched with a surrogate, because couples outnumber surrogates. It has been my experience that when a program does not have a waiting period, it is not unreasonable to assume that its surrogates are not being screened in a thorough manner. It is clear that unsuitable surrogates are much less likely to be accepted by an open program where there is more careful screening and where good relations between the program and surrogates and the surrogate and couple are held to be of greater importance.

The Brookside program, the largest program in the United States, has been in business for thirteen years and has arranged hundreds of successful matches between surrogates and couples, resulting in close to three hundred births. The Brookside and other open programs make a concerted effort to treat their surrogates well and do not cater to their couples to the same degree as closed programs. Couples desirous of closed contracts are turned away, and all couples must provide medical proof of their infertility. In addition, couples are expected to uphold certain responsibilities toward their surrogate, and failure to do so may result in expulsion from the program. For example, couples are expected to telephone their surrogate regularly. Telephone calls once a week are considered the norm, and couples are also expected to maintain written contact with their surrogate throughout the period of insemination and pregnancy. Once a pregnancy is confirmed, personal contact or telephone or written correspondence is expected to intensify in direct correlation to the progression of the pregnancy.

All communication, written and spoken, is direct, that is, the Brookside program does not monitor or screen any telephone calls or letters between surrogates and couples. Both surrogates and couples are given each other's home address and telephone number. Surrogates and couples are initially introduced to each other after the program's psychologist has matched them according to similar interests, hobbies, personalities, and phenotype, in hopes that they will enjoy each other's company during the pre-birth period. If couples live near their surrogate, it is expected that they will accompany her to doctor's appointments, whenever possible, and extend invitations to lunch, dinner, and other social engagements and outings. Failure to take their responsibilities toward their surrogate seriously resulted in one couple's being telephoned by the director of the Brookside program and warned that failure to keep in regular contact with their surrogate (even though she was not yet pregnant) could result in their being dropped from the program. As this and other policies and practices indicate, the Brookside program's approach to surrogacy has been greatly influenced by the resident psychologist's view of the importance of the psycho-social component of surrogacy. That is confirmed by the program's unwillingness to arrange closed contracts and other financially advantageous options.

The most serious complaint I received from surrogates at the Brookside program involved the difficulties they experienced in setting limits with what they defined as overbearing couples. One surrogate, for example, complained of an adoptive mother who had tried to control and limit the types and quantities of food she consumed. The situation continued for four months until the surrogate felt that she could not bear it any longer. "It was ruining my life and my family's life," she said, until she finally confided in the program's psychologist, and the psychologist immediately intervened. The surrogate's failure to recognize her right to privacy and her failure to complain to the resident psychologist until months had passed, even though she had been encouraged to do so, is disturbing. This complaint, serious as it is, is minor when compared to the problems experienced by Drake program surrogates, and it hints at the degree of abuse that can occur in closed programs where the services of a psychologist are not offered and the rights of surrogates not given priority. Another important choice afforded surrogates at the Brookside program is the right to request a few hours alone with the child while in the hospital "to say their good-byes," which is not permitted in the Drake program. The director and psychologist at the Brookside program advise all their couples not to create any undue stress for their surrogate, to shield her from anxiety whenever possible, and to speak to someone at the center first if they experience any problems with their surrogate. Couples are also instructed not to argue in front of their surrogate.

An additional difference between open and closed programs is revealed in their payment schedules. In the Brookside, Allen, and Wick programs, surrogates are paid a monthly sum of approximately $1,100 rather than being given the full sum at the time of the child's birth, as they still are in the Drake and Harper programs. Although monthly payments may have been initially instituted to improve public relations, as we have seen, they also serve as a boon to surrogates in the event of a miscarriage because the surrogate has at least been paid until that point in her pregnancy. In the event of a stillbirth, the Brookside program's policy is to issue the final payment, another benefit that is not offered by closed programs.

Although the majority of surrogate mother programs can be classified as either open or closed, some programs—notably, the Frick and the Harper—are willing to arrange either an open or a closed contract, according to the couple's wishes. Programs such as these two resemble closed programs in a multitude of ways. In the interest of clarity, when I refer to the open programs I mean specifically the Wick, Allen, and Brookside, and when I refer to closed programs I mean the Drake, Harper, Frick, and Smith. A program's willingness to arrange either an open or a closed contract appears to be directly related to the profit motive. Based upon the Harper program's policy of allowing couples to make decisions about the use of amniocentesis and similar practices, it is perhaps not surprising that the director will also arrange a closed contract for couples who request it. In 1990, I was informed by a program director that the Frick program had been involved in seven out of the ten legal suits brought against the industry to date, including the Baby M case. Another program director explained this high number of suits by characterizing the Frick director's attitude toward surrogacy as "money, pure and simple. He makes no excuses about it." Chesler reported that the Frick psychologist also appeared to hold an uncharacteristically relaxed approach toward surrogate selection, concluding that surrogates are a "self-selecting group" and that the program can "safely accept 499 out of 500" applications (Chesler 1988:56), thereby dispensing with rigorous screening methods. The Frick method of selection is strikingly different from the Brookside program's screening process, wherein the psychologist accepts approximately one surrogate out of every twenty applicants, a 5 percent rate of acceptance, as compared to the Frick's acceptance rate of 98 percent.

The Wick, Harper, and Allen programs all claim to accept between one and three surrogates out of every ten applicants, twice as many as the Brookside. The accuracy of these statistics can be confirmed in part by the presence of a waiting list, that is, when a couple is told that they must wait a certain period of time to be matched with a suitable surrogate and couples are informed at the time they interview with a program of the approximate waiting period. The Brookside informs its couples that they may have to wait up to one year to be matched with a surrogate, whereas the Allen and Wick programs usually advise couples of a three-to-four-month waiting period. In the Drake, Harper, and Frick programs, there is no waiting period for couples at all. Clearly it is more difficult to match couples and surrogates in the open programs than in the closed programs because the success of the arrangement is greatly dependent upon the compatibility of all the parties; nevertheless, given that throughout the industry there are more couples looking for a surrogate than there are surrogates looking for a couple, one would expect that some degree of screening would be advisable.

Size is an important determinant that shapes and influences the inner workings of a surrogate mother program. In the surrogate industry, size is not measured solely in terms of sheer number of staff (although this is one variable) but rather in the number of yearly contracts, the number and kind of services offered by the program, and, most important, the number of live births each year. As of 1990, the Allen program reported between thirty and forty total births, averaging approximately two to four per year. For the Wick, the total in early 1994 was ninety-three live births, with approximately twenty arrangements made per year. The Brookside, the largest program, has had almost three hundred births since 1980.

Over the course of this study I found that a couple's preference for a large or small program is determined by several factors. Couples who choose, for example, the Brookside program, which is large, often describe it as being "professionally run." When asked what they mean by this phrase, they usually say that someone is always available to field their phone calls and answer their queries twenty-four hours a day. In the Brookside program all the legal contracts are handled by the center, whereas in smaller programs legal work is referred to outside consultants, area lawyers. The Brookside program also has a resident psychologist on staff who is available in the office during regular office hours and is also available on twenty-four-hour call. Smaller programs such as the Wick employ psychologists as outside consultants; they have other responsibilities and commitments and are not readily available to clients without notice.

One of the defining features of smaller programs is that they tend to display more flexibility and are less constrained by hard and fast rules, a factor that some couples preferred over the larger programs' policies. For example, the Wick and Allen programs both allow their surrogates the option of having home or self-inseminations (whereas the Brookside program does not allow this option). The reason cited by both of these small programs is "convenience," since the surrogate does not have to keep an appointment at a physician's office. In light of the historical medicalization of childbirth (Michaelson 1988), it is interesting to note that the Wick and Allen programs, both administered by women, are to my knowledge the only two now permitting the option of home insemination. Home inseminations can also be understood to empower surrogates by demedicalizing the procedure, giving the surrogates added control over their reproduction, as feminist self-help theories have amply demonstrated. Inseminations are, however, routinely performed in the office of a physician, and the use of home insemination is not considered a viable option at the Brookside program and others. When questioned about the Brookside's policy barring this practice, the director described it as "unprofessional."

Before selecting a program, nearly all the couples in my sample conducted some research, for example, reading available literature, attending infertility group meetings, calling programs, and requesting to see program literature, as well as visiting programs and interviewing directors. The administrative style of an individual director was often a decisive factor in a couple's final selection of a program. Couples who chose larger programs reiterated that the program made them feel that "everything was taken care of" or that "everything was under control." Couples who selected smaller programs often mentioned that they chose them because the larger programs seemed "too impersonal," but they also attributed their choice of a smaller program to a desire to develop a more personal relationship with the director. Ultimately, individual preference appears to play a significant role in whether a couple selects an open or closed, personal or impersonal, large or small, program.

In contrast to couples, surrogates usually enter the first program they contact and they do not as a rule research the program they contact beforehand. It would seem that the difference in educational background between couples and surrogates is revealed in the degree of research and the degree of control they appear to exercise over the decisionmaking process. Surrogates who had been employed by closed programs often informed me that they selected them because they did not know that open programs existed, and every surrogate I interviewed who had been in a closed program and later learned of and was accepted into an open program reported having had a qualitatively better experience there. It is, however, important to bear in mind that no matter how egalitarian a program's policies toward its surrogates, the couples are always accorded a greater advantage. Even in the most egalitarian of programs, such as the relatively "surrogate-centered" Wick program, anecdotes attesting to the flexibility about guidelines and greater degree of control granted to couples can be found. For example, I was told about an adoptive mother who was wearing padding to simulate a pregnancy at the

Wick program, which open programs generally prohibit. The Wick program encourages couples to tell the child about its origins, and surrogates are led to expect that couples will do so, yet in spite of the surrogate's feelings of disappointment, the director did nothing to interfere with the adoptive mother's plan to keep the child's origins a secret and to pretend that it was her own biological child conceived through conventional methods.

An additional component of a program's size is its total operating expenses. A small program like the Wick has little overhead because it is housed in the director's home and accrues few or no advertising costs: Its director relies largely on word-of-mouth to attract new surrogates and increase business. Surrogates were paid a standard sum, ranging from $10,000 to $12,000, an amount that did not change for ten years. When questioned about this sum, the Brookside psychologist suggested that there might usefully be an increase to $15,000 to offset "cost-of-living expenses" but advised against offering surrogates more than this amount because it might result in a "woman denying her true feelings and doing it just for the money."[9] The Frick is the only program that mentions remuneration in its advertising copy for surrogates, using the phrase: "Please state your fee." It is therefore presumably possible for a surrogate at the Frick program to be paid more than the traditional sum, but it is also possible for her to be paid less. Since the Frick program did not participate in my study, I was unable to determine why they advertise the surrogate fee as a negotiable one. One explanation might be that the phrase "Please state your fee" serves to alert potential surrogates to the fact that this is paid employment, especially in view of the fact that all programs report receiving numerous telephone inquiries from potential surrogates who are unaware that remuneration is provided. The advertisement might also be designed to attract as many potential surrogates as possible, and once initial contact has been established, the program may then inform the surrogate of the standard industry fee scale, which is nonnegotiable outside of that range.

Advertising costs represent a large percentage of the budget for some programs, especially large ones. Programs routinely advertise in newspapers, although the assistant director at the Drake program claimed that it does not advertise for either couples or surrogates. All other industry personnel with whom I spoke greeted that claim with a great deal of skepticism. It seems possible that since the director is a physician, infertile couples are referred to him through infertility specialists, but the practice of relying on references from colleagues rather than formal advertising strategies would require a great deal of professional networking. University IVF clinics are similarly dependent upon referrals from

FIGURE 1.1   Sample Ads for Surrogate Mothers

BABY MAKES THREE

Give the gift of life, help a childless couple become a family. Carry a child for an infertile couple.

Call Monday - Friday
1-800-
Mothers only, please

It's not just the money, it's the life experience. Surrogates in our program are joined with wonderful recipient parents and compensated with the highest fees.

You will be well cared for, respected and your legal rights will be protected while you carry the embryo of an infertile couple. Help a couple's dream come true.

Become A Surrogate!

Extremely rewarding emotionally and financially.

Insurance preferred, but not required.

other physicians, since those clinics are not permitted to advertise; they
are at a distinct disadvantage in competing with privately owned IVF
clinics (Bonnicksen 1989:27). And even though it is possible that the
Drake program is able to rely upon referrals for couples, its claim not to
advertise for surrogates seems less likely. Open programs as well as programs like the Harper receive referrals from their former or current surrogates, but this kind of referral, I would argue, occurs with much less
frequency in closed programs because of high levels of surrogate dissatisfaction.

Unlike smaller programs, the Brookside maintains extensive records
and statistical profiles of its client and surrogate base, and for every surrogate selected into the program the program reports spending approximately $3,000 in advertising. The Brookside advertises in more than
thirty newspapers, casting a wide net, with advertisements slated for
quite diverse publications. Advertising is considered one of the most important means by which to attract surrogates and couples and to increase revenue, and it is made the subject of serious study by most programs. The vital part played by program advertising was illustrated at an
information-gathering session of the California legislature when anti-
surrogacy panel members discussed a possible recommendation to the
California legislature that surrogate mother programs be prohibited
from advertising. The opponents of surrogacy knew that prohibition
would effectively eliminate commercial surrogacy since without it few
couples or surrogates would know where to locate or how to contact
these programs.

Advertising copy is carefully worded to attract or target the select
group of women who will ultimately choose to become surrogates. For
example, when the Brookside program changed its advertisements from
the then-standard type in the industry, "Surrogate Mother Wanted," or
"Help an Infertile Couple," to "Give the Gift of Life,"[10] the number of responses from potential surrogates increased significantly. As one staffer
remarked, "We got tons more responses; it was really amazing." The
phrase "Give the Gift of Life" poignantly appeals to women's desire to
appear altruistic, a phenomenon that will be discussed in greater detail
in Chapter 2. Figure 1.1 shows some of the actual ads run by surrogate
mother programs and individual surrogacy consultants throughout the
United States.

Another difference between the larger and smaller programs is shown
in the range of services offered. At the Brookside program, for example,
the following services are made available to couples: in vitro fertilization
(IVF), the process of taking a fertilized ovum (which has been fertilized
outside the female body in a petri dish) and implanting it into the womb
of the ovum donor or into a host womb; zygote interfallopian transfer

(ZIFT),[11] the placement of an embryo into the fallopian tube so that it can descend and implant in the uterus in a manner that closely imitates "nature"; gamete interfallopian transfer (GIFT), a process whereby an unfertilized ovum is placed in the fallopian tube and semen is injected into the fallopian tube so that fertilization occurs inside the woman's body and approximates more closely than ZIFT the process that occurs during "natural" fertilization; and an egg donor program. Personnel from programs that offer a more limited range of services differ in opinion as to the efficacy of these methods of insemination. For example, the director of the Allen program expressed skepticism about the use of IVF, ZIFT, and GIFT, procedures she viewed as a "rip-off that simply prolongs the couple's infertility while charging them outrageous sums of money per attempt."

Success rates with the use of these procedures at the Brookside program are, however, reportedly twice those reported by The American Fertility Society, a degree of success the program attributes to a number of factors. Current statistics on the IVF rate of success compiled by The American Fertility Society are based upon a population of women that suffers from a history of infertility, usually women over thirty years old who have not given birth and who have taken various synthetic hormones in an effort to conceive. As reported by the Society of Assisted Reproductive Technology and The American Fertility Society, the live birthrate for IVF (based on data collected in 1991) is 15.2 percent (1993), however, IVF clinics have consistently inflated their rates of success (Bonnicksen 1989:56).

Surrogates receiving IVF at the Brookside program are, in contrast, women in their childbearing prime who have no history of infertility or difficulty conceiving, who have not been given hormone therapy, and who have previously given birth (that is, they have what are referred to in the industry as "experienced uteruses")—all factors that, according to the Brookside program, contribute to its high rate of success. Nevertheless, each attempt costs approximately $7,000, and with only a one-in-four chance of successful implantation, a couple can expect to accrue an average bill of $21,000 in addition to the initial $44,800. Tables 1.1 and 1.2 list the actual costs for traditional surrogacy, that is, artificial insemination and gestational surrogacy (in vitro fertilization or IVF).

Although the difference in cost between traditional surrogacy and gestational surrogacy appears to be $1,256.00, the figure of $44,800 for IVF includes the cost of only one implantation attempt ($7,000), and the procedure has a success rate of 28 percent as of 1994. A more accurate estimate would include the additional estimated cost of three more implant attempts, raising the statistical rate of success to slightly more than 100 percent. Based upon the program's own statistical probabilities,

TABLE 1.1   Estimated Average Costs for Artificial Insemination

$ 8,300.00	Retainer
$ 12,000.00	Surrogate fee
$ 8,300.00	Center upon contracting surrogate, including legal and administrative fees
$ 300.00	Estimated cost of life insurance for surrogate
—	Estimated costs of cryobank Fed. Ex./fertility center (if using frozen sperm)
$ 4,044.00	Inseminations and ultrasounds (sex selection, add $600) for 6 months
$ 1,900.00	Initial screening of surrogate
$ 500.00	Prepayment to OB/GYN
$ 750.00	Maternity delivery cost (assuming 80% ins. coverage)
$ 500.00	Maternity allowance for clothes
$ 2,100.00	Monthly exp. allowance—11 months, $200 x 6 = $12,000 (inseminations), 100 x 9 = $900.00 (nine months of pregnancy)
—	Medical insurance (required if surrogate has no coverage)
—	Lost wages due to cesarean section (approx. $500)
$ 550.00	Adoption court filing fees
$ 4,050.00	Psychological fees
$ 250.00	Legal counsel for surrogate
$ 43,544.00	Total Estimated Cost

TABLE 1.2   Estimated Average Costs for In Vitro Fertilization

$ 8,300.00	Retainer
$ 10,000.00	Surrogate fee
$ 8,300.00	Center upon contracting surrogate, including legal and administrative fees
$ 300.00	Estimated cost of life insurance for surrogate
$ 2,000.00	Initial screening of surrogate
$ 500.00	Prepayment to OB/GYN
$ 500.00	Implantations—per cycle surrogate fee
$ 6,500.00	In vitro process—per cycle (includes lab fees, fertility drugs, ultrasounds, and hospital costs)
$ 750.00	Maternity/delivery cost (assuming 80% ins. coverage)
$ 500.00	Maternity allowance for clothes
$ 2,300.00	Monthly exp. allowance—10 months, $500 x 1 month = $500.00 (1 implant), $200 x 3 = $600.00 (1st 3 months of pregnancy) $200 x 6 = $1,200.00 (last 6 months of pregnancy)
$ —	Medical insurance (required if surrogate has no coverage)
$ 550.00	Court filing costs
$ 4,050.00	Psychological fees
$ 250.00	Legal counsel for surrogate
$ 44,800.00	Total estimated costs

this would increase the price by an additional $21,000, raising the total to $65,850. It is, however, important to bear in mind that there is enormous variability in the rates of success with gestational surrogacy (IVF), and couples have been known to spend in excess of $200,000. Researchers have observed that there is a general reluctance on the part of individuals who avail themselves of IVF to "stop treatment even after repeated failures to have a child" (Sandelowski 1991:30). The Brookside program director, as I observed in an intake interview with a prospective couple, makes it clear to couples that they should be prepared to spend significant sums of money if they decide to pursue gestational surrogacy and that the decision as to when to desist in their attempt or "toss in the towel," as he phrased it, is theirs alone. He cautioned one couple considering IVF that they could spend their "life savings and end up with nothing," as compared to the success rate of 95 percent they could expect with traditional surrogacy.

All programs offer their couples the option of sex selection; however, the procedure is not commonly selected by couples, nor is it generally encouraged by the open programs for two reasons: Because sex selection requires that the androsperm or the gynosperm be separated, the rate of conception is consequently reduced by half. As Chapter 3 will reveal, couples who have chosen surrogacy usually have a long history of infertility treatments and as a consequence do not wish to compromise conception or prolong the process any more than necessary. Program staff also point out that sex selection is not encouraged because the surrogate may experience feelings of inadequacy for having conceived what is perceived to be the "wrong sex." It is unclear precisely how often the option of sex selection is chosen in the closed programs, but it remains an underutilized option in the open programs.

All surrogate mother programs also offer couples the option of a paternity test once the child has been born; however, like sex selection, paternity tests are rarely requested. I learned of only two cases out of approximately one hundred births where the couple requested that a paternity test be performed. The primary reason given by couples for not selecting the procedure is that they feel confident that the child is theirs. Given that the surrogate must abstain from intercourse with her husband throughout the insemination period (which may be as long as six months to one year), such a degree of certainty about paternity would not seem to be warranted. The issue of paternity and paternity testing will be discussed at greater length in Chapters 3 and 4.

Although the larger programs are theoretically able to offer more services to their surrogates and couples than are smaller programs, one of the potential obstacles facing larger ones is the perception that their size may encourage an assembly-line approach to surrogacy. The likelihood of experiencing this problem is greater in programs such as the Frick, Drake, and Harper, which recruit their surrogates from all over the United States rather than from local areas, as the Brookside, Allen, and Wick tend to do.[12] A program that recruits from its own area incurs little cost associated with transportation, lodging, and meals, aside from having to reimburse surrogates for mileage, meals, and any lost work time. When a program recruits surrogates from other areas, however, the more quickly they can fly a surrogate in to interview her, complete her medical tests, match her with a couple, and have her visit a physician to begin inseminating, the lower their costs. An example of this cursory style of intake was revealed to a staffer at the Brookside program by an ex-Frick surrogate. One week after the surrogate completed and mailed in her written application to the Frick program, which arranges both open and closed contracts, she was flown in to meet with the program's psychologist, given a physical examination (where blood samples, urine samples, and so on, were taken and sent to the lab), and introduced to a prospective couple. The couple and surrogate immediately liked each other, and according to this surrogate, since it was determined that she was ovulating, she was inseminated later the same day, before the lab had even completed its tests, although test results such as HIV might have resulted in very negative consequences.

Despite the greater tendency for the larger, closed programs to engage in shortsighted practices such as these, which can and do victimize surrogates and which focus on profit rather than prudent courses of action, abuses also occur in the smaller and open programs—although with somewhat less frequency. It is important to bear in mind that abuses, when they do occur, overwhelmingly involve surrogates rather than couples. It should be remembered, however, that surrogates are at this time in great demand; in other words, the surrogate is in a position to make demands and exercise control over her situation that she would theoretically not be able to make should there be an overabundance of women interested in becoming surrogates.

The most troublesome instances of abuse perpetrated against surrogates tend to occur in closed programs. As we have seen, the director of the Drake, a closed program, reportedly proposed that labor be induced early so that his vacation plans would not be altered; and pregnant surrogates were left stranded with the responsibility of deciding how to deal with their pregnancies and their relationship with the couple when the Smith program filed for bankruptcy. Moreover, as mentioned earlier, the Harper program permits couples to decide whether a surrogate should undergo amniocentesis, and the Drake program removes the infant from the surrogate immediately after its birth.

The two most infamous cases of negligence occurred in the Frick (a program that will arrange either open or closed contracts) and the Drake (closed) programs. The Diane Downs case illustrates the shortcomings of the Drake program's approach to surrogacy and its tendency to view surrogates as a means to an end. When Downs applied to become a surrogate, two separate psychological evaluations indicated that there was evidence of "psychopathology" (Rule 1988), but a third psychologist recommended accepting Downs into the program. Downs was later convicted of the murder of one of her own children and of the attempted murder of her two remaining children, both of whom survived the attack but were left permanently disabled. The Frick program's meteoric rise to fame, or notoriety, began with the Baby M case. The following psychological report by Dr. Joan Einwohner, a clinical psychologist employed by the Frick program to evaluate the psychological health of potential surrogates, deserves to be quoted:

> I do have some concern about her tendency to deny feelings and I think it would be important to explore with her in somewhat more depth whether she will be able to relinquish the child at the end. ... She may have more needs to have another child than she is admitting. Except for the above reservation, Ms. Whitehead is recommended as an appropriate candidate for being a surrogate volunteer. (as quoted in Chesler 1988:177)

Why a surrogate mother program would accept a woman who might have unresolved needs to have another child and who might thus experience difficulty parting with a child is perplexing since programs profess to avoid accepting women who exhibit either of these two propensities. Given the Frick program's record of legal difficulties and its emphasis upon arranging contracts as quickly and cost-effectively as possible, the psychologist's reservations about Mary Beth Whitehead might have been dismissed as too slight to be heeded. Industry personnel frequently apprised me of the Frick program's poor legal record and expressed concern that its poor business practices would adversely affect the reputation of the industry as a whole. One program director opined that the director of the Frick program had in fact "single-handedly shut down surrogate parenting in New Jersey and Michigan."

By 1992, four states had laws effectively banning surrogacy: "Arizona bans surrogacy contracts, and Kentucky, Michigan, and Utah ban payment to a surrogate. Five states (Florida, New Hampshire, New York, Virginia, and Washington) ostensibly ban payment to surrogates, but ... [they] allow surrogates' expenses to be paid." Eight states, Florida, Kentucky, Michigan, New Hampshire, New York, Utah, Virginia, and Washington, prohibit payment to an intermediary, a third party, such as a program, although Florida and Virginia permit compensation for lawyers who are advising couples and/or surrogates on contractual issues pertaining to surrogacy (Andrews 1992:50).

Altering Cultural Norms: The Control of Information and the Balance of Power

All programs, regardless of whether they are open or closed, large or small, administered by lawyers, physicians, psychologists, or others, alter prevailing cultural norms concerning the relationship between the surrogate and the child and the surrogate and couple. Some program directors are more directive, sometimes bordering on heavy-handed in their approach, a style that is usually reflected in the remarkably consistent, almost identical responses given by their surrogates during interviews. Certain sets of questions in particular elicited strikingly similar responses from surrogates. For example, when these surrogates were asked, "Whose baby is it?" they typically responded, "It's theirs [the couple's], no doubt about that." And when asked what first motivated them to become a surrogate, they frequently responded with typically "altruistic" responses: "To help an infertile couple have a child," or "I know how important my kids are in my life; I know what they must be going through." There is little doubt that when surrogates first contact a program they are already aware that certain responses to questions such as, "Why do you want to become a surrogate?" are culturally appropriate and that certain others are not. There are, however, differences produced by the degree of coaching that psychologists and program directors exert over surrogates reflected in their responses to questions such as these. As will be shown in Chapter 2, the surrogate's ability to frame her motivations is complex, and since culturally sanctioned motivations tend to be highlighted, it is difficult to ascertain what other motivations surrogates are reluctant to articulate.

As we have seen, one of the most important psychological determinants used by programs in the selection of a surrogate is whether she will be able to part with the baby once it is born. Programs invest a great deal of time in the anticipation of and prevention of a scenario in which a surrogate will not part with the child, or in which she will experience an overriding sense of loss when parting with the child. One of the primary means by which this determination is made is through the administration of standard psychological testing; in addition, experienced directors and psychologists have interviewed hundreds of potential surrogates and are thus able to decide, on the basis of experience, who is or is not likely to be a viable candidate based on her life history. Inter-program guidelines are also utilized for this purpose. Once a surrogate is officially accepted into an open program, the primary role of the program is to shift whatever potential there is for a surrogate to bond with the child away from the child and onto the couple. Programs accomplish this in part by emphasizing the couple's indebtedness to the surrogate and their overwhelming desire for a child; they also focus on the surrogate's responsibilities to the couple.

However, little of this type of preventive reinforcement is provided by closed programs, where the only information the surrogate is given is that she is having a baby for an infertile couple who is desperate for a child of their own. It would seem quite important that the surrogate candidate be inclined to give up the child without encouragement in a closed program, a fact that makes the acceptance of a candidate like Mary Beth Whitehead all the more surprising. In closed programs, someone on the staff typically telephones surrogates on a monthly or semi-monthly basis, and surrogates and couples correspond with each other and speak on the telephone, which creates a degree of limited and monitored contact, but interaction occurs in a much more abbreviated fashion and at a much less intimate level than in the open programs, where therapy sessions, both individual and group, are considered important.

All programs use essentially the same terms when referring to participants, thereby providing an important means by which to reconceptualize the surrogate arrangement, family, motherhood, and so on. The surrogate, for example, is always referred to as "the surrogate," or "the surrogate mom." As mentioned earlier, surrogates, when asked how they felt about this term, reply that they would rather be called surrogate than "birth mother" because, as one surrogate stated it, "that's what I am." She reasoned, as did all the surrogates with whom I spoke, that the term "mother" should be reserved solely for the woman who is going to raise and nurture the child. The adoptive mother is referred to as either "the adoptive mother" or "the mom," and the husband is referred to as "the father" or "the dad," which he is in the American system of reckoning descent; thus kinship terminology is routinely employed even prior to the conception or birth of the child.

Both couples and surrogates are encouraged by the open programs to act toward each other in certain stylized or idealized ways. Surrogates receive one kind of instruction and couples another. For example, surrogates all express noticeable concern about the feelings of the adoptive mothers who, unlike themselves, are infertile. Since the majority of surrogates explicitly express the view that having children is one of the most important experiences in a woman's life, it is not difficult for programs to reinforce the empathy of these women for another woman who is incapable of sharing in this experience, the adoptive mother. Surrogates very often attempt to protect the adoptive mother from undue worry or anxiety. An example of this is an instance in which a surrogate was experiencing light bleeding during the pregnancy and was concerned that she might be at risk of having a miscarriage. Despite her concerns, she was careful to conceal this information from the adoptive mother. Programs also foster surrogates' empathy for the couple, portraying couples (not inaccurately in the majority of cases) as composed of individuals who have suffered a great deal of pain, anxiety, disappointment, and unhappiness owing to their infertility. In conveying this message, programs hope to create in their surrogates not only a heightened degree of sensitivity, caring, empathy, and consideration for their couple but a sense of responsibility and mission as well. As one surrogate said: "After the miscarriage, after seeing the couple's pain and shock, I see how come people jump off bridges. I felt like a real failure. I have three children ... but it was their last chance" (*Los Angeles Times*, March 22, 1987, pt. 4).[13]

Since directors tend to view their role in surrogate motherhood as a mission or calling, it is not difficult for them to convey this belief to their surrogates. With this kind of reinforcement and encouragement being provided by programs, surrogates often come to regard themselves as providers of the last opportunity for their couple to have what they consider a complete and full life, a life with children. The surrogate thus perceives surrogacy to be the "last chance" for these couples, just as couples pursuing IVF perceive that technology to be their "last chance" (Modell 1989).

The importance of a child in the couple's life is used by the programs as a means of instilling in their surrogates the significance of what they are doing, the great degree of responsibility it entails, and the injustice they would commit in keeping the child. Surrogates are keenly aware that the primary fear of any couple is that the surrogate may change her mind and decide to keep the child. Programs therefore openly address this issue with their surrogates, emphasizing that keeping the child would constitute an egregious act, reminding them that keeping the baby would constitute a terrible, perhaps even insurmountable blow in the lives of these emotionally exhausted and vulnerable couples. As one surrogate noted, "I constantly tell her [adoptive mother] not to worry, that the baby is hers." Programs make use of phrases such as "destroying their lives" to emphasize this point, a practice that—while serving to reinforce a surrogate's responsibility to her couple—could also be viewed as a form of emotional coercion.

The power and the responsibility of the surrogate are two themes that are continually reinforced by programs and reflected in the surrogates' descriptions of themselves. By portraying the surrogate as the heroine or as the actor rather than the acted upon, programs are able to facilitate a high degree of commitment on the part of their surrogates. As one surrogate stated it: "I have made an obligation that is so sacred. [The couple] has wanted a child for so long. They are going to be as pregnant as I am. To deny them a child would be the worst thing I can imagine. After all, what right do I have to keep the child?" (*San Diego Union* 1982:D-7).

Surrogates often describe themselves as the vehicle through which a couple's dream can finally be fulfilled or, conversely, through which that dream can be destroyed. Programs reiterate (most often through individual and group therapy sessions) that the surrogate has been entrusted with an enormous amount of power and responsibility. Programs also facilitate a surrogate's desire to part with the child by emphasizing just how crucial her contribution is to a couple's future happiness. With this two-pronged approach of making the surrogate feel that if she kept the child it would destroy the lives of the couple, and fostering the idea that she has the power to make their lives joyous, a program encourages the surrogate's wish to part with the child.

Parting with the child is also described as giving "the ultimate gift," one that many women would not ever be able to give someone else. Casting surrogacy as the ultimate act of love serves to counteract conventional or traditionally held views that to keep and nurture the child is the best way to show love to a child to whom one has given birth. The following statement by a surrogate, with its almost fairy tale or mythic quality, is fairly common: "Twenty years from now I want to say, long ago I had a baby for someone who wanted a child very much. I hope he will grow up realizing how special he is. I hope he will know that there is a woman out there who cared enough to have him and give him up" (*San Diego Union* 1982:D-7).

It is important to note the extent to which the ideas and beliefs that surrogates express and programs reinforce are culturally sanctioned. Surrogates and programs are, for example, aware that to cast reproduction in a materialistic light would contradict a number of cultural norms, not the least of which is that reproduction is traditionally undertaken out of "love" and not out of a desire for "money" (Schneider 1968). Programs thus normalize or standardize surrogacy by reinforcing certain culturally embedded ideas that participants share. They construct the surrogate motherhood experience and then articulate that experience in culturally palatable ways.

Couples may receive less reinforcement about how to view surrogacy in the form of therapy, but they also receive encouragement and advice as well as instructions from the programs about how to treat their surrogate and how to view her situation. At the same time that programs take special care to remind their surrogates about their couple's pain, couples are instructed to strive to create the best possible impression of their marriage for the benefit of their surrogate. Specifically, they are advised against arguing or engaging in any type of negative or unpleasant exchange in their surrogate's presence. Programs advise the couple about the importance of creating and maintaining the image of being a loving and devoted couple who has the ideal marriage (except for their inability to have a child) and is ready to take a child into a perfect, idyllic home. The couple is also informed of or forewarned about the surrogate's beliefs on certain issues where it is known they may differ. For example, they are sometimes told about the surrogate's ideas as to whether a mother should work outside the home when her children are young. They are also instructed to avoid topics on which they would be likely to disagree with their surrogate, abortion being a common one. To my knowledge, the converse, in which a surrogate would be warned about a couple's beliefs, never occurs.

Just as surrogates are instructed to be caring and considerate to their couples, couples (in the open programs) are instructed to be caring and considerate to their surrogates. Traditionally, programs try to instill in their couples a sense of empathy for the surrogate; for example, the Brookside director tells couples, "Your surrogate is pregnant with your child, she has swollen feet, a backache ... she has enough to deal with without your problems, that is what we are here for, call us first." Prescribed ways in which couples are encouraged to demonstrate their appreciation for their surrogate are by calling her on the telephone, writing her letters, and, as we have seen (if they live within a few hours' drive), accompanying her to doctor's appointments, inviting her to lunch, dinner, and other social events, taking Lamaze class with her, and so on. They are also expected to be present in the delivery room when the child is born, if at all possible.[14] In the Wick program, the father has even, on occasion, been assigned the task of cutting the umbilical cord, to literally sever the tie between the child and the surrogate, an act that carries many psychological and symbolic overtones as well.

In addition, programs also offer their surrogates monthly or semimonthly support groups (sometimes mandatory) and usually plan parties for them on major holidays. The importance of surrogate support groups is twofold: First, they provide surrogates with an opportunity to meet with other women who, like themselves, have elected to become surrogates. This, as one director of a surrogate mother program noted, is because "the surrogate that is in a vacuum will keep the child. By providing surrogates with a group of people who are experiencing what she is, there is no need to feel like a freak" (*San Diego Union* 1982:D-1).

Support groups also provide surrogates with a feeling of solidarity, the opportunity to compare notes on the treatment they are receiving from their couples and program staff, and to work in concert to effect reforms. Thus, although support groups may provide reinforcement for the program's goals, they also provide a setting in which surrogates can compare experiences and empower themselves in a way that they could not if they were kept isolated from one another in their homes. In addition to offering peer support, the support group can also serve as a form of social control, exerting peer pressure upon its members. Thus, if a surrogate is experiencing doubt or anxiety, the group is there to help her to regain her sense of purpose, and if and when the group encounters what it perceives to be a more serious problem, members have been known to relay that information to the program director/psychologist. For example, when a woman in the Allen program revealed to her support group that she felt she deserved more money because her couple was wealthy, members alerted the director to her feelings. Support groups thus serve as an early-warning system to programs of possible problems among their surrogates.

Programs, because they are engaged in a process of normalizing the surrogate mother experience for both their couples and their surrogates, use inclusive, colloquial language, describing their surrogates as "great gals who want to give something to someone else" and their couples as "regular folks who want a baby just like everyone else." They offer all their participants reassurance that although the arrangement may be unusual or novel to them, the program has been involved in numerous successful contracts over many years and that those contracts have overwhelmingly resulted in happy, healthy children being born into wonderful homes. Programs reinforce these impressions by displaying photographs of happy couples smiling in the delivery room with a child in their arms and their surrogate by their side and photographs of couples with their children at birthday and holiday parties. IVF clinics, in a similar effort to humanize the clinic or office environment and to advertise their successes, feature bulletin boards labeled "Our Babies," on which they show photographs of children, with thank-you notes from grateful parents (Bonnicksen 1989:26). It is common for surrogate mother programs either to display these photographs in prominent areas, often in the director's office, or to place photograph albums in their waiting rooms or conference rooms so that both surrogates and couples can observe the happy results of these unions. These photographs are willingly sent by couples to program directors with the knowledge that they will be shown to others. When couples visit a program, they are shown photographs of other couples with their children, and their subsequent decision to send photographs of themselves with their children is understood to be their way of offering other couples the support they themselves received when they first contacted the program.

Both couples and surrogates have been instructed from the outset that once the child is born they should "terminate" their relationship in order to allow the couple "to get on with being parents" and to allow the surrogate to "pick up the pieces of her life," as the Allen director stated it. Like many of the recommended guidelines in the surrogate motherhood process, this is only a suggested directive, but it is one to which couples usually adhere more rigidly than do their surrogates. Once the child has been born, couples and surrogates visit each other much less frequently and also have less frequent communication via telephone or letter. The typical program ideal is for couples and surrogates to exchange yearly cards, the couple sending a photograph of the child for the holidays and/or for the child's birthday with a short note detailing the child's maturation process, for example, whether she or he is walking or talking. In return, surrogates also often send photographs of themselves with their families. Many surrogates are quite content to receive yearly or semi-annual correspondence from their couple, but many other surrogates have no wish to terminate their relationship with their couple. It is interesting to note that it is the bond between the couple and the surrogate, so carefully fostered by programs to substitute for the surrogate and child bond, that surrogates most often mourn. It is often difficult for couples to bow out of these relationships gracefully and compassionately, and at such times they may be forced to appeal to the program's guidelines. My research shows that the couple most readily relates to their surrogate as "the woman who is carrying our child," and once she gives birth, they are ready to begin parenting without her assistance. The surrogate, however, relates to the couple more as friends with whom she feels a bond and from whom she has received gratitude, kindness, consideration, and respect; to the surrogate's way of thinking, that relationship should not change or end once the child has been born, no matter how well she has been prepared for this eventuality by the program.

In addition to suggesting that couples and surrogates terminate their relationship once the child has been born, the open programs also strongly recommend that couples tell the child the truth about its birth origins. As the Allen director explained this process, "If you keep it a secret there is an implication of shame." Based upon extensive research on the issue of disclosure in the adoption process, there can be little doubt that it is in the best interest of the child that she/he be told the truth (among others, Snowden, Mitchell, and Snowden 1983; Tizard 1977). Programs inform couples of these findings and strongly advise them to inform their children of their surrogate origins, but the programs have, of course, no means by which to enforce this recommendation. Couples are, as a matter of course, questioned as to their intentions when they initially contract with a program, but there are on record instances in which couples deliberately withheld their true intentions from programs. The frequency with which this occurs is not known, but considering how desperate many of these couples are to have a child, it would not be surprising if couples withheld their true intentions, knowing that an unwillingness to tell the child about her or his surrogate mother might compromise their acceptance into an open surrogate mother program. The Drake program (a closed program) recommends that couples tell their children of their origins, but it is unlikely that closed programs are as emphatic on this point as open programs since their overall approach to couples is markedly less intrusive and since closed programs strive to make all aspects of the arrangement as effortless as possible for the couple.

The ease with which I was able to find instances in which this and other program guidelines were flouted illustrates how the balance of power often tilts in favor of the couples. For example, in the previously mentioned case of the adoptive mother who was pretending to be pregnant and planning to tell everyone that she herself gave birth to the child, nothing was done to alter her plans. In another instance, I interviewed an adoptive mother enrolled in an open program who said that she was not sure if she would ever tell her child of its origins because of a "purely selfish reason: I have not come to terms yet with my own infertility." In another case, a father appeared unannounced at a director's home after the birth of his child and asked to be given his file. He informed the program director that he had not telephoned in advance because he did not want her to have time to make a copy of the file and he wanted to ensure that all evidence of the surrogate arrangement would be erased, and it was. These three examples illustrate not only the negative effects that may result from inadequate screening of couples but also the leverage that can be exerted by the couples (as clients) and the leeway that they can expect as compared to that of the surrogate, whose only leverage, significant though it is, is to keep the child.

Even though a concerted effort is made in the open programs to match couples and surrogates who are compatible and who will over the course of their relationship develop genuine feelings of appreciation and affection for each other, these expectations cannot always be fully realized. In these instances programs may withhold from or release information to their couples and their surrogates in order to maintain control over and redirect the course of the arrangement. As the Brookside psychologist rather frankly stated it, "I decide the flow of information."

Despite the fact that programs can decide to withhold information from either the surrogate or the couple or both, in the majority of cases that I observed, the couple receives much more information than does the surrogate, and fewer restrictions are placed upon the couple's access to information. There is little doubt that the primary reason for this is that the couple is considered the client and the surrogate an employee of the program. It may also be relevant in this context to note that couples, unlike surrogates, are the peers of program directors in the sense that they are usually professionals whose financial status and educational background are the same as or superior to those of the directors.

Examples of the channeling and controlling of information by the programs abound. For instance, an adoptive mother who was in favor of a woman's right to have an abortion was matched with a surrogate who was opposed to abortion. With the exception of this one emotionally charged issue, they were deemed compatible, and it was decided by the program director that the match was "good enough" to warrant a degree of information control. In this case, the surrogate remained unaware of her adoptive mother's stance on this issue throughout the pregnancy, whereas the adoptive mother was fully informed of the surrogate's beliefs and was advised to avoid the subject when and if it should arise. In another instance, an adoptive mother who had once had an abortion and was now infertile was advised to withhold this information from her surrogate because her surrogate had expressly stated a desire to bear a child for someone who had never conceived. Adoptive mothers frequently state that when their surrogates mention an issue with which they disagree, they "simply drop it." Questioned further about this response, they inevitably reply that they feel constrained by the fact "she is still carrying our child."

Although programs tend to favor their adoptive couples with respect to information sharing, it must, however, be acknowledged that they also protect their surrogates and act as their advocates against overbearing couples who attempt to place restrictions upon or make what are considered unreasonable demands on their surrogates (a degree of protection that would not exist in a private arrangement). The previously discussed case of the adoptive mother who tried to control what her surrogate ate, how much she ate, and so on, is a problem typical of those encountered by surrogates in open programs. In most cases, once the surrogate has informed the program of her problem, the couple is instructed to desist from such behavior. Another common complaint cited by surrogates is that couples phone them "too often," and here again, once a program has been informed, couples are advised to phone less frequently.

In addition to enlisting program aid to assist them in their relationships with their couples, surrogates frequently attempt to empower themselves by rebelling in whatever ways they can (in addition to their one proven form of control, threatening to keep the baby). For example, a surrogate who had agreed to undergo amniocentesis then adamantly refused to inform her couple as to the sex of the baby, evasively stating that she "wanted them to be surprised." The director told me that she merely advised the couple to "let it go," but since the director knew the sex of the child, it seems unlikely that she did not share this knowledge with the couple. This is a prototypical example of how the surrogate is allowed to rebel, within limits, by the program and couple in concert. The attitude adopted by programs in these instances is that the surrogate does not pose a real threat unless she tries to keep the baby and must therefore be humored through these lesser rebellions.

In another case, a surrogate who intended to reenlist in the Brookside program told me that she would not become a surrogate for a second time for less than "$25,000" because, as she said, "It is worth it and that's what I need for a down payment for a house," exhibiting a somewhat unusual degree of interest in remuneration. When questioned about the likelihood of this prospect, the program psychologist informed me that although they would welcome an opportunity to reemploy an experienced surrogate, they had no intention of giving her that sum and might instead propose a counteroffer: For example, an opportunity to be matched with a couple whose expertise in the field of real estate could serve as remuneration in the form of advice or information. Through instances such as these, it becomes fairly clear that the balance of power in the surrogate mother contract rests squarely with the program and the couple, even though surrogates are presently in demand and there are numerous examples of surrogates attempting to shift the balance of power.

Although some programs, especially the closed programs, overwhelmingly favor their couples, it should be noted that even such couple-centered arrangements offer surrogates some degree of protection from the exploitation and abuse that can and does occur with great frequency in privately arranged surrogate mother contracts. Most open program contracts do appear to offer satisfying and rewarding experiences to both the couples and the surrogates in the majority of cases—in spite of the publicity generated by unsuccessful arrangements such as the Baby M case.

It should also be noted that although couples are accorded a privileged position, they are nonetheless completely reliant upon the surrogate because "contracts to bear a child place most of the risks on the prospective adoptive parents" (Winslade 1981:154). The surrogate must give up her legal right to custody, a factor that ultimately depends upon whether she chooses to honor her agreement. It is beyond the scope of this study to address the complex legal issues raised by surrogate motherhood, but it is important to note that in state legislatures where the issue is raised, the current tendency is to permit surrogacy in its noncommercial form, that is, by banning the role of the program or a third-party broker. This legislation is understood to have been devised in order to minimize the potential exploitation of surrogates and to belie the suggestion that surrogacy is "baby selling," but it may in fact have the opposite effect; do-it-yourself, private, or noncommercial surrogacy arrangements have, at least in the state of California, resulted in numerous custody disputes (Andrews 1992:48). The governor of California recently vetoed the most comprehensive legislation passed to date, a bill (it will be reintroduced in 1994) that was reflective of how surrogate mother programs such as the Brookside are working with their state legislatures, offering their expertise to establish laws that address with fairness the concerns of all parties. The bill discussed by the California legislature included provisions for the payment of all medical expenses and legal fees for surrogates, a crucial benefit largely ignored by other states, as well as a mandate that term life insurance be purchased for the couple and life and health insurance for the surrogate. It also outlined the "testamentary rights of the child and the options available to the surrogate should one or both of the intended parents die during her pregnancy" (Andrews 1992:46). According to the bill, the couple would have to take custody of the child at birth irrespective of any mental or physical defects, and the couple and the surrogate would have to undergo psychological counseling at the couple's expense for a minimum of thirty days before execution of the contract and two months after the birth. Both couple and surrogate would have to have medical evaluations before execution of the contract. With gestational surrogacy, the couple is considered the legal parents of the child, whereas with traditional surrogacy, once the surrogate is inseminated with the father's sperm, he is recognized as the legal father, but the social mother must adopt the child under California stepparent adoption laws. The court, in the event of a dispute between a surrogate and a couple, will consider the "intent of the parties in entering the contract, but the best interests of the child shall prevail. Even when the surrogate is awarded custody after a dispute, the intended father remains the legal father" (Andrews 1992:46). The surrogate, however, is defined as the "sole party to control the pregnancy and she may choose the necessary physicians" (Andrews 1992:46). (See Appendix B for an example of a legal contract.) In June 1993, in a precedent-setting decision, the California Supreme Court upheld a gestational surrogacy contract, *Anna Johnson v. Mark and Crispina Calvert*, Case #SO 23721, and concluded that whereas both the gestational and the biological mother could under California law claim maternal rights to the child, the court rendered its decision not on the basis of genetic relatedness or on the basis of who carried the child to term but rather upon the intent of the parties. This decision and its implications will be discussed in greater detail in Chapter 4.

In the fifteen states that had laws on surrogate motherhood in the early 1990s, "few address[ed] the ... issue of who should be given custody of the child when a surrogate changes her mind" (Andrews 1992:50), a rather surprising omission. In only eight states were there provisions to account for gestational surrogacy in a satisfactory way. Most often, the laws forbade paid-surrogacy contracts (Andrews 1992:50).

The decisions of three states, Arizona, North Dakota, and Utah, to view the surrogate and her husband as the legal parents of the child produced by a surrogacy contract are incompatible with the intentionality of the parties. As will be discussed in Chapter 4, the decision to view the surrogate's husband as the legal parent is inconsistent with American kinship ideology as well.

To summarize, the practices and approaches of surrogate mother programs are subject to numerous influences, not the least of which is the director's personal approach. Though programs offer their couples greater latitude than they offer their surrogates, they do provide the structure needed by both surrogates and couples. The most pronounced differences among programs are manifested in a comparison of the practices of the open and closed programs; not only do the open programs provide surrogates with a more equitable arrangement, but they also encourage couples to inform the child of its origins. Surrogacy programs appear to provide a much-needed structural and social matrix for their participants; when individuals are forced to pursue surrogacy without the expertise provided by these programs, the results are often disastrous, as reflected in the legal record. The complexities of surrogate arrangements require the services of programs such as these, in particular to maintain appropriate boundaries between participants, to offer support through groups and individual support services, to provide mediation services for the couple and surrogate, and to ensure that all the elements of the contract are respected. As the following chapters will reveal, third-party reproduction is a complicated interactional process, and all of these services are essential if positive results are to be achieved.

Surrogate Mothers

*P*ERHAPS THE MOST INTRIGUING QUESTION posed by surrogacy is why women elect to participate in surrogate motherhood. In order to begin to answer this question, it is necessary to analyze the surrogate's experience of the surrogate process, that is, her stated and unstated motivations. The tendency to cast surrogates' motivations into dichotomous, often antagonistic, categories such as either altruism or monetary gain may reveal more about American culture than it does about surrogacy itself. In the final analysis such dichotomous categories fail to address questions raised about why this unique group of women elects to participate in surrogate motherhood and fail to illuminate the nuances of the surrogates' decisionmaking process.

Feminist interest in the role of procreation and motherhood has come to occupy an important theoretical niche. It has provided a framework with which to understand not only the position of women in society but also "the relationship between procreative beliefs and the wider context (world view, cosmology, culture) in which they are found" (Delaney 1986:495; Delaney 1991; Strathern 1992a; Rapp 1990; Ginsburg 1987; Modell 1989; Dolgin 1993; Martin 1987). Moreover, although both the private versus public and the nature versus culture dichotomies have since come to be understood as informed by our own "history of gender relations" (Lamphere 1987:22), they remain salient features in Western society (Abu-Lughod 1986:30)

An understanding of the role of women's work and the separation of domestic work from the public sphere is of critical importance in any analysis of surrogacy. The American family is but one part of a set of symbolic oppositions in which the family is associated with nurturance and is thus placed in opposition to the world of work and business (Collier, Rosaldo, and Yanagisako 1982:39), an idea that may ultimately be traced back historically to the cult of true womanhood (Cott 1977; Pleck and Cott 1979; Kessler-Harris 1979). The split between the public and private domains reflects the dialectical relationship that developed between home, "the private realm where women are most in evidence, where 'natural' functions like sex and the bodily functions related to procreation take place, where the affective content of relationships is primary," and work, "where 'culture' ... is produced, where money is made, [and] work is done" (Martin 1987:15–16). Although the split between public and private domains has been a cultural attribute of many state-based systems at least as far back as the ancient Greeks, it became markedly apparent at the time of the industrial revolution. That is when the workplace and the home became two distinct arenas (no longer in the same location) and consequently acquired new and separate meanings. As production for exchange "eclipsed production for use, it changed the nature of the household, the significance of women's work within it, and consequently women's position" (Sacks 1974:211).

In this sense, we can see how it is that women who become surrogate mothers bridge the domestic and public spheres through their work: They enter the public domain through paid employment while they reify their roles as mothers, wives, nurturers, and homemakers in order not to threaten either their own or their family's self-definition. Within this context, surrogacy is understood as work that links the domestic and public spheres. Although reproduction in American culture has traditionally been associated with the domestic sphere, surrogate motherhood transforms reproductive work, specifically motherhood, bringing it into the public realm of paid employment. Thus the boundaries of the family and work are altered when women contract to bear children for infertile couples so that they too may have a family.[1]

Motivational Factors of Surrogate Mothers

Until now the image of surrogate mothers has been principally shaped by media, legal, and scholarly portrayals of them either as motivated by monetary gain or as unwitting, naïvely altruistic victims of the patriarchy, mothers who have been coerced into giving up their babies. Current studies of the surrogate population tend to focus, at times exclusively, upon surrogates' stated motivations for becoming surrogate mothers (among others, Parker 1983). Although surrogates' stated motivations are certainly of interest and importance, if we are to form an understanding of their decisionmaking processes in all their complexity, we must seek out other possible motivations rather than accepting their reasons a priori.

The stated motivations of surrogates are often expressed in what can be described as a scripted manner, reflective of culturally accepted ideas about reproduction, motherhood, and family, and reinforced by the programs. Aside from these stated motivations, there are also many unexplored, unstated motivations, which constitute a significant component of a surrogate's decision to choose surrogacy as a means by which to attain fulfillment in her life.

The most widely discussed and least understood member of the surrogate arrangement is the surrogate herself. This widespread interest in the surrogate may stem in large part from curiosity about her as someone whose behavior represents a departure from the biologically deterministic models and constructs that continue to surround motherhood itself, for example, ideas such as in utero bonding and the "instinct" to mother.

When I began my research I found that many surrogates reported having considered becoming a surrogate for an infertile couple even before having learned that programs for this purpose existed. Most surrogates reported having first learned of surrogacy through the media, in particular through popular daytime "talk shows,"[2] such as Oprah Winfrey's, and evening news-magazine programs, such as "60 Minutes" or "20/20," or through ads placed in the "personals" section of newspapers, most often those placed by surrogate mother programs; some learned of it through friends, and still others from their husbands. Once a woman has decided that she would like to learn more about becoming a surrogate, the first step in the realization of her goal is for her to make a telephone call to one of the surrogate mother programs listed in newspaper ads or in the yellow pages of the telephone directory.

A typical encounter between a potential surrogate and a member of a program's staff is illustrated by the following description of the Brookside program's procedure. A member of the center staff who is responsible for answering all incoming phone calls from potential surrogates, in addition to future correspondence with them, fills out a sheet containing initial information about the caller, including age, marital status, and number of children. A letter and informational packet are then mailed to the potential surrogate (see Appendix C for sample phone intake form and letter to prospective surrogate). Included in this packet are newspaper accounts describing successful surrogate births that have been arranged by the center as well as a more detailed application form (see Appendix D). Once a surrogate has completed this form, she returns it to the center, where it is reviewed by an assistant. If on the basis of this initial review, the applicant is considered suitable, an appointment between the potential surrogate and the staff and psychologist is arranged in order that any and all questions she might have about the surrogate process can be addressed and that she can be interviewed in person. If the surrogate is considered suitable, the next step is a psychological evaluation of the candidate—on the same day, if her schedule permits. This includes an in-depth interview with a psychologist, who also administers a number of psychological tests, for example, the Minnesota Multiphasic Personality Inventory (MMPI), with the choice of psychological tests varying from program to program.[3] Psychological testing is followed by a complete physical examination, including a gynecological exam. In addition, prospective surrogates are given a series of blood tests: for blood sugar levels, venereal disease, HIV, and other communicable diseases.

Once a surrogate has been accepted by the program, the psychologist constructs a short biographical sketch of her, including her most salient personality traits as well as her reasons for wanting to become a surrogate (a description the surrogate does not see)[4] (see Appendix E); in addition, the surrogate also writes a short statement about herself to be sent to a prospective couple (see Appendix F). It is only after careful consideration as to the compatibility of the surrogate and couple that this information, along with a photograph of the surrogate, is sent out to the couple with whom she is tentatively being paired.

The criteria used to match surrogates and couples in the open programs are numerous, and the process is a complex one that combines an analysis of personality profiles, surrogate and couple expectations, and the impressions of the psychologist and/or director as to the likelihood of a successful match. In addition to phenotype, that is, the physical similarity of the surrogate to the adoptive mother, shared personality traits and interests are also of keen importance in the open programs. For example, an extroverted, sociable surrogate is ideally matched with an extroverted couple whose hobbies and interests are similar to those of the surrogate.

The quantifiable data collected from formal surrogate interviews reveal that surrogates are predominantly white, working class, of Protestant or Catholic background; approximately 30 percent are full-time homemakers, married, with an average of three children, high school graduates, with an average age of twenty-seven years.[5] In addition, 98 percent report that they have completed their own families. Table 2.1 indicates surrogates' educational levels and employment. Although couples are primarily upper-middle class and surrogates are primarily working class, surrogates view their decision to become a surrogate as an informed choice and do not articulate any experience of class inequity in relationship to couples, even when questioned extensively about this issue. (See Chapter 3 for further discussion.)

Surrogates who are employed outside the home tend to work in the service sector. The average family income of married surrogates is $38,700. Unmarried surrogates' income level ranges from $16,000 to

TABLE 2.1 Educational Level and Employment Experience of Surrogates

Educational Level	Employment
5 years of college	Full-time nursing student
B.A./1/2 M.B.A.	Homemaker (former sales representative)
B.S.	Nurse
B.A.	Homemaker (former secretary)
B.A.	Owner, housecleaning co.
A.A.	Freelancer
2 years of college	Merchandiser
2 years of college	Receptionist
2 years of college	Telephone operator
2 years of college	Tax examiner
1 year of college	Computer operator
1 year of college	Part-time secretary
1 year of college	Homemaker (former computer programmer)
High school	Part-time cashier
High school/trade school	Homemaker (former nurse's aide)
High school	Day-care provider
High school	Dog trainer
High school	Full-time college student
High school	Accounts payable clerk
High school	Motel night auditor
High school	Homemaker
High school	Homemaker
High school	Homemaker (former dispatcher)
High school	Day-care provider
High school	Day-care provider
High school	Sunday School teacher
G.E.D.	Homemaker (former reservations clerk)
11th grade	Homemaker (former cocktail waitress)

$24,000. Women from middle- or upper-middle-class backgrounds do not generally enroll in surrogate mother programs because, it has been theorized, they have educational and employment options available to them that are not as readily available to working-class women. As will be shown, surrogates stress the idea that surrogacy is women's work, elaborating upon the symbols of motherhood and the importance of women's reproductive role.

Rather than seeing surrogacy as a job, surrogates as a group tend to view surrogacy as a vocation or calling, an important means by which both to express and to fulfill themselves. This belief is easily reinforced by program directors and psychologists, who also see themselves as having a special mission to help infertile couples. Most surrogates report feeling a sense of jubilation upon first hearing about surrogacy, often claiming to have been astonished to learn that surrogacy was not merely a privately held fantasy about helping infertile couples but an actual arrangement in which they could have a part. As the following quotations reveal, surrogates tend to have envisioned themselves as such even before knowing that surrogacy programs or formal arrangements existed. Betty, aged twenty-nine, a nurse and mother of one child, who has been in a long-term relationship for eight years, related her impressions upon first hearing about surrogacy:

> *I thought it sounded like something I'd like to do and I could do very well. It planted a seed in my mind. To most women it doesn't hit a chord; for me it did. I always thought I could follow a blind person around and see for them with words, and surrogacy is like that. You don't just sit down and say I should do this; you just know.*

Another surrogate explained that when she told her grandmother of her plans to become a surrogate, her grandmother revealed that she had considered the idea of surrogacy during her own childbearing years, and she expressed wholehearted support for her granddaughter's decision. Accounts such as these from surrogates and other women in their families who had privately imagined surrogate motherhood are not uncommon. Those stories were frequently related to me by industry personnel as confirmation that surrogacy is not without historical precedent, that "surrogacy has been around for a long time," or that "there is a lot more of it than people are aware of," although it would be difficult to confirm or deny the validity of this commonly held or folk belief in the surrogate industry. What is clear is that when a surrogate receives family support, particularly from an older female member of the family who personally views surrogacy as a viable choice, it gives the surrogate a sense that although others may find her decision to participate in surrogacy objectionable, odd, or socially unacceptable, there is a precedent for the idea of surrogacy within her own family. She uses this as a form of validation for her decision. Surrogate programs reinforce this idea, most often through casual conversations with surrogates, in order to give surrogates a sense that they are part of a shared wider community and to elaborate upon the idea that their behavior is consistent with positive cultural values such as altruism.

Hilary Hanafin reported in a clinical study of surrogates that in her experience there are two categories of women who become (or wish to become) surrogates. Approximately two-thirds of them can be categorized as "conservative" or "traditional" women who subscribe to conventional beliefs about sex roles and women's proper role in the family, the importance of having children, being good mothers, good wives, and so on. For the most part, they are, Hanafin suggested, women who have not done anything that would be considered unconventional or unusual during the course of their lives. The other one-third, in contrast, are women whom Hanafin described as "nontraditional" or "independent," who have chosen to become single mothers and/or to participate in nontraditional activities such as crewing and racing sailboats or joining the military. Hanafin based her analysis upon her dissertation findings (Hanafin 1984) and her research as the resident psychologist at the Center for Surrogate Parenting. This portrayal, although accurate in the sense that it establishes a distinction between the two types of surrogates, proved to be inaccurate for my sample in that less than 5 percent of the surrogates interviewed and observed could be considered "nontraditional" according to Hanafin's definition of that term.

The surrogates in the present study chose to become surrogates for several, often equally important reasons.[6] One of the reasons most frequently cited in media accounts is the desire for remuneration, and surrogates acknowledged that remuneration was one of their considerations, although they consistently denied that receiving remuneration was their primary motivation (nearly all surrogates stated—repeatedly—that although money was initially of some importance, its importance decreased over time, as the pregnancy progressed), and they frequently protested that no one would become a surrogate for the money alone because, they reasoned, it simply "isn't enough."[7] As mentioned earlier, many directors report that surrogates telephone their programs unaware that payment is involved, a phenomenon that would seem to reinforce surrogates' claims that remuneration is not their primary motivation, as does the fact that Jan Sutton, the founder and spokeswoman for a group of surrogates in favor of surrogacy, stated in her testimony before an information-gathering session of the California legislature, "My organization and its members would all still be surrogates if no payment was involved."

The following examples are typical surrogate responses to questions concerning the importance of payment with respect to the decision to become a surrogate. Fran, aged twenty-seven, divorced, with one child, and currently working as a dog trainer, explained her feelings about payment in this way:

> It [surrogacy] sounded so interesting and fun. The money wasn't enough to be pregnant for nine months.

Andrea, aged twenty-nine, is married and has three children. She is a high school graduate and works as a motel night auditor. She did not believe that remuneration motivates most surrogates. As she said here:

> I'm not doing it for the money. Take the money: That wouldn't stop me. It wouldn't stop the majority.

Sarah, aged twenty-seven, attended two years of college, is married, has two children, and works part-time as a tax examiner. Here she explained her feeling about remuneration:

What's 10,000 bucks? You can't even buy a car. If it was just for the money you will want the baby. Money wasn't important. I possibly would have done it just for expenses especially for the people I did it for. My father would have given me the money not to do it.

The issue of remuneration is of particular interest in that although surrogates do accept monetary compensation for their reproductive work, the role of compensation is multifaceted. The surrogate pregnancy, unlike traditional pregnancy, is viewed by the surrogate and her family as work, and that view is informed by the belief that work is something that occurs only within the context of paid occupations (Ferree 1984:72). It is interesting to note that surrogates rarely use the money they earn for themselves. Not one of the surrogates I interviewed spent the money she earned on herself alone; the majority spent it on their children, for example, college education funds, and others spent it on improvement for their homes, gifts for their husbands, a family vacation, or simply to pay off "family debts."

One of the primary reasons that most surrogates do not spend the money they earn on themselves alone appears to stem from the fact that the money serves as a buffer against and/or reward to their families, particularly to the husband, who must make compromises as a result of the surrogate arrangement. One of those compromises is that he must abstain from sexual intercourse with his wife from the time she begins inseminating until a pregnancy has been confirmed (a process that takes on average three to four months but may take as long as one year). The fact that a surrogate does not have to leave the home on a routine basis or in any formalized way in order to earn money is attractive to both the surrogate and her husband, but as a consequence of her employment, she has less time to spend with her family because of doctor's appointments, therapy sessions, and social engagements with her couple. Thus surrogates use the monetary compensation they receive as a means by which to procure their husbands' support for their decision. Surrogacy is viewed by surrogates as a part-time job in the sense that it allows a woman, especially a mother, to have, as one surrogate noted, "the luxury of staying home with my children."

Surrogates' devaluation of the amount of money they receive as insufficient to compensate for "nine months of pregnancy" can be understood to fulfill two functions. This view is, of course, representative of the cultural belief that children are priceless (Zelizer 1985). In this sense, surrogates are merely reiterating this widely held belief when they devalue the remuneration they receive. As mentioned earlier, when the Brookside program changed its newspaper advertisements from "Help an Infertile Couple" to "Give the Gift of Life,"[8] the new formula attracted the type of woman the program wished to attract and Brookside received a considerably larger volume of response from prospective surrogates. The ad that pointed to the profound significance of a surrogate's action struck a chord with surrogates because it recognized that their act is not one that can be compensated monetarily and because it cast surrogacy in a poignant and life-affirming context.

An underlying function served by surrogates' dismissal of the importance of remuneration is reflected in the following quotes. Fran, who was quoted earlier dismissing the importance of money, here offered a more revealing account of her decision to become a surrogate mother:

> *I wanted to do the ultimate thing for somebody, to give them the ultimate gift. Nobody can beat that, nobody can do anything nicer for them.*

Stella, aged thirty-eight, who is married and has two children, noted:

> *They [the couple] consider it [the baby] a gift and I consider it a gift.*

Carolyn, aged thirty-three, who is married, has two children, and owns a house-cleaning company, discussed her feelings about surrogacy:

> *It's a gift of love. I have always been a really giving person, and it's the ultimate way to give. I've always had babies so easily. It's the ultimate gift of love.*

Thus, when surrogates define the children they are reproducing for couples as a "gift," they are also tacitly suggesting that no amount of money would ever provide sufficient compensation. As Rubin summarized Mauss's pioneering work on this subject: "The significance of gift giving is that [it] expresses, affirms, or creates a social link between the partners of exchange ... confers upon its participants a special relationship of trust, solidarity and mutual aid" (Rubin 1975:172).[9]

As in the practice of exogamy, where the gift is a wife, the result of exchanges such as the one that takes place in surrogacy is "more profound than the result of other gift transactions, because the relationship established is not just one of reciprocity, but one of kinship" (Rubin 1975:172). Thus, when surrogates minimize or dismiss the importance of money, they are on the one hand reiterating cultural beliefs about the pricelessness of children, and they are on the other hand suggesting that the exchange of a child for money is not a relationship of reciprocity but one of kinship. Even though they are discouraged from thinking of the relationship to the couple as permanent, surrogates recognize that they are creating a state of enduring solidarity between themselves and their couples. This belief complicates the severing of the surrogate's relationship with her couple once the child has been born even though she knows in advance that the surrogate-couple relationship is to be an impermanent one. Surrogates' framing of the equation as one in which a gift is given thus serves as a counterpoint or a reminder to their couples that one of the symbolically central functions of money, namely, the "removal of the personal element from human relationships through its indifferent and objective nature" (Simmel 1978:297), may be insufficient to erase certain relationships, and that the human relational element may continue to surface despite the monetary exchange. This tendency to deemphasize remuneration has also been found among baby-sitters (*passepike,* or girls who "look after" children) in Norway. Marianne Gullestad reported that even though remuneration is important to these girls, they share in a cultural ideology that devalues the importance of payment for such a service. For this reason, when asked, the girls say that "they do not look after children for the sake of money, but because they are fond of children (*er glad i barn*)" (Gullestad 1992:119).

Of all the surrogates' stated motivations, remuneration is the most problematic. On a symbolic level, of course, remuneration detracts from the idealized cultural image of women/mothers as selfless, nurturant, and altruistic, an image that surrogates do not wish to lose; in addition, if surrogates were to acknowledge the money as a fair and equal exchange or compensation for their reproductive work, they would lose the sense that theirs is a gift that cannot be compensated monetarily.

Another reason cited by surrogates was altruism, specifically, a feeling of empathy for couples who are infertile. Many surrogates reported having felt empathy for the plight of an infertile couple they knew personally. In a fair number of instances, this relationship with an infertile couple corresponded chronologically with the first time surrogates considered the idea of surrogacy. Some surrogates even reported having offered to become a surrogate for a couple they knew personally, without the assistance of a program, but did not do so because either they or the couple thought the process might jeopardize the friendship or simply become "too complicated."

The empathy surrogates feel for an infertile couple appears to be related to the importance they attribute to the experience of having children in their own lives. Surrogates frequently reported that they have a desire to share this joy, to help someone else to have a child. In Britain, for example, commercial surrogacy was outlawed in 1985 with the passage of the Surrogacy Arrangements Bill (Wolfram 1989:189), and the situation has been framed in moral terms: "The symbol of the 'pure' surrogate who creates a child for love was pitted against the symbol of the 'wicked' surrogate who prostitutes her maternity" (Cannell 1990:683). The idea of "pure" versus "wicked" surrogacy and, correspondingly, good versus bad surrogates, is predicated on the belief that altruism precludes remuneration.[10] The overwhelming acceptance of the idea of unpaid surrogacy (both in the United States and abroad) can be attributed to the fact that it "duplicates maternity in culturally the most self-less manner" (Strathern 1991:31). Of the fifteen states that now have surrogacy laws the "most common regulations, applicable in 11 states ... are statutes voiding paid-surrogacy contracts" (Andrews 1992:50). But perhaps even more important, the rejection of paid or commercial surrogacy may also result from a cultural resistance to conflating the symbolic value of the family with the world of work, to which it has long been held in opposition, drawing together those two spheres through the agency of the surrogate, who bridges them through her reproductive work. In the Baby M case, for example, the most "decisive issue" was one of "payment to the surrogate" (Hull 1990b:155), but the 1993 precedent-setting decision of the California Supreme Court (see Chapter 1) focused not upon remuneration but rather upon intent, and the effect this will have on the practice of surrogacy in the United States will be profound (to be discussed in Chapter 4.)

Another motivation offered by surrogates was a desire to reexperience the joy and ease of being pregnant. Christine, aged twenty-eight, married, with two children, a full-time homemaker and gestational (IVF) surrogate, explained:

I love being pregnant and I didn't want to raise another child. I have easy pregnancies.

Andrea, who previously stated that eliminating commercial surrogacy would not prevent the majority of women who become surrogates from becoming unpaid surrogates, here discussed her feelings about pregnancy:

As the kids got older I wanted to become pregnant again. I want to be pregnant [but] I don't want more kids. I really love being pregnant; I'm healthier. Normally I feel fat, [but when] I am pregnant there's a reason for it.

Here the focus of the surrogate shifts away entirely from the end product of a pregnancy, a child, and is instead focused on the process of "being pregnant" as its own reward—a reward quite apart from that provided by remuneration or the joy of giving a couple a child. A very odd assessment, this intriguing explanation appears to be related to the idea that when one is pregnant one is fully female, physically and obviously a mother, and rewarded for being so. Several surrogates told me that they experience their surrogate pregnancies differently from their traditional pregnancy, specifically, that they received more attention for their surrogate pregnancy. As the above quotes reveal, a surrogate pregnancy appears to create for these women an experiential shift: Surrogacy allows them to enjoy the physical, psychological, and social dimensions of pregnancy without having to incur the responsibility of raising "more kids"; in this way, they do not have to "raise another child" in order to experience and enjoy pregnancy.

An additional reason offered by Parker's informants for their desire to become surrogates is the belief that surrogacy provides them with an opportunity to assuage the guilt they may be experiencing for having had an abortion or having put a child up for adoption (Parker 1983), although none of the surrogates in my study mentioned this idea to me.

Contrary to surrogates' stated motivations for choosing surrogacy, I found numerous instances that contradicted what they had said or that revealed the complexities and difficulties they had encountered. Based on the data gathered in this study, it can be concluded that it is not the ease of pregnancy that informs a surrogate's decision to become a surrogate; neither is it, as surrogates often state, that they "enjoy being pregnant" or that "pregnancy is a breeze," although for some this may be true. It is clear that surrogates have experienced miscarriages and ectopic pregnancies, have had difficulty conceiving, and have been given infertility drugs, synthetic hormones to expedite conception, and that none of these obstacles discourage or dissuade surrogates. For example, Jeannie, aged thirty-six, divorced, with one child, and employed as a free-lancer in several different fields, described her experience of an ectopic pregnancy while she was a surrogate in this way:

I almost bled to death: I literally almost died for my couple.

Nevertheless she was inseminating a second time for the same couple.

Fran, who earlier had described her reason for becoming a surrogate as motivated by her desire to do the "ultimate thing for somebody" rather than a desire for remuneration, discussed how difficult her surrogate delivery was:

I had a rough delivery, a C-section, and my lung collapsed because I had the flu, but it was worth every minute of it. If I were to die from childbirth, that's the best way to die. You died for a cause, a good one.

The Wick director reported having had a surrogate in her program who had miscarried and was again inseminating for the same couple, something that is, she said, "not all that unusual." In the Wick director's experience, when a surrogate has a miscarriage or experiences difficulty conceiving, she frequently reports feeling like a "failure," and as a result, her motivation to become pregnant and/or deliver a healthy child is strengthened and her efforts are redoubled.

The number of difficult conceptions, ectopic pregnancies, and miscarriages contradicts the notion frequently put forth by surrogates themselves and by industry personnel that pregnancy is for surrogates overwhelmingly a problem-free and positive or pleasurable experience. For example, one surrogate who had experienced a miscarriage while pregnant with one of her own children miscarried again while pregnant with a surrogate child. It appears that the desire on the part of some women to become surrogates often takes precedence over the risk pregnancy poses to their own health. It was the presence of these difficult conceptions, miscarriages, and ectopic pregnancies, coupled with the scriptlike quality of their idealized depictions of conception, pregnancy, and childbirth, that led me first to begin to formulate a hypothesis that would account more fully for all the motivations of the surrogates, both stated and unstated. Over time, I developed the idea that surrogacy provides women who are predominantly working class with the opportunity to transcend the limitations of their roles as wives/mothers and homemakers while concomitantly attesting to the satisfaction they derive from these roles. My hypothesis accounts for some of the contradictory statements made by these women.

Surrogate programs take women whose lives revolve around their home and children or women who, when employed, view their employment as a financial necessity, a job rather than a career, and immerse them in an unfamiliar and interesting world filled with social interaction, beginning with the initial screening process, application forms, psychological evaluations, and physiological tests and continuing through a number of social interactions with professionals, couples, and other surrogates. From the moment she establishes the initial telephone contact with the program, a surrogate is made to feel important and special by the program staff. The fact that programs are selective and may reject other women as unsuitable candidates reinforces a surrogate's sense of achievement when she is accepted and further contributes to her sense of uniqueness. The process thus takes a woman, most often one living in a nuclear family, functioning at times semi-exclusively in the home, and catapults her into a more public and social life without threatening her homemaker/wife/mother role because, like many occupations dominated by women, surrogacy can be seen as an extension of the "housewife, wife, or mother roles" (Chodorow 1978:180).

The majority of surrogates can be described as women who have assumed traditional sex roles in that they are married and often employed as full-time homemakers; they perform the chores and tasks associated with the home and children: cleaning, grocery shopping, laundry, cooking, and child care. As Chodorow found, "Childcare is considered ... [a woman's] crucially important responsibility ... [while] her work outside the home ... is not considered by her as important to her self definition in the way that her housewife role is" (Chodorow 1978:64); professing a love of children thus provides surrogates with an incontestable, socially acceptable motivation. Chodorow's finding illustrated how these stated motivations provide a noncontroversial way for surrogates to describe their relationship to surrogacy. Their husbands are usually employed in full-time jobs outside the home and when at home perform the "outdoor" chores traditionally performed by men, such as mowing the lawn, taking out the garbage, and doing household repairs. When surrogates are employed outside the home, they tend to consider their incomes as supplementary to the income of their husbands, as pin money, for example, to "make ends meet" or "to buy the little extra things."[11] Many surrogates who are employed outside the home express a desire to be full-time homemakers, perhaps because even when they have outside employment, it is not very rewarding or highly paid work and they continue to maintain primary responsibility for the maintenance of the household and the care of their children.

Once a surrogate is selected by a program, her life no longer revolves around her family and her home, although she is still essentially at home and available as a mother and wife. Her sense of place and her social network are greatly enlarged as she receives telephone calls from the program, rushes to keep doctor's appointments, meets with prospective couples (she may even be flown to other cities to meet couples), and later on attends (in the open programs) surrogate support-group meetings, monthly or semi-monthly, attends (in some programs) individual therapy sessions, is taken out socially by her couple, may receive gifts from her couple for herself and her children, and is telephoned regularly by her couple, receives cards and letters from them, and attends holiday parties and other social events hosted by the program. Her sense of importance is also enhanced when she tells others about her new and unusual work. Once a surrogate meets, selects, and is selected by her couple and begins insemination (another rite of passage that confers additional status upon her), the couple becomes central to her life, adding yet another steady source of social interaction and stimulation.

The entire surrogate experience serves to alter the balance of power in a surrogate's personal life, giving her entree to a more public role and creating new and exciting demands upon her time. Her time can no longer be spent just caring for and nurturing her own family because she is performing an important task, helping an infertile couple to start a family of its own, an activity that, unlike an ordinary job, cannot be regarded as unfeminine, selfish, nonnurturant, or ambitious. In this sense, we can see how surrogacy assists surrogates in their efforts to transcend the limitations of their domestic roles by highlighting "their differences from men ... [b]y accepting and elaborating upon the symbols and expectations associated with their cultural definition" (Rosaldo 1974:37), for example, motherhood. The enormity of this task provides the surrogate an opportunity to do more than care for her family alone, and surrogates often report feeling that they are undertaking a task laden with importance, a project that fills them with a sense of pride and self-worth. Sally, aged thirty-three, has a B.A., is married, has two children, and is a full-time homemaker. In the following passage, she discussed how surrogacy provided her with a feeling of unique accomplishment:

Not everyone can do it. It's like the steelworkers who walk on beams ten floors up; not everyone can do it, not everyone can be a surrogate.

Celeste, aged twenty-eight, is married, has one child, and provides day care at her home. She too discussed the feeling of accomplishment and the sense of mission surrogacy provided for her:

I know when I make a commitment I can stick with it. I am really proud of myself. It's like some people want to climb Mt. Everest, surrogacy is like that. You are driven and you feel so good when you do it. I am really proud of myself!

The decision to participate in surrogate motherhood is articulated by surrogates in terms of the sense of pride, confidence, and control that surrogacy comes to represent for them. For most surrogates, patterns of conventional female behavior are for the first time altered in their lives when they become surrogates and again when they part with the baby. Without seeming to, the surrogate is nonetheless challenging her husband and family's claims as well as traditional definitions of motherhood.

Motherhood in the United States tends to be defined as an innately biological process (Sternglanz and Nash 1988:15); this view, coupled with the romanticized 1950s American image of the full-time mother and homemaker, creates an idealized norm that carries with it the belief that "any variation from the natural biologically determined model will lead to disaster" (Sternglanz and Nash 1988:15). In this context, a surrogate's actions can be understood as a radical departure from traditionally held beliefs surrounding motherhood and reproduction.

It is not surprising then that surrogates claim it is their love of children that motivates them to become surrogates; but one study indicated that although love of children may be their stated motivation, surrogates may have other reasons less acceptable to themselves, their families, and society. Resnick (1989), for example, has found that surrogate mothers, as compared to a control group of mothers, are in fact less nurturant of their own children than the control group. When surrogacy is framed in this fashion, as a love of home and family, the surrogate is viewed (and is able to view herself) as selfless and her motivation is held to be beyond reproach, an image also reinforced by the surrogate program and her couple. A surrogate mother's experience of surrogacy occurs, it should be remembered, in the structured context provided by the program. The image of the selfless mother thus provides surrogates with a conceptual framework that does not threaten culturally acceptable definitions of motherhood.

The surrogate process also provides surrogates with social contacts who serve as their allies, people with power, influence, and social connections whom these women might not otherwise meet. Just as one can be stigmatized by associating with a person from a stigmatized group (Goffman 1963), a surrogate may, by virtue of her contact with an educated, wealthy couple, benefit positively through her close association with them. For example, as mentioned earlier, a couple may be in the real estate business and be able to provide the surrogate with valuable information in the future, or if a member of the couple is a lawyer, the surrogate knows that she will have access to legal advice should she ever need it. It is not unusual for couples from open programs to say, as one couple did, that although they no longer maintain the same degree of contact with their surrogate as they did during the insemination process and pregnancy, in the event that "anything happened to our surrogate, we are there for her."

The protective role adopted by the couple in relationship to the surrogate further contributes to her new sense of self-importance, security, and well-being. Since the surrogate is carrying a baby for this couple, the couple expresses its gratitude in a multitude of ways, one of which is by remaining her loyal and devout allies throughout the process and even afterward. In ways that are immeasurable, the balance of power in a surrogate's marital relationship and home life almost certainly shifts, first, in response to her being at least partially removed from the province of the home and by the fact that she is earning an income, and second, because she has established these outside social contacts or advocates through her association with the program and the couple. The psychologists, lawyers, and doctors that she meets through the program are often among the few professionals she may know on a personal and professional level. Although work continues to be narrowly defined as something motivated solely by economic factors, and noneconomic factors, such as freedom from the monotony of staying at home or the desire to gain recognition or financial leverage in the family in order to affect the balance of power, are routinely excluded from that definition of work (Ferree 1984), it is clear that for surrogates, surrogate work involves more than remuneration.

This shift in the balance of power is most clearly revealed when we consider that a surrogate's husband must sign a consent form stating that he will abstain from having sexual intercourse with his wife until a pregnancy has been confirmed, an example of how the surrogate gains control over her reproduction both in terms of her sexual relationship with her husband and in electing to give up the baby. This newfound sense of freedom from their husbands and their families is reflected in the following quotes. Carolyn, who earlier described the surrogate child as a "gift," here explained her sense of independence from her husband on the subject of surrogacy:

> It was harder on my husband: He'd ask me, "Can you give up this baby? I don't think I can," he'd say. I told him, "It doesn't matter what you think."

Sally, who compared surrogates to "steelworkers," also considered the decision to become a surrogate a personal one. Here she mentioned her mother's displeasure with her husband for supporting Sally's decision to become a surrogate,

> My mother and husband went at it after the birth and she said, "How could you let her do it?" Like he really had a say in it.

Celeste, the day-care provider, also discussed how her husband's friends did not understand why her husband had supported her decision to become a surrogate, framing it in the language used by pro-choice advocates,

> My husband's friends didn't understand why he let me do it. It's my right to do what I want to do with my body.

In this way, the surrogate's belief in her right to make autonomous decisions about her reproduction also represents a decline in the "culturally legitimated authority" (Yanagisako 1987:116) of her husband and her family. It is interesting to note that surrogates and couples both utilize feminist pro-choice language concerning a woman's right to control her own body, although many surrogates are personally opposed to abortion. Specifically, surrogates frequently state that "it's my body," and "it's my right to do what I want with my body," when confronted with an anti-surrogacy position. Surrogates consistently view opponents of surrogacy as hostile and misguided adversaries, as individuals who have an incomplete understanding of surrogacy and who are therefore unable to appreciate a woman's right to participate in surrogate motherhood, in much the same way as individuals who are pro-choice view those who are opposed to abortion. When questioned about their feelings concerning individuals who are opposed to surrogate motherhood, surrogates typically say, "Give me fifteen minutes with someone and I know I can turn them around."

Surrogates and Their Couples

Programs reinforce a surrogate's feeling of specialness from the beginning of the process, but once a surrogate has become pregnant, the open programs transfer a great deal (though not all) of this responsibility for reinforcing her sense of achievement to the couple. Once a surrogate has been matched with a couple, she experiences what could be understood as a rite of passage; the match functions as both the literal and the symbolic moment at which she becomes a surrogate mother. As we have seen, if the couple lives nearby, it is not uncommon (and is in fact somewhat encouraged and expected by the programs) that they invite their surrogate (and at times her family) to social events such as lunch or dinner, carnivals, and other outings, and that they give gifts to both the surrogate and her children. Surrogates and couples frequently mention with enthusiasm the social or recreational aspects of their relationship with each other. Nora, aged twenty-nine, two years of college, divorced, with two children, who had given birth as a surrogate eighteen months earlier, described her enjoyment of the social, emotional, and remunerative benefits of her relationship with her couple:

They were pretty well off and they spoiled me rotten.

Fran, the dog trainer, who was in the process of being inseminated at the time of the interview, described interests and activities in which they engaged as equals:

We talk on the phone everyday. Every other weekend we go to my son's ball game and swim at their pool. She [the adoptive mother] introduced me to sailing. I'm training their dog right now.

Melissa, aged forty, a college graduate and adoptive mother, who was initially "scared" about having a relationship with her surrogate, talked about the ways in which they socialized, a fairly representative level of interaction in open programs:

> *During the pregnancy, we took her [surrogate] out with her husband and her kids for dinner, movies, and museums once a month.*

This feeling of specialness conferred upon surrogates by couples, programs, and the process itself is often later conferred by extension onto the surrogate children conceived for the couple. For example, as Celeste explained:

> *These kids are so loved they are going to grow up and solve the world's problems.*

Another surrogate, Judy, aged twenty-six, was divorced and had no children of her own (she put her first child up for adoption). She was working as a merchandiser and said of the surrogate child,

> *This baby is one of God's special children, and I'm glad I'm in on it.*

Couples and surrogates talk over the phone during the pregnancy an average of twice a week, and even when they live in another city, couples often fly in to attend doctor's appointments with their surrogates. Contact between surrogates and couples increases in direct proportion to the progression of the pregnancy; this increase in contact between couples and surrogates is undertaken, as mentioned in Chapter 1, in response to the specific directives of the open programs. Once the baby has been born, it is not uncommon for the couple to give the surrogate yet another present, a final and very special gift, such as an expensive vacation (for example, one couple sent their surrogate and her husband on a two-week, all expenses paid trip to Hawaii) or an expensive piece of jewelry, to express their gratitude in yet another way. Molly, aged thirty-two, a homemaker with two children, pregnant with a second child for the same couple, at the time of the interview, received a ring with the baby's birthstone. Another surrogate, Mary, said:

> *She [the adoptive mother] gave me a heart-shaped necklace I still wear.*

With respect to a surrogate's interpersonal relationships, the importance of the couple in her life and, in particular, the importance of the adoptive mother cannot be overstated, as exemplified by the following case in which Alicia, aged thirty-two, who is married and has two children and who is a full-time homemaker and a gestational surrogate, discussed her relationship with the adoptive mother:

> *I had a closeness with Jane [the adoptive mother] that you would*
> *have with your husband. She took [the] Lamaze class and went to*
> *the delivery room with me.*

Chesler (1988) suggested that surrogates may be described as seeking the experience of being mothered through the attention they receive as surrogates. And the couples and the program do "mother" the surrogate in the sense that they protect her and shield her from unpleasantness whenever possible and reward her for what she is doing. Hanafin, the Center for Surrogate Parenting program's psychologist, in her efforts to develop a surrogate profile, described the typical surrogate as a woman who has "mothered" everyone in her life, including at times even her own mother, father, or husband, and of course her own children. Additionally, according to Hanafin, the surrogate can be described as taking leave of or saying good-bye to her own fertility through the surrogate process. Although the majority of surrogates have completed their own families and have no plans to have more children of their own and in this sense surrogacy could be said to represent a final act of reproduction to them, the increasing number of surrogates who are repeating surrogacy would seem to contradict this theory. I would suggest that surrogates may instead be making use of their fertility in new ways, for example, fertility for excitement or remuneration, and pregnancy without the cares of child-rearing responsibilities.

The caretaking behavior exhibited by surrogates, perhaps best exemplified by their protective behavior toward the adoptive mother, can be understood as part of what has been described as the "feminine personality structure," in which it is common for women to view themselves in relation to others (Chodorow 1974:44). Surrogates frequently relate stories about feeling "protective" toward the adoptive mother or wanting to "shield her" from unnecessary pain and suffering, as illustrated by the case of Theresa, aged thirty-seven, married, with two children, who experienced light bleeding (and later miscarried) but resisted telling her adoptive mother because, as she stated:

> *I didn't want to worry her, if it had turned out to be nothing then*
> *there would have been no point in worrying her.*

The director of the Harper program told me that she believed that "surrogates also want to create not only a child but a mother as well," specifically, to transform an infertile woman into a mother. Hanafin, in contrast, viewed the surrogate's desire to become a surrogate as an extension of her own mothering role, a role that is central to her identity as well as her life-style.

Clearly the issue of mothering is central to the surrogacy phenomenon, as surrogacy involves the act of reproduction, but none of these theories, "to mother," "to create a mother," or "to be mothered," provides a satisfactory explanation for the surrogate's motivations. One of the difficulties posed by the task of evaluating surrogate motivations is that surrogates tend to cite, as mentioned, somewhat scripted responses. They also exhibit familiarity with other surrogates' reasons and with media preconceptions and often appear to be reacting to negative publicity. It does not appear to matter whether a program was open or closed, large or small; negative experiences do not seem to affect surrogate perceptions of surrogacy: Surrogates' commitment to surrogacy could best be described as unwavering. It became increasingly clear that if a complex rendering of surrogate motivation was to be attained, it would be necessary to take into consideration those aspects of surrogacy that result from the cultural embeddedness of certain ideas, for example, the culturally appropriate and sanctioned motivations offered by surrogates and the program reinforcement of those motivations, most notably, the image of surrogates as "giving," and of children as "priceless."

Trying to determine whether surrogates were coming to programs already in possession of these ideas or whether programs were providing surrogates with a scripted response proved difficult. It was clear that since surrogates and programs draw from the same cultural repertoire, surrogates would have arrived with many of these ideas already formed. They are aware, for example, that drawing attention to those aspects of surrogacy that are transgressive, such as procreation outside of marriage, would, of course, render surrogacy unpalatable. Focusing instead upon those aspects of surrogacy that can be accommodated by preexisting values, beliefs, and ideology, such as the importance of creating a family or the idea that surrogates are selfless and nurturant, is a means of ensuring that surrogacy will be more readily accepted or accommodated and one that surrogates are quite ready to reinforce. Programs help to standardize, or regularize, surrogacy by instructing their surrogates and their couples how to avoid or minimize its transgressive or culturally inappropriate elements; for example, programs encourage the formation of bonds between surrogates and adoptive mothers in order to avert lingering suggestions of adultery; and they generally profess to prohibit unmarried women and men from engaging the services of surrogates in order more closely to approximate the appearance of a "traditional" family. Nevertheless, in spite of the best efforts of programs, surrogacy still calls into question numerous closely guarded beliefs con-

cerning reproduction, motherhood, fatherhood, and family, and participants are therefore more than willing to emphasize those aspects of
surrogacy that are most consistent with American values. For this reason, the surrogate emphasizes her love of "mothering," of children, and
of family without prompting when she enters a program, and she continues to do so with the encouragement of the program.

One of the more interesting aspects of the surrogate's relationship to
mothering is that she uses the act of reproduction as a means of remov-
ing herself from the limitations of the role traditionally assigned to
women, caretaking or mothering, by simultaneously employing and
transcending that reproductive role. The surrogate chooses pregnancy
as an occupation because it is a skill she is confident she possesses. Giving birth is something surrogates as a group view as a considerable skill,
something that only women are able to do, and something that only fertile women can do, which lends it an even more special quality since giving birth is socially valued but it is not financially rewarded. Surrogates
often express the idea that what they are doing is special, that giving
birth is an act that should be rewarded both monetarily and with social
recognition and public appreciation. Surrogates often proudly boast of
their skills in this area. Elizabeth, aged thirty, married, with two children,
is a day-care provider. She described surrogacy (or giving birth) as something that not every woman can do:

I knew this was something I could do well.

Mary, aged thirty-seven, who is married, has three children, and works
part-time, recalled that her husband considered her talented or skilled
in giving birth:

*My husband told me, "This is something you can do," and I knew at
that moment he was right!*

The surrogacy experience also appears to offer these women confirmation of the cultural importance of childbirth, work that they always
believed to be of profound significance and worth but for which they did
not receive the amount of attention they garnered as a surrogate, when
they carried a child for a couple. The recognition these women receive
for their surrogate role thus confirms and reinforces their belief that
motherhood is of profound importance and that giving birth is a talent
or a skill. Although motherhood in the United States has also been associated with "negative meanings of powerlessness and isolation" (Tiffany
1982:119), surrogate motherhood, like other assisted reproductive technologies and like reproduction in general, also partakes of "older cultural terrains, where women interpret their options in light of prior and

contradictory meanings of pregnancy and childbearing" (Rapp 1990:41). In this way, surrogacy becomes a form of public or publicly acknowledged motherhood that confers upon the surrogate feelings of empowerment, status, and value—rewards that her private mother role does not generally give her. And although a woman's "biological processes, including childbearing, are viewed as constraints rather than as sources of power and autonomy" (Tiffany 1982:119), they also contain rewards, and the surrogate parlays her childbearing capacity in such a way as to maximize the benefits of motherhood.

Gestational Surrogates (IVF)

Gestational surrogates (surrogates who do not contribute an ovum) differ from traditional surrogates (who are the child's biological mother) in that the former believe they would be unable to part with a child who was genetically related to them. However, in addition to the normal risks that accompany pregnancy, surrogates who select IVF incur additional risks owing to the complications that may arise with the implantation of several embryos and the prospect of multiple births. Nevertheless, as the technological aspects of IVF are improved, there is little doubt that this method will become more and more commonplace in the surrogate industry. And although the Allen director described this service with the colloquial term "rip-off," arguing that its costs clearly outweighed its potential benefits since success rates were poor (under 10 percent at that time as compared to the 95 percent success rate reported with traditional surrogacy), as we have seen in Chapter 1, success rates for IVF are based on statistics derived from a population of infertile women.[12] The Brookside program claimed to have a pregnancy rate of 17.6 percent and a live-birth rate of 14 percent, a success rate it attributes to having implanted embryos in a population of woman who are young, healthy, and comparatively drug-free, with no history of infertility, rather than the traditional candidates for this procedure, which helps to explain the statistical discrepancy. It should also be noted that the Brookside program's high rate of success is based upon a fairly small sample size.

Surrogates in the IVF program receive, in addition to the standard fee, a payment of $500 per implant attempt even if the biological mother's and the surrogate's cycle do not synchronize (i.e., no implant attempt occurs) because the surrogate must visit a doctor on a daily basis to have her hormone levels checked and may be given synthetic hormones. The principal controversy surrounding the technologies of IVF, GIFT, and ZIFT, excluding the arguments of those who are simply opposed to surrogacy in any form, centers primarily upon the allowable number of eggs or embryos implanted into a surrogate's womb. The number of twins, triplets, and other multiple births produced is markedly higher for the above procedures than it is with traditional reproduction because, with the process of superovulation, for example, between ten and twenty ova may be flushed. The problem, however, arises in response to the number of eggs or embryos implanted; according to the Brookside psychologist, the average number of implanted embryos is three. However, even though she does not believe in implanting more than four, it is not unusual for a physician to implant five or even six embryos in the interest of improving the rate of success. Additionally, because frozen embryos do not have as high a rate of success as newly retrieved ones, if five embryos have been fertilized, there is a distinct possibility that the physician will implant all five rather than freezing one or two.[13] If more than two embryos begin the process of mitosis, the surgeon will selectively terminate all but two.

Surrogates who choose IVF even after they have been informed of the risks do so because, although they wish to help an infertile couple, they believe, as we have seen, that they could not part with a child that is biologically related to them. One of the gestational surrogates interviewed stated that she could not give up a baby that was "half hers," an interesting formulation in view of the fact that traditional surrogates do not consider the child their own, an issue that raises many interesting questions concerning beliefs about kinship, genetic relatedness, and pregnancy. The woman who becomes a traditional surrogate disavows the importance of her biological link to the child and instead focuses her attention upon the role of the adoptive mother, whereas the gestational surrogate acknowledges the biological link in traditional surrogacy. For example, prior to the advent of these and other technologies, society was able to assume safely that the child a woman was gestating was her own genetic child; it was also assumed that she would begin to bond with that child in utero (Snowden, Mitchell, and Snowden 1983). However, with the advent of reproductive technologies, the "organic unity of fetus and mother can no longer be assumed" (Martin 1987:20), and it remains to be seen just how the knowledge that a child is not genetically hers might alter a woman's perception of her pregnancy. A great deal can, of course, be learned about in utero bonding through the study of surrogates' responses to the fetus, in particular, how the intentionality of the woman serves as a powerful determinant in her perception of her pregnancy.

Currently, the Warnock Report (a British government–commissioned study on reproductive technologies) concluded that the gestational surrogate should be considered the biological mother of the child, and the Glover report (a European study) concluded that the gestational surrogate bears a "biological" tie to the child. Although an effort is being made to expand the definition of biological relatedness to include the physiological process of pregnancy, the theory being that ovum contribution is but one aspect of biological motherhood since without the womb, the embryo/fetus/child could not develop and survive, we know that gestational surrogates choose IVF precisely because for them it eliminates the issue of genetic relatedness. The effort, however, to expand our definition of biological relatedness, which has until now depended upon a genetic component, runs contrary to the Euro-American emphasis on biogenetic relatedness, in which genetic parents are legally and socially considered the "real" parents. As one gestational surrogate said of traditional surrogacy,

I know [that] my husband and I couldn't give up the baby.

Surrogates who elect to participate in IVF surrogacy agree in advance to undergo amniocentesis if it is requested; quite often, the ovum is being retrieved from a woman who is in one of the high-risk groups (usually age). In this way, in the event of a detectable birth abnormality, the surrogate has already agreed in advance to abort if necessary, and there is no need to negotiate this step later on.

The three gestational surrogates and twenty-five traditional surrogates questioned about this issue (some of whom were opposed to abortion for themselves) acknowledged that they would, if so advised by a physician, undergo amniocentesis or other tests and an abortion if that was the couple's decision. The primary reasons for agreeing to abort an abnormal fetus cited by surrogates are that they do not regard it as their own and that because the couple would raise the child, that decision could only be made by the couple; in short, surrogates do not believe that they have the right to make such a profound decision about a child that they do not consider their own and that they will not be rearing.

Surrogates' Perceptions of the Child

One of the most interesting aspects of a surrogate's perception of the fetus she is carrying is that it is not her child, and this belief holds true whether it is half her genetic contribution, as it is in traditional surrogacy and in a traditional pregnancy, or not genetically related to her at all, as in gestational surrogacy. On the one hand, surrogates consistently regard anti-surrogacy efforts as attempts to exercise control over their bodies, but they do, on the other hand, distinguish between their own bodies and the embryo/fetus/child. The perception that the child is not her own tends to shape a surrogate's entire experience of surrogacy. In the case of gestational surrogacy, when she is, in fact, not the genetic mother of the child, her decision to allow the couple to decide the best course of action in the event of a genetic abnormality is perhaps more understandable than in the case of traditional surrogacy. (For a more extensive discussion of these issues, see Chapter 4.) It is essential in this context to bear in mind that a surrogate is a fertile woman, usually with children of her own, who does not wish to bear a child of her own. She does not become a surrogate in order to have a child of her own and has instead gone to great lengths to conceive a child for another couple, and when this intention is taken into consideration,[14] it sheds some light on the subject of why the surrogate does not consider the child her own. Andy, aged thirty-nine, divorced, with two children, a full-time nurse, framed the issue of relatedness in this way:

Parents are the ones who raise the child. I got that from my parents, who adopted children. My siblings were curious and my parents gave them the information they had, and they never wanted to track down their biological parents. I don't think of the baby as mine; it is the parents, the ones who raise the child, that are important. *[Emphasis mine]*

Pam, a Smith program ex-surrogate, expressed a belief shared by many of the surrogates about their pregnancies:

If it wasn't for this couple I wouldn't be pregnant.

Kay, aged thirty-five, divorced, with two children, added:

I never think of the child as mine. After I had the baby, the mother [adoptive] came into the room and held the baby. I couldn't relate that it had any part of me.

The traditional surrogate thus downplays the significance of the genetic relatedness she shares with the child (the same degree of relatedness she shares with her own children) and focuses instead upon the importance of nurturance and parenting. The gestational surrogate chooses IVF precisely in order to eliminate the genetic component, and she is always the first to point this out, as Alicia, who is a thirty-two-year-old IVF surrogate, did:

The baby isn't mine. I am only carrying the baby.

Celeste, a gestational surrogate who gave birth to twins, asserted that she did not feel any appreciable bond or connection toward the babies because of her lack of a genetic link to them and that she viewed this as a positive aspect of IVF surrogacy:

They didn't feel like my babies. I didn't want to care for them. The next day I held them for a few seconds. If I had any feelings about it I could have dealt with it but I didn't.

In an interesting twist on the issue of genetic relatedness, Christine, also a gestational surrogate, stressed the certainty attained with IVF that the child was not hers, something that is very important to IVF surrogates:

With IVF you know it's not your child.

The traditional surrogate's pregnancy is also one that is made possible by the belief that she is carrying the couple's child rather than her own. She arrives at this idea by reasoning that intentionality or choice is involved, saying to herself, for example, If I wanted a child I would have had one, but I did not want a child. Both traditional and gestational surrogates ignore or minimize the biogenetic and biological aspects of pregnancy. As Alicia, a traditional surrogate, expressed it, in a phrase indistinguishable from that one would expect to hear from an IVF surrogate:

I am strictly the hotel.

Jeannie, another traditional surrogate, expressed the sentiments of many surrogates when she stated:

I feel like a vehicle, just like a cow; it's their baby, it's his sperm.

Mary, aged thirty-seven, who is married and has three children, also separated biological motherhood from social motherhood, describing her relationship to the baby as having ended with its being an "egg" (parallel to the way a man might feel about semen donation), the emotional component having been eliminated by choice:

I don't think of the baby as my child. I donated an egg I wasn't going to be using.

It should be noted that a woman's ability to separate herself from her pregnancy and child is greatly facilitated and reinforced by the surrogate program (especially in the open programs), in particular by the resident psychologist. However, surrogates appear to be already convinced that a surrogate child is not the surrogate's child when they first contact a surrogate program. As we have seen, they often express the belief that surrogacy is something that not everyone can do, that it requires certain qualities or virtues such as independence, strength, courage, and self-knowledge; as one surrogate noted, "You really have to know yourself." It is the ability or strength to be able to separate oneself from the pregnancy/child that surrogates consider a prerequisite of surrogate motherhood, and since this belief represents a departure from traditional ideas and beliefs surrounding pregnancy and motherhood in American culture, the open program's role is to provide support for this idea through therapy, support groups, and so on. Programs (usually closed) that dispense with the need for the various kinds of psychological reinforcement provided by the open programs are thus more likely to encounter surrogates who desire to keep the child. Another factor responsible for disputes is that closed programs dispense with the more rigorous screening methods employed by the open programs.

The Smith Program

In December 1988, the director of the Smith program informed me that his surrogate mother program (a closed program) was no longer in business and that on the advice of his attorney he would not be speaking with anyone about his program, but the following spring, in May 1989, I was able to establish contact with three Smith ex-surrogates. During the course of my interviews with these three women, the importance of a program's structure, in particular, the importance of psychological-support services and the consequent reinforcement and structure they provide for surrogates, became clear to me.

All three surrogates had no prior knowledge that the program was in financial distress when "out of the blue," as they said, they all received a form letter one Friday afternoon informing them that the program was bankrupt. All the pregnant surrogates (those with whom I spoke were all pregnant) were given the "option" of developing relationships with their couples, and all other, nonpregnant, surrogates were told that their contracts with their couples were officially terminated. The remaining five pregnant surrogates then formed their own support group because all support services had also been terminated (the Smith program, though closed, had recruited surrogates from the local area and had offered its surrogates support services). As one surrogate said, in reference to the "option" she was given of continuing or discontinuing her contract with her couple:

Some option, what choice did we have? We were pregnant.

They all discussed the awkwardness they experienced in having to meet their couples again without someone from the program serving as an intermediary. They had previously met but were not maintaining the close or regular contact encouraged in open programs; the abrupt closing of the program thus forced them into an unfamiliar degree of close contact.

Aside from the obvious lack of concern for the welfare of surrogates displayed by the Smith program, what is of great interest here is the fact that all three of the Smith program surrogates said that they had experienced or expected to experience a tremendous sense of loss when they gave up the baby. They also assured me that the other two surrogates in their support group of five shared these feelings. On this subject, Stella said:

I first saw the baby again at two weeks and it was really hard. I cried and cried. The pain was really intense, but I never regretted doing this.

Pam, another Smith program ex-surrogate, stated:

You have nine months with the child, but it's how you choose to handle those feelings that counts. There will be a tremendous amount of grief and sadness and yet it's not right for me to raise this child. I don't have the energy. If it wasn't for this couple wanting this child, I wouldn't be pregnant. There are nights I wake up crying and I see this is going to be hard.

What is unique about these statements is that with the exception of the Smith surrogates, none of the surrogates interviewed for this study expressed grief or sadness about parting with the baby (although they expressed sadness at the loss of the couple's attention and the surrogate role). I suggest that the reason the Smith program surrogates experienced this loss is twofold. First, in the open programs the surrogates and couples interact frequently. As the director of the Allen program stated:

The surrogate bonds with the couple and not the baby; when the surrogate gives up the baby, she doesn't feel separation anxiety from giving up the baby but from losing her couple.

None of this is left to chance; as discussed in Chapter 1, it is carefully planned by the programs. The semi-monthly or monthly therapy offered by the open programs (mandatory in some of them) is designed to maintain the desired state of mind or attitude toward the process.

Although the Smith program surrogates had met their couples (unlike surrogates in the more strictly run closed programs), they had not been permitted, as they are in the open programs, to interact closely or regularly with them. Nevertheless, even in the midst of expressing grief over this loss, these surrogates interjected disclaimers such as "I never regretted doing this" or "if it wasn't for this couple wanting this child I wouldn't be pregnant." This case illustrates that when the support ser-

vices are removed and the structure of the program dissolves, it is difficult, if not impossible, to maintain the prescribed and desired boundaries between the surrogate and her child; hence, surrogates report
feelings of loss, pain, and despair when parting with the child.

Post-Birth Experience

As a consequence of the bond established between surrogates and couples in the open programs (to be discussed in more detail in Chapter 4),
many surrogates reported feeling disappointed in the behavior of their
couples after the baby was born, even though they were advised in advance that their relationship to their couple would be greatly attenuated
if not terminated at that point. As one surrogate noted:

*I felt they had been my friends, but after they got what they wanted,
they weren't.*

The disappointment experienced by the surrogate upon the termination
of this relationship clearly has to do with the loss of close contact with
the couple, but it also has to do with the loss of the surrogate role. Once a
woman ceases to be a surrogate, the feelings of specialness conferred
upon her by the role are also removed. She is on her own, no longer in
contact with the program or in close contact with the couple. It appears
that nothing the program says or does can adequately prepare her for
this situation, which may explain why many surrogates reported that
they wished their couples had been (and continued to be) more verbally
expressive to them about how special they are. Surrogates wished to be
reminded of this repeatedly, especially after the child was born, when
they returned to the—by contrast—somewhat mundane world of full-
time unpaid housework and child care or a low-paying job.

As Christine, a twenty-five-year-old IVF surrogate, stated:

*I am an attention grabber, I love the attention of being pregnant. It
was a big letdown after nine months of attention. Everyone in the
hospital wanted to see what a surrogate looks like. I felt depressed
after the birth. I was the center of attention. Three days after the
birth I had a crying fit and on the fifth day I was crying all night. I
took pills to stop the milk.*

One of the strategies employed by surrogates to counteract the afteref-
fects of the termination of surrogacy and/or to prolong the surrogacy
experience is to discuss their experiences with virtually anyone who will
listen, to relive it through talking about it. They discuss their experiences
on television and on the radio, they give interviews in their local news-

papers, and many of them express a desire to write a book about their experiences. As mentioned earlier, none of the directors of open programs seemed overly concerned about the privacy of surrogates because, as they all acknowledged, surrogates as a group, unlike couples, do not wish to remain anonymous; on the contrary, they appear to enjoy sharing their experience with interested parties, including journalists, co-workers, and even casual acquaintances.

In publicizing her experience, a surrogate enhances her feelings of importance and also establishes a public record or media chronicle of her experiences to which she may return when she is no longer a surrogate. Through this documentation and publicizing of her act, the surrogate extends and prolongs her surrogate role. The Allen director noted that after the child is born, the couple must "get on with being parents" and then added, with an interesting slip of the tongue, that the surrogate "needs to pick up the pieces of her life." But the surrogate often has little inclination or desire to return to her pre-surrogate existence and frequently expresses a desire to continue her surrogate experience.[15]

Another of the ways in which many surrogates "pick up the pieces of their lives," in addition to reliving the experience in the media, is by repeating their surrogacy experience, occasionally for the same couple. One of these repeat surrogates who was in the Wick program refused to grant me an interview because, as the director informed me, the surrogate feared that I would consider her "addicted to the program" because she was repeating for the fourth time. The Wick director acknowledged that all of the surrogates currently enrolled in her program at that time wished to repeat the program, and the Harper director also stated that all of her surrogates wished to repeat the program. The Wick director acknowledged that, with the advent of repeaters, there is growing concern that some surrogates may run the risk of becoming "addicted to the excitement."

In spite of the reservations expressed by some program staff about repeat surrogates, the fact that they have a number of surrogates who would like to repeat the program is often cited by program directors with a great deal of pride, as if surrogates' desires to repeat the process were the measure of a successful program. A fairly large percentage of surrogates, at least 65 percent of those with whom I spoke, are either repeating surrogacy for a second time or if it is their first time, have plans to repeat the experience in the future. No doubt the "excitement" provides a partial explanation for this desire to repeat. Another explanation offered by the programs is that if a surrogate has had a positive experience with her couple, she will most likely want to repeat the process for her couple. Repeat surrogates revise their explanations about motivation as well, from "wanting to help an infertile couple" to "wanting to give the couple's first child a sibling, so she won't be lonely." This remarkable shift away from helping the couple to improving the perceived quality of the first child's life is a fairly common occurrence among surrogates. As I understand it, when surrogates refocus their intent onto the idea of creating a sibling for the first child, they provide themselves with an additional altruistic reason for continuing their surrogate role, and they reassess their situation in light of the first child's birth. Since they have already "helped" an infertile couple to have a child, they have in essence expired the parameters of that motivation and they must go on to a second and, like their first, incontestable motivation.

This desire of surrogates to repeat the surrogacy process is a phenomenon that first began to appear in the late 1980s. According to directors, surrogates did not express a desire to repeat the surrogate experience before that time. The shift in surrogates' perception appears to be in part a response to programs' approaches to this issue and also in part to growing societal familiarity with the idea of surrogacy. Although not all programs profess to welcome this change, all of them are currently permitting it. For example, the Brookside psychologist informed me that a "red flag goes up" when a surrogate mentions wanting to repeat the program and that she has "serious reservations" about repeaters, but in spite of her reservations, her program is permitting the practice. The Brookside psychologist also said that there were, to her knowledge, very few surrogates in her program who wished to repeat and that those who did so usually acted at the couple's request. However, although the Brookside program's rate of repeat surrogates was lower than that of the Wick and Harper, the desire to repeat was not as rare as the psychologist suggested: Close to 30 percent of the program's surrogates, when questioned, expressed a desire to repeat.

It would appear then that when surrogates are permitted, and even encouraged, to repeat the process by a given program, the profit motive of the program must be taken into consideration. An experienced surrogate who has been through the process once before is considered a known quantity, a reliable and "proven" candidate. As we have seen, the initial screening process relies primarily upon psychological and physiological testing, yet no amount of testing can guarantee that a woman will become a successful surrogate; a successful surrogate, according to the programs, is someone who experiences surrogacy positively and who willingly parts with the child. The ultimate proof that someone is or is not a "good" surrogate can only be revealed through the process itself. After a surrogate has been accepted on the basis of tests, the program's original evaluation of her is then either confirmed or called into question during the insemination process, pregnancy, and final parting with the child, a long and involved process (or period of evaluation) that makes the prospect of repeat surrogates a welcome one to programs, despite the reservations of some directors and some staff members.

One of the repeat surrogates interviewed, Lauren, aged twenty-nine, a high school graduate and homemaker, had participated in three different surrogate programs. Her experiences illuminate why women who choose surrogacy are frequently motivated to repeat the process. Her first experience in the Drake program, a closed program, was a negative one, and she was particularly distressed by the fact that she knew very little about her couple. After three months of trying unsuccessfully to become pregnant, Lauren was referred to an infertility specialist who prescribed Clovin (a synthetic hormone) for a single day. Lauren contended that after the first day, the director of the Drake program instructed her, against the infertility specialist's instructions, to continue to take Clovin, which she did. When her couple learned about the use of a synthetic hormone, they were, in Lauren's words, "furious," not out of concern for her health, but because they believed it to be an indication that she was infertile. Subsequently, they requested to have their contract with her declared null and void.

Lauren was then matched with a second couple, who she later found out had not been diagnosed as infertile and who had hired a surrogate for the sake of "convenience." After the baby was born, the nurses removed the child from Lauren immediately, as they had been instructed. According to Lauren, the adoptive mother never "even thanked me for what I did." She claimed that when she called the couple four days after the birth to inquire about the baby's health, something that is permitted by programs, "she [the adoptive mother] chewed me out." The adoptive mother told the surrogate: "I never want her [the child] to meet you; I'll never encourage her." Lauren was understandably disturbed by this experience; as she described it:

I sat around and cried a lot that year. They send me fuzzy pictures of her.

Inasmuch as it is considered the norm for couples to send a photograph of the child to their surrogate on major holidays or on the child's birthday, the practice of sending "fuzzy" or out of focus and therefore unrecognizable photographs is a means by which some couples appear to fulfill their agreed-upon post-birth responsibility while disguising the identity of the child.

Nonetheless this surrogate's negative experience in the Drake program did not deter her from later signing up with the Frick program. At the Frick, she received monthly phone calls from the program's psychologist, calls that she felt were somewhat cursory, more a means of "checking up on me than [being] genuinely interested in me." However, she was able to speak with her couple on a weekly basis and consequently described her experience in the Frick program as satisfactory or "okay." When I interviewed her, Lauren was enrolled in the Brookside program, and she rated her experience there as superior to her previous ones.

It is difficult to assess why a woman who had had such a negative first experience, having been subjected to both program and couple abuses in the Drake program, would remain in the program and allow herself to be matched with a second couple rather than quit after being unable to conceive for her first couple, and once the experience was completed, continue to search for another surrogate mother program in which to enroll. Perhaps a partial explanation is that when a surrogate does have a negative experience in a program (most often a closed program), she may nevertheless derive sufficient feelings of specialness from her participation in these programs to make the overall experience seem worthwhile, especially through the attention she derives from her family and friends for having done something so unusual. Though the extent to which the closed programs attempt to confer feelings of specialness upon their surrogates pales in comparison to the efforts of the open programs, being a surrogate in a closed program still confers upon surrogates a feeling of uniqueness by virtue of the fact that they are serving as surrogates, a novelty that allows others to see them as special. And for the surrogate in a closed program, the experience, when compared with her daily routine, is still somewhat exciting and rewarding in spite of its drawbacks. If surrogates were fully informed about the existence of open programs, it seems unlikely that they would choose to enter closed programs. Open programs offer greater rewards in terms of personal satisfaction and fulfillment to their surrogates than do closed programs, whose priority is to cater to their paying client, the couple.

Surrogates who desire to "repeat the program" and the programs that permit them to do so are motivated by a number of different factors. All the programs currently allow surrogates to repeat, and it is clear that programs have little if any incentive to reject a repeat surrogate. Since programs do not view women who wish to become surrogates as deviant, they therefore have no reason to believe that repeating the process is deviant in any way, although, as we have seen, the Brookside psychologist viewed this desire as potentially problematic. Some programs have established upper limits to define what they consider to be unhealthy patterns of repeating surrogacy. For example, the Harper director stated that "two times is the limit; she needs to get gratification elsewhere in her life." The Wick program has had a surrogate repeat the program four times, and the Brookside program accepted Lauren, the surrogate who had been in two different programs prior to undertaking her third surrogate pregnancy with them. As with the other guidelines established by programs, these guidelines are also subject to the whim of the director and may change at any time.

Surrogate programs are for profit, and considering the significant sums of money spent by the larger programs in advertising for surrogates, suitable surrogates are a highly prized commodity, a fact supported by the one-year waiting list at the Brookside program. Unlike the psychologist for the Frick program, who stated that surrogates are a self-selecting group (Chesler 1988), the Brookside director claimed to accept only 5 percent and the Harper director claimed to accept 20 percent of those who apply; other programs fall somewhere within this range. Thus it is not likely that repeat surrogacy will be discouraged by these programs unless adverse publicity causes them to establish new, stricter guidelines on this issue.

In conclusion, Ferree's argument that the definition of work must be expanded to include noneconomic variables is particularly apt in the case of surrogates. Studies have suggested that full-time homemakers experience the "trauma of eventlessness, the absence of stimuli, [and] challenges," and that this "threatens mental well being" (Margolis 1984:246–247). Surrogacy provides women with the excitement and validation that their private roles as mothers and wives do not provide in adequate measure, although surrogates claim to prefer to stay at home. Surrogates attempt to reinforce the boundaries of their traditional roles, as can be seen in the selfless or altruistic idiom they prefer, for example, "to help" an infertile couple, "to share" the experience of parenting, and "to give life." The selfless idiom allows them to achieve their objectives in a nonthreatening way, in a manner that does not challenge the status quo in which women are said to be care givers and nurturers. From the surrogate's perspective, the element of remuneration must be dismissed since it detracts from her motive and places her actions in a less favorable light. In addition, her dismissals of remuneration reinforce the idea that both the child she creates and her gift of that child to the couple are priceless.

In this way surrogacy allows a traditional woman to achieve a certain degree of autonomy, independence, and newfound personhood without threatening her current relationships. The surrogate's decision not to mother the child, a decision that may appear incomprehensible within the context of the values associated with motherhood in American culture, is for her always a given; it provides her with a cathartic experience in which she breaks out of the role that has been a primary one for her, that of mother. In order to break out of this role without threatening her traditional beliefs about sex roles, reproduction, and family and the traditional views of those around her, she must do so within the confines, or parameters, of the female domain of motherhood and reproduction.

Thus, without threatening the structure that constrains her, she creates a small window onto other possible ways of being.

The high number of surrogates who are desirous of repeating their surrogate experience is testimony to the fulfillment and satisfaction they receive from their experiences. The surrogate, through her actions, can be understood to embrace both the traditional and the nontraditional at once. A surrogate participates in reproduction, a traditional sphere of women's work, but is inseminated with the semen of a man other than her spouse, a man with whom she has no emotional relationship or attachment, and she is also parting with a child who is genetically hers (as closely biologically related to her as her own children) or, with gestational surrogacy, creating a new category of motherhood. In this sense, what was conventionally considered an inextricable chain of events linking marriage, intercourse, pregnancy, childbirth, and motherhood has been altered by the advent of surrogacy and other reproductive technologies. The fact that a surrogate becomes pregnant with the intention of parting with the child contradicts the (often biologically deterministic) ways in which women's reproduction has been understood. Surrogates do not want to mother a child; they want instead to be socially rewarded for having made a valuable contribution, made to feel special, and, at least for a short time, made the center of attention for having accomplished something that they consider to be of tremendous value and importance, giving birth to a child.

Fathers and Adoptive Mothers

$\mathcal{T}$HIS CHAPTER, based upon seventeen interviews with individual members of commissioning couples, provides an analysis of the ways in which fathers and adoptive mothers perceive surrogacy. In all cases, the interviewed spouse was asked to supply information about her or his spouse's age, educational background, religion, and income in order to maximize the sample of quantifiable data on couples. On the basis of these interviews, I found that couples initially respond to the idea of surrogacy less readily and less enthusiastically than surrogates. As the following material will reveal, the way in which a couple conceptualizes the viability of surrogate motherhood as a personal remedy to their childlessness is greatly dependent upon where they are on what I refer to as the "fertility continuum." Prior to interviewing at a program and entering into a contract, couples tend to have read about and conducted research into the practice of surrogacy, comparing and evaluating the various surrogate mother programs. My research revealed that during the course of researching programs and eventually contracting with a single program, couples tend to select one of two styles of relating to their surrogate: the "pragmatic" or the "egalitarian."

There is in the literature on surrogate motherhood a paucity of data on couples who elect to have a child with the help of a surrogate mother. As we have seen, surrogate motherhood calls into question traditionally held beliefs concerning the inviolability of the chain of events linking marriage, conception, pregnancy, and parenthood. Researchers have shown only minimal interest in studying the motivations of couples who choose surrogacy as a way to remedy their childlessness. This contrasts with the great degree of interest researchers have exhibited on the subject of the motivations of women who become surrogate mothers. The reason for this paucity of data on couples appears to be twofold. First, the couples' motivation has been viewed, in the debate for and against surrogate motherhood, as relatively uncomplicated, namely, to have a child that is biologically related to at least one member of the couple, in this case, the father. This motivation has been tacitly understood to be consistent with ideas about American kinship, in particular, the emphasis on the primacy of the blood tie. My research confirms that primary motivation. However, the couples' decision to participate in surrogate motherhood is a novel one within American culture, forcing them to devise their own strategies for coming to terms with their surrogate relationship, with some assistance from the programs.

The second and more practical reason why limited data now exist on the couples is the fact that media and researcher access to the couples is somewhat circumscribed. In order to locate and interview couples, one must first gain the confidence and trust of the program directors, which is not always possible. Many of the directors are reluctant to allow their programs to be studied. As I mentioned earlier, the Allen director refused a request to ask her couples if they were willing to participate in this study and the Frick director refused to participate in the study at all. The difficulty of gaining access to couples through the programs is also related to the importance programs place upon their couples' needs and desires. Since the couples are the programs' clients, anything that could potentially jeopardize that relationship is not permitted. Closed programs, in particular, tend to attract individuals who want to minimize their contact with their surrogates, and the entire relationship is consequently shrouded in secrecy.

The following material is based upon interviews with seventeen individual members of couples (eight husbands and nine wives) from the open surrogate mother programs, seven individuals from the Wick program and ten individuals from the Brookside program. Statistics on the actual number of couples who have pursued a surrogate solution to their childlessness are based upon information provided by programs. In 1988 the Office of Technology Assessment concluded that there had been "600 surrogate mother arrangements ... to date" (OTA 1988) in the United States, and that there are approximately 100 arrangements per year (OTA 1988). The director of the Brookside program estimated that there have been between 5,000 and 10,000 surrogate births, the majority of which were private arrangements; however, statistics on the actual number of couples who have pursued a surrogate solution are difficult to obtain because only those arrangements that result in live births are included in the database. Second, many programs simply do not maintain accurate statistical records. The third problem with these estimates is that some program directors tend to inflate the actual number of successful arrangements since the more contracts a program has arranged, the more successful it appears to would-be clients.

At the Brookside program I was given access to master lists of couples and allowed to select from them without restriction. I selected couples from both rural and urban areas and from every major geographical region in the United States, and I was able to interview two European couples, one couple from Britain, whom I met, and one couple from France (in which the husband was American and the wife French), whom I interviewed by telephone, as well. I was also able to include two couples who, unlike the majority of couples, found the costs of surrogacy financially burdensome. I was also allowed to sit in on three three-hour intake interviews at the Brookside program: two with prospective couples and one with a prospective surrogate and her husband.

Because I found that couples choose one of two strategies of relating to their surrogate, either a pragmatic or an egalitarian approach, I have selected individual members of each type to illustrate these differences. Prior to the birth of the child, all the couples follow the instructions of their programs as to the proper way to behave toward their surrogate. Once the child has been born, pragmatists redefine their relationship to their surrogate as one of acquaintanceship, in accordance with program guidelines that suggest that the relationship between couple and surrogate be terminated except for cards and photographs on the child's birthday, and occasional cards and letters during the major holidays. Egalitarians, in contrast, continue to treat their surrogate as a friend, in defiance of the program's guidelines.

All the couples contacted agreed to participate in this study because they wished to assist in developing a more extensive body of data on couples like themselves and they also wished to dispel the negative media stereotypes surrounding surrogacy as a whole, in particular, those concerning couples. These stereotypes tend to characterize the couples (especially the husband) as comprising individuals who, owing to their class privilege, are accustomed to purchasing whatever they desire, and in this instance they wish to buy a baby.[1] In addition to these images of the couple, the wife is often viewed as the pawn of her husband, less involved in the decision to choose surrogacy, and motivated by feelings of inadequacy and guilt because of her infertility. Most of these images were not borne out by my fieldwork with couples, and they were particularly untrue of egalitarians, whose concern for the well-being of their surrogate and evident compassion for her were marked. Nevertheless, the stereotype was of some concern to all of the couples because they would like to see surrogacy become a more socially acceptable remedy to involuntary childlessness so that their children's lives will not be marred by social disapproval.

As Table 3.1 reveals, the couples as a group are upper-middle-income, educated professionals, in their late thirties and early forties. Although

TABLE 3.1 Educational Level and Current Employment of Adoptive Mothers and Fathers

Surrogate Mother Program	Husband's Educational Level	Age	Employment	Annual Income ($)	Wife's Educational Level	Age	Employment	Annual Income ($)
Wick	*Ph.D.	45	Professor	50,000	Ph.D.	n.a.	Psychologist	n.a.
Wick	*M.B.A.	35	Advertising	90,000	H.S.	40	Advertising	30,000
Wick	*B.A.	30	Law Student	n.a.	*B.A.	35	Stock broker	20,000
Wick	*M.A.	44	Engineer	55,000	B.A.	42	Homemaker	n.a.
Wick	J.D.	44	Lawyer	75,000	*J.D.	42	Lawyer	n.a.
Wick	M.B.A.	50	Business	150,000	*B.A.	45	Homemaker	n.a.
Brookside	*B.A.	38	Real Estate	150,000	*B.A.	40	Homemaker	75,000
Brookside	*B.A.	33	Sales Rep.	50,000	3 yrs. college	41	Homemaker	n.a.
Brookside	M.D.	n.a.	Physician	n.a.	*A.A	n.a.	Decorator	15,000
Brookside	Ph.D.	36	Researcher	60,000	*M.A.	33	Nurse	30,000
Brookside	Ph.D.	39	Professor	30,000	*M.A.	42	Teacher, p.t.	30,000
Brookside	*D.D.S.	39	Dentist	180,000	*M.B.A.	40	Executive	80,000
Brookside	B.A.	40	Banker	75,000	*B.A.	40	Architect	25,000
Brookside	*B.A.	43	Artist	85,000	H.S.	40	Bookkeeper	85,000

* Interviewed

n.a. = not available

this information is not reflected in the table, all of the couples in my sample are Caucasian, as are the majority of couples who choose surrogacy. Of the nine adoptive mothers for whom financial data were available, three, or 33 percent, earned less than $30,000 and six, or 67 percent, earned more than $30,000 per year. Six of the eight interviewed husbands (75 percent) and seven out of twelve husbands for whom financial data were available (58 percent) earned $75,000 a year or more. The average combined family income is in excess of $100,000. According to the information available, the average age of wives is 40.4 years, and that of husbands is 35.3 years.[2] A comparison of surrogate and couple statistics reveals pronounced differences in educational background and employment (see Table 2.1) and income level (ranging from $16,000 for unmarried surrogates to $38,700 for family income of married surrogates).

Class Differences

Theorists opposed to surrogate motherhood might cite differences in the class backgrounds of surrogates and couples as yet another reason that surrogate motherhood is problematic. As we have seen, class differences do appear to be present, but it proved to be extremely difficult to persuade informants, either surrogates or couples, to discuss these differences in a forthright manner. Since surrogacy challenges so many of our ideas about "traditional" reproduction, the importance of class differences may have been of diminished significance in the minds of participants. Both surrogates and couples tend to deemphasize those aspects of surrogacy that are controversial, problematic, or that represent a departure from tradition, a strategy that may carry over to the area of class as well.

When couples are questioned about class differences, they tend to gloss over them, referring to their surrogate and her husband as "people," implying a shared sense of humanity, redirecting the focus of their relationship to their commonality. Typically, when questioned about class differences, surrogates also dismiss them as unimportant. One surrogate, however, when questioned about class differences, alluded to the advantages of the couple by emphasizing an area in which she was superior to the mother:

I am fertile and she [the adoptive mother] isn't.

The issue of fertility thus serves as a leveling device for perceived, if unacknowledged, inequities between couples and surrogates. I would suggest, tentatively, that all surrogates view their fertility to some extent as a resource that provides them with a decisive handicap or advantage in their relationship with the couple. From the surrogate's perspective, the couples' material success pales in comparison to the unhappiness their infertility and ensuing state of childlessness create in their lives. They are portrayed by the programs as wonderful people who would make great parents, but it is clear that their happiness hinges upon their ability to have a child. It is interesting in this connection to note that members of Concerned United Birthparents (CUB), like surrogates, describe themselves as individuals who are fertile and who therefore possess "something adoptive parents lack" (Modell 1986:654). Couples, because their relationship to their surrogate is firmly centered on what is lacking in their lives, rather than on their economic, educational, and social privileges, are regarded in the surrogate context as individuals who are unfulfilled and faced with a tragic impediment to the attainment of complete happiness. The issue of infertility thus serves as a pivotal and multifaceted issue in the surrogate arrangement, especially as it pertains to class differences between couple and surrogate.

All the adoptive mothers in this sample had been diagnosed as infertile. The causes of their infertility ranged from the common diagnosis of nonspecified infertility, that is, no discernible cause, to blocked fallopian tubes, to the results of surgery following cancers of reproductive organs. The adoptive mothers had all spent several years attempting to conceive, availing themselves of the most advanced reproductive technologies; many of these medical procedures not only have a relatively low rate of success, but they are also painful, invasive, potentially dangerous and expensive. One adoptive mother, Susan, aged forty-two, who was working on her doctorate and teaching part-time, had a hysterectomy at the age of twenty-seven, was married at thirty-eight, and was still grieving over her inability to have children. She said that she was unable to look at a pregnant woman without crying. She summarized her experience of undergoing infertility treatments before her hysterectomy:

> *I don't know how I went through what I did. It was awful, not only the physical frustration but the humiliation and the emotional pain.*

Tom, aged forty-three, a successful British artist, described the difficult years during which his wife was undergoing infertility treatments:

> *Seventeen years we tried. Nine in vitro attempts. They never proved Patty [wife] was infertile. They took a pint of my blood to inject into her to stop her antibodies from attacking my sperm, but it didn't work.*

Jane, aged forty, an architect, described her years of trying to conceive:

Compared with the stress of infertility, surrogacy was a pie in the sky. My attitude about childbirth is it's a difficult job. When you're infertile for a while it becomes obsessive, it's my vanity. A lot of women don't come to terms with their infertility. I did.

After years of pain, frustration and disappointment, surrogacy was for these couples a final chance to have a healthy infant who was genetically related to at least one member of the couple. The meaning of having children for these and other couples results from the shared cultural ideal described in a national survey as the "desire for love and affection and the feeling of being a family" (Zelizer 1985:4).

Adoption

Approximately 35 percent, or six of the seventeen couples, had attempted or considered adoption. They felt, however, that the adoption process was riddled with problems and in many cases was not able to meet their needs. In 1983, for example, there were 50,000 adoptions but an estimated 2 million couples who wanted to adopt (OTA 1988:1). A major obstacle posed by an adoption solution is the length of the waiting period, which can be as long as five to six years (Kadushin 1980). Because couples usually discover their infertility late in life, their age may constitute a major barrier to "agency-defined desirable limits" (Kuchner and Porcino 1988:25; Deutsch 1983), a phenomenon that has also been noted in Britain among IVF couples (Franklin forthcoming). Years of infertility treatments can also delay the age at which a couple pursues the adoption solution, as can the pattern of delayed childbearing exhibited by these couples. That pattern corresponds to the new life-style in which many individuals prefer to focus on their careers in their twenties and thirties and postpone beginning their own families until later in life when they have achieved a degree of economic and/or professional success.

Regardless of the validity of such adoption agency policies, there are many more couples attempting to adopt than there are available infants, and agencies are therefore in a position to select couples they consider most suitable, based upon their own criteria. An additional barrier in the adoption process is posed by the discriminatory practices of some private adoption agencies. Many private adoption agencies are affiliated with the Catholic Church (as a consequence of its opposition to the use of all forms of contraceptives as well as abortion), and these agencies prohibit non-Catholic couples, for example, Protestants and Jews, from adopting.

Another difficulty posed by adoption is cost. In states that allow private adoption—California, for instance, allows only private adoption—the financial costs can be as high as $50,000 (Blank 1990:75), more than the cost of surrogacy. One of the most emotionally difficult and frustrating aspects of private adoption is that after a couple has negotiated all the contractual procedures, and in some cases paid the living expenses of a woman for nine months (the amount paid is determined by the individual woman's circumstances), up to 50 percent of birth mothers change their minds, often at the last minute, and decide to keep the child. Researchers have concluded that there is an underlying assumption held by many social workers that the biological mother should, irrespective of her actual chances for successful parenting, raise the child (Tizard 1977:238) and that this belief may influence the outcome of cases such as these. The results of this policy are that these children often spend time in and out of institutions and foster care for years until they are often too old to be successfully adopted (Tizard 1977).

An additional problem with adoption is the shortage of healthy white infants, a shortage that may have been created by the legalization of abortion, a reduction in the social stigma associated with single motherhood (Tizard 1977; Snowden, Mitchell, and Snowden 1983), the availability of more effective birth control methods, and the increased availability of financial support services for birth parents (Modell 1986). When questioned whether couples who insist on adopting only a white infant are practicing a form of racism, surrogate directors often point out, as the director of the Allen program did at an American Civil Liberties Union (ACLU) meeting, that this is a social problem for which everyone shares responsibility:

> It is not, nor should it be the sole responsibility of the infertile to remedy this particular societal problem. Every one of you in the audience should ask yourselves why you haven't adopted one of these children. You don't have to be infertile to adopt.

As Tizard, a psychologist, stated, we as a society place "great value on children as individuals," but "we accept very limited responsibility for any but our [own] biological children" (Tizard 1977:2). The further complexity of the issue is revealed in the recommendation of the Association of Black Social Workers that minority children not be placed in white homes. These are just a few of the difficulties that the adoption solution poses for infertile couples. Many couples who eventually choose surrogacy have either studied adoption and rejected it as a solution or have attempted to adopt and been unsuccessful.

Surrogacy also offers the infertile many benefits that adoption does not. Specifically, with surrogacy, a couple can select the woman who will be the child's biological mother and become very familiar with her personality, her likes and dislikes, her worldview and physical attributes. The knowledge that a woman is drug- and alcohol-free throughout the pregnancy, for example, which is of increasing importance as more is learned about fetal alcohol syndrome (Dorris 1989) and HIV transmission, is information that cannot always be gained with adoption. Even with the recent increase in gestational surrogacy, where the physical attributes of the surrogate are of minimal importance, the couple still is able to gain access to information about the physical and psychological history of the surrogate. At the Brookside program, for example, both surrogates and couples are provided with a sheet explaining the importance of genetic screening and are required to fill out a questionnaire on hereditary illnesses (see Appendix G). In the case of adoption, the identity of and history of the father of the child often remain unknown, whereas with surrogacy the biological father also serves as the child's social father.

Another positive feature of surrogacy is that many women who decide to put their children up for adoption agonize over that decision, sometimes for their entire lives, whereas with surrogacy the pregnancy is not (as it usually is in adoption) an unwanted one. It has been suggested that adoption is made possible by a "sub-class of relatively powerless adults" who are producing but unable to raise children (Tizard 1977:2), an opinion shared by organizations such as CUB that contend that social workers and the legal system "regulate the marketing of children from the powerless to the rich and powerful" (Modell 1986:654).[3] With surrogacy the surrogate's pregnancy is a desired one, and the surrogate does not, in the majority of cases, agonize over her decision to part with the child because it was her intention to do so from the beginning.

Couples' Initial Impressions of Surrogacy: The Fertility Continuum

There are, as I have attempted to illustrate, numerous factors that eventually culminate in a couple's decision to choose surrogacy over other options. However, a couple's degree of receptivity to the idea of surrogacy can usually be found to be in direct correlation to where they are situated on the fertility continuum: from not having been able to conceive a child after one year of unprotected intercourse (the medical definition of infertility) to having attempted many of the available reproductive technologies without success. Specifically, if a couple still retains a degree of optimism that they may conceive through reproductive technologies, surrogacy is not held to be a suitable remedy to their childlessness. Although there are couples who respond to surrogacy as most surrogates do, that is, with immediate acceptance of the idea, many more couples do not, and it may take them years to view surrogacy as a potential solution to their own infertility, although they may consider it an acceptable option for others. Even when a couple's first response to surrogacy as an abstract concept is positive, they usually do not consider it a personal solution or they continue to believe that it requires further research and study.

Of the individuals interviewed as to their first impressions of surrogacy, twelve (seven wives and five husbands) viewed it positively; five (two wives and three husbands) viewed it negatively; and two (wives) viewed it neutrally or could not recall their initial impressions (seventeen people were interviewed, but occasionally a spouse provided information about a noninterviewed partner). The process of accepting surrogacy as a personal option is, in most cases, a slow one that includes gradual shifts in perception. Couples (ten individuals, or four wives and six husbands) tended on the whole either to have read about surrogacy or to have learned of it at infertility conferences; three individuals (wives) learned of it through the media, two individuals (one wife and one husband) did not recall how they heard of it, and two individuals (husbands) heard about surrogacy from a friend. Surrogates, by contrast, usually learned about surrogacy through a television program or were told about it by a friend or their husband; surrogates usually saw it immediately in a positive light and wished to participate personally in it. They also tended to enroll in the first surrogate program they contacted, unlike the couples I interviewed, all of which researched several of the programs before making a final decision. What follows are some of the retrospective accounts of initial impressions of surrogate motherhood given by individual members of couples.

Susan, the forty-two-year-old doctoral candidate, described her first impression of the idea of surrogacy:

> *I first read about it in Ohio in 1974 and I remembered [that] my impressions were positive but I didn't see it in a personal light. I thought of it as a great thing for a woman to do for someone else and I didn't have any moral objections to it.*

Don, aged thirty-five, who has an M.B.A. and is employed in marketing, also considered surrogacy first as an abstract idea rather than as a personal solution:

> *We first read magazine articles about it in the press five years or so ago. Both of us are very liberal and we said that's interesting to know it's going on. I never thought of it as personal though.*

Karen, aged forty, who has an M.B.A. and is an executive in a research and development firm, recalled wanting to study surrogacy further:

I read about it seven or eight years ago in a magazine article. It sounded like a good option and one we should investigate so we went to the library.

David, who is thirty-nine and a dentist, remembered initially being disconcerted by the idea of surrogacy:

You're scared of the unknown and these are uncharted grounds.

Patricia, aged forty-two, an attorney, was concerned that the surrogate would want to keep the baby:

I first learned of it either through the Mary Beth Whitehead story or when I was referred to the Wick program through a resource group [fertility group] because I was interested in IVF. My first impressions were that it was a good compromise between adoption and my desire to become pregnant. But I had a fear of a Whitehead repeat.

James, aged thirty, a law student, remembered feeling uneasy about the idea of surrogacy:

We were really apprehensive when we first heard about it. I first learned about it when I was looking through the yellow pages under adoption and called the Wick program by mistake. She explained what it was. We decided to explore other options because surrogacy cost a lot of money.

Many couples who were initially opposed to surrogacy as a personal solution to their childlessness later experienced what can be understood as a gradual reevaluation of surrogacy. This occurred as their frustration with infertility treatments and the adoption process increased.

Tom described the effects of seventeen years of infertility on his view of surrogacy:

At first I couldn't believe it. It comes on slowly in incremental steps. So much is invested in it [to have a child], it becomes a way of life. It's been a major factor for the last ten years. The more you invest the more determined you become. ... We needed some type of success.

Bill, aged thirty-three, who is employed in the sales field, described his shift of perception:

The first time I heard of surrogacy I was against it. Then I heard the director of the Frick program speak at a RESOLVE meeting [infertility group].

Even after surrogacy was accepted as a viable solution by these couples, some resistance to the idea often remained and occasionally even continued throughout the experience. In spite of the fact that there appears to be a correlation between a couple's position on the fertility continuum and their response to surrogacy, it is not unusual to find couples who have essentially abandoned all hope of being able to conceive but who continue to find the idea of surrogacy unsuitable. Such confusion about or resistance to surrogacy may be traced, at least in part, to the American kinship belief that a family is created through the process in which the wife is transformed into the genetrix and the husband into the genitor, as each makes her or his equal genetic contribution to the creation of the child. It is interesting to note that husbands, in particular, frequently expressed initial resistance to the idea of surrogacy even after their wives proposed it as a solution, because husbands felt that surrogacy was not in their wives' best interest. Many husbands reported experiencing a "protective" feeling toward their wives and concern that they might feel "left out." The husbands believed that surrogacy might provide a less than "fair" solution since the child would not be genetically "half her child." The scientifically promulgated view that a child receives 50 percent of its genetic material from its mother and 50 percent from its father has great salience for important American cultural valuations about equity, equality, and fairness. To create a child that is genetically related only to one parent in the context of a current relationship (unlike the case with stepchildren) produces a sense of imbalance or inequity.

Ed, a forty-five-year-old college professor, expressed the following fairly representative degree of concern about his wife's role:

I wondered if my wife would feel [that] she wasn't in on it. I felt really weird about another woman having my child.

Tom, whose wife Patty had undergone nine unsuccessful in vitro attempts while the cause of her infertility continued to remain unspecified, said:

We would have preferred to adopt than have surrogacy but we were too old. Initially I favored adoption because we would have started out equally. She [his wife] was pro-surrogacy and I was anti-surrogacy.

Bill, who changed his mind about surrogacy after hearing the Frick director speak on the subject, initially wanted to continue with infertility treatments rather than pursue a surrogate solution:

My initial reaction was [that] we should still try the infertility treatments. I felt [that] if we couldn't conceive we'd adopt. We didn't want six years of waiting for adoption. Lucille [his wife] felt it would be easier to bond with the baby knowing it was mine.

Research on IVF populations has revealed that wives and husbands who are pursuing IVF treatments seek equal involvement in the process, reasoning that together they should have "either all or no biological continuity with a child" (Modell 1989:134). For this reason, they view adoption as a more desirable solution than either donor insemination (DI) or surrogacy (Modell 1989). They tend to view surrogacy and donor insemination as disruptive of the "cultural fabric of reproduction" and to believe that IVF, unlike surrogacy and donor insemination, "uphold[s] cultural values about family, sexuality" (Modell 1989:135). It is clear that IVF participants still retain the hope that a pregnancy and subsequent birth are possible, unlike couples participating in surrogacy, the majority of whom have already unsuccessfully availed themselves for many years of IVF and other reproductive technologies. Unlike IVF couples, those who choose surrogacy have lost their "cultural faith" in the idea that "persistence in the pursuit of a goal ultimately pays off" (Sandelowski 1991:41) in the form of a baby that is biologically related to both of them. Couples who espouse these viewpoints are understood to do so because they lack personal knowledge of the difficulties associated with the adoption process and retain belief in the idea that biogenetic relatedness is unacceptable unless it is shared by both parents. Findings derived from studies of IVF couples and of couples who have chosen a surrogate solution indicate that there is much to be learned through an analysis of individual attitudes and beliefs concerning reproductive technologies, especially when attention is paid to where they are with respect to the fertility continuum.

Program Selection

Once couples have overcome any initial reluctance to consider surrogacy an option, usually in response to intensifying frustration over the failure of infertility treatments and increasing familiarity with the subject of surrogacy, they then begin to research the various programs in earnest. As mentioned earlier, couples often conduct research by reading articles and books on the subject of surrogate motherhood,[4] telephoning programs to request program brochures, and making appointments to meet with directors of programs. Then, based upon a program's or director's approach, they choose the program that best suits their preferences and needs. (See Appendix H for sample telephone intake form that is filled out by a member of the staff, at most programs, when a couple calls to inquire about surrogacy. See Appendix I for a sample prospective parents questionnaire that couples are asked to fill out.)

Although I was unable to interview couples who had selected and contracted with closed programs, I did interview four couples who had researched closed programs and rejected them in favor of an open program. The primary reason they chose an open program over a closed program was that in their opinion closed programs exploit, or "use," surrogates, a practice that these couples considered "unacceptable." The decision to choose an open program was thus made in spite of the fact that closed programs place fewer demands and restrictions upon couples. The following examples illustrate the kinds of concerns couples expressed about the closed programs they researched.

Susan, who chose an open program and has since developed a very close relationship with her surrogate, Betty, had been trying since the birth of her daughter to "sort out" what kind of post-birth relationship she should have with Betty. Her husband was more conservative than she was and more cautious about the type of relationship she and Betty should continue to maintain. Susan described her initial feelings about program selection with respect to the degree of surrogate contact:

> We looked into the Smith [closed] and Brookside [open] programs.
> In the Brookside program there is a lot more contact with the
> surrogate. In the Smith program you exchange letters with your
> surrogate but the only time you meet is in court [to finalize custody
> and adoption]. My husband was a little nervous about going with
> the Brookside program because of all the contact, but now we are
> both glad we did. After all, we are all in this together.

Don and his wife, who had initially read about surrogacy in a magazine article and considered it interesting but not "personal," later faced a diagnosis of nonspecified infertility (the wife's). They tried in vitro fertilization once, unsuccessfully, and she visited numerous fertility specialists, none of whom was able to offer them the promise of success with existing treatments or procedures. They then began researching surrogacy programs in earnest. As Don described the process:

We bought New Conceptions *[Andrews 1984a] and called all the centers and received letters from them and spoke with the director of the Grey program [closed program] who wasn't very positive and chose the Wick program [open program] because she keeps it small and personal. The Brookside program [open program] felt more like a machine.*

Richard, a forty-three-year-old computer engineer, and his wife tried to have a child for "seven or eight years." They underwent IVF procedures four times at a cost of $4,000 to $5,000 per attempt, and the cause of Richard's wife's infertility remained nonspecified. According to Richard, the years of infertility created a "heavy emotional strain and it was very hard on her." Richard emphasized the relational component in the surrogacy process, something that he felt couples should be more aware of when choosing a program:

Be careful about the program … it's a major thing. You can't approach it as a business arrangement; there is significant emotional involvement.

It is not difficult to understand why some couples choose closed programs since, as we have seen, little is required of them. Moreover, many of the difficulties that can arise in open programs, such as having to avoid discussing political and emotionally charged topics with one's surrogate or having to terminate one's relationship with one's surrogate after the child is born, are avoided in the closed programs.

Couples often make their final decision about which of the programs to select after having visited the program offices and met with the director. Tom, who was initially uninterested in surrogacy although his wife favored pursuing that course of action, recalled that after his wife sent for and received an information packet from the Brookside program, he continued to urge caution, saying:

Let's take this one step at a time. We'll visit the center and see him [Brookside director] on his own ground. We'll know if it's a sham or a harebrained scheme or not.

At the Brookside program, for example, a couple first meets with the director, at which time legal questions and concerns are reviewed. They then meet with the resident psychologist, who explains to them the process of selecting surrogates, answers their questions about that process, and asks them specific questions about why they are pursuing a surrogate solution, especially what type of surrogate they are looking for, or how they would describe their "wish list." Afterward, the medical coordinator explains to them the details of the medical tests all surrogates receive, how the insemination process takes place, and so on. Finally, they meet with an administrative coordinator, whose job it is to explain the details of insurance coverage, management of their finances, and other administrative details. At the Brookside program, the couple is not permitted to sign a contract immediately; they are asked to take the contract home, review it, and then make an informed decision. The entire process takes three to three and one-half hours.

Once a couple has selected an open program, they begin the process of being matched with and introduced to a prospective surrogate. After an initial face-to-face meeting, couples and surrogates are free to accept or reject one another. It should be noted that introductions in the open programs are made only between individuals who the psychologist or director believes will prove compatible, based upon variables such as phenotype, personality, hobbies, and interests. It is unclear whether couples and surrogates are more, less, or equally discriminating when selecting each other, but I did learn of a case in which a couple and surrogate were accidentally introduced, that is, they had not been matched by the psychologist. In this case the couple found the surrogate suitable, but she rejected them as her couple. I would theorize that couples, because of the years of frustration over their infertility, may be more inclined than the surrogate to expedite the process and might thus be more willing to accept any surrogate whom the program has already screened and identified as compatible.

Interestingly enough, all the programs in this study reported a marked and unexpected increase in the number of inquiries from both prospective couples and surrogates[5] in direct response to media coverage of the Baby M case. What is more, according to industry personnel with whom I spoke, no negative impact was experienced by the Frick program (which had arranged the contract between Mary Beth Whitehead and the Sterns). Perhaps publicity of any type increases the public's familiarity with the availability of surrogacy and reduces uncertainty, one of the principal barriers to be overcome by couples.

Pragmatists and Egalitarians

My study revealed that in the open programs one can discern two distinct types of couples once they have been matched with surrogates and have begun to interact with them.[6] The first type of couple I call "pragmatists," or individuals who adhere rather rigidly to the program's guidelines, in particular, to the amount of time to be spent socializing with one's surrogate and to the recommendation to terminate the relationship once the child is born. Eight of the seventeen individuals interviewed were pragmatists.

All programs recommend eventual termination or severe attenuation of the surrogate-couple relationship, but the recommendation remains a suggested course of action rather than a directive. This policy cannot be enforced, although clearly some program directors, for example, the Allen director, place more emphasis on the importance of terminating the relationship than others, and that appears to influence the outcome of this prescribed course of action.[7] In lieu of the formerly close and friendly relationship, pragmatist couples send their surrogates greeting cards for the major holidays, usually enclosing a photograph of the child along with a short note listing the child's recent achievements and/or experiences. The recommended post-birth relationship can best be described as one of acquaintanceship, and this limited degree of contact is considered appropriate and acceptable and is encouraged by all programs.

The following are examples of pragmatist relationships. David, the thirty-nine-year-old dentist, and his wife tried to conceive for several years until she was at last diagnosed as having early menopause and it was determined that she had "no ovarian tissue left." The couple made plans to adopt a child and received word of the approval of their application from the adoption agency at the same time as they entered into a contract with a surrogate mother program. Two months after their surrogate child was born, they were offered a child through the adoption agency. They were, however, unable to accept it because of financial constraints and the fact that they already had an infant to care for. In the following passage, David was discussing his early concerns about close contact with and eventual attenuation of contact with their surrogate in terms that suggest that he might have been more suited for a closed than an open program:

> I wondered how secretive we should be, at the beginning. We kept our address and our phone number secret at first, then we changed. Some people even use fake names! We met our surrogate in the city and would contact her through the center. After she was pregnant, we visited her twice at their home. The option is you can get as close or impersonal as you want. My main concern was how to end the relationship. ... Our surrogate was very friendly and called to see how the baby was. She supported my wife. I was scared during the pregnancy.[8]

Barbara was forty-five years old and a full-time homemaker. She tried to have a child for six years before she was diagnosed with blocked fallo-

pian tubes and later with early menopause. She explained her feelings
about her post-birth relationship with her surrogate:

> *Our contact with our surrogate is basically letters and holiday*
> *cards. We are there if something traumatic happens to her. But I*
> *couldn't handle living in the same town as her because when you*
> *meet it should be by choice. She [surrogate] told me she would call*
> *and perhaps visit, but then it was put off. Life is complicated*
> *enough and it's expected that they [surrogates] will lead their own*
> *lives. I didn't tell anyone locally until a month before she [daughter]*
> *was born because I didn't want to hear other people's fears.*

When Patricia, the forty-two-year-old attorney, was diagnosed with
nonspecified infertility, she and her husband initially attempted in vitro
fertilization but decided that at "$8,ooo per attempt it was too expen-
sive." Here she described how she envisioned her post-birth relationship to her surrogate, illustrating the pragmatic couples' extensive reli-
ance on program policies to guide their behavior:

> *We didn't want any continuity to the relationship. After the baby is*
> *born we will send pictures. [The director] makes this part of the*
> *program very strong ... when the baby is born you go your separate*
> *ways.*

There are, I would suggest, several explanations for couples' acceptance of the programs' directive to terminate the relationship with their
surrogate. First, it allows couples to avoid any difficulties that continua-
tion of the relationship might pose. Although programs recommend that
the child be informed of its origins, the timing of that announcement is
left up to the couples. Pragmatist couples fear that if they continue close
contact with the surrogate, the child will have to be told about the circumstances of her/his birth, perhaps sooner than they had planned. For
example, Susan expressed concern that if she continued an active relationship with their surrogate, Betty, she would be forced to explain her
surrogate's biological link to the child earlier than she and her husband
thought was appropriate. Second, unless the relationship is terminated
early on, some couples fear that the surrogate will eventually come to
know the child intimately and perhaps grow to love her/him and wish to
keep her/him. As we have seen, the primary fear of all couples during
the pregnancy period is that the surrogate will change her mind and
want to keep the child; continued close contact after the birth might, in
some couples, trigger renewed fear of this prospect.

The other type of couple, which I call "egalitarians," displayed a much
different attitude toward their surrogate. Nine of the seventeen individu-

als interviewed could be defined as "egalitarians," people who viewed their surrogates in what can be described as a warm and caring, sometimes loving, way rather than in a fearful or suspicious way. For example, those who live out of state talk with their surrogates on the telephone every few months after the birth. In one case, a couple's stated objective from the outset was to locate a surrogate to whom they could relate as peers, thereby increasing the likelihood of forming and continuing to maintain a close relationship with her and her husband after the birth of the child, which they did. What follows are examples of egalitarian attitudes. Bill, who changed his mind about surrogacy after hearing the Frick director speak at an infertility meeting, had been struggling with the issue of infertility for years. He and his wife had been trying for over a year to have a child when she was diagnosed with blocked fallopian tubes. She then underwent four hours of tubal surgery to correct the problem, and she had to recuperate in bed for the next three months. Two other surgical procedures were attempted as well as hormone therapy, all to no avail. Bill's discussion of his feelings about their post-birth relationship to their surrogate bore the marks of the egalitarian approach, a relaxed and flexible attitude:

> *I would have no objection to it [relationship with their surrogate]. If it was more comfortable for Jamie [surrogate] to break ties, that would be okay too. We have a really good rapport with Jamie and Chris [surrogate's husband] and send her a birthday gift every year. We tiptoed around during the pregnancy and we still do it. Part of the joy of doing this for her is knowing that she did something for us. Harriet [program psychologist] didn't encourage continued contact.*

Susan's description of her concerns about maintaining a close relationship to her surrogate was also less fearful than that expressed by pragmatist couples:

> *The type of relationship I have with Betty [surrogate], I am sorting it out. I am comfortable with maintaining a relationship but to what extent we want our daughter to have contact with her I don't know. Part of me wants it completely open so that Chris [daughter] knows her as Betty and another part of me says that I don't want to make a mistake. My husband is a little more skeptical than me.*

Lucille, thirty-eight, a health-care provider, described the warm post-birth relationship she developed and maintained with their surrogate. She exhibited the degree of concern for the surrogate's feelings typical of egalitarians:

*We look at our surrogate and her husband as friends, we send her
pictures. We look forward to seeing them, we don't want to put
pressure on them [surrogate and husband]. While there are
educational differences, as people we are very similar.*

Richard, who cautioned other couples against approaching surrogacy
as a business arrangement (exhibiting egalitarian concern about feelings and emotions rather than rules and policies), discussed his post-
birth relationship to their surrogate in these terms:

*We knew we wanted to maintain the relationship with Brian's
[son's] biological mother all along. She is a lot like Kathy [wife]. I
don't want to say thank-you very much and good-bye; we met two
very nice people.*

The overriding concern of egalitarians is the perceived immorality of
"using" someone, and it is important to them not to behave in an uncaring fashion or to be viewed by society as uncaring people who engaged
in a financial transaction without regard for or acknowledgment of the
emotional component in the agreement. One of their greatest concerns
is that their surrogate not be treated as a means to an end. They believe
that the best way to accomplish this is to continue to maintain a relationship with the surrogate after the birth. The continued relationship is
thus understood by the couples as evidence of or a testament to their in-
tegrity.

Pragmatists, however, do not offer any explanation for their severance
of the relationship with the surrogate except to reiterate that that is what
programs recommend and that termination is something that they and
their surrogate agreed upon from the outset. I would argue that a program's recommendation to terminate the relationship between surrogate and couple after the child has been born serves to attract couples
who might otherwise have been candidates for a closed program. These
couples demonstrate the agreed-upon degree of appreciation for their
surrogate throughout the period of insemination and pregnancy, no
more and no less, yet the knowledge that they will terminate the relationship once the child is born allows them to overcome any apprehen-
sion they may experience initially about close contact with their surrogate. The recommendation to terminate the relationship once the child
is born serves to assuage any residual fear or guilt about the prospect of
discontinuing close contact with the woman who is the biological
mother of their child. The very fact that they are participating in an open
program reinforces pragmatists' belief that they are treating their surrogates well. They select open programs because they view the anony-

mous way in which surrogates are treated in closed programs as unacceptable and unethical, even though they tend to also view some aspects of closed programs as more desirable.

One issue that unites both egalitarians and pragmatists is their shared concern about how society views surrogacy and how societal attitudes will affect their children's lives in the future. The primary concern of both pragmatists and egalitarians is how best to explain their child's surrogate origins to her or him and at what age.

In conclusion, although the surrogate process may be, from the couple's perspective, motivated by an active desire to have a child that is biologically related to at least one member of the couple, a couple's process of decisionmaking about whether to pursue a surrogate remedy to their childlessness is slow and gradual, affected by a number of other factors. These include the age at which they first recognize and finally come to accept their infertility; the restrictions, waiting periods, and financial expenses they encounter in the adoption process; and the availability of healthy white infants. Moreover, there are numerous issues raised by surrogacy, such as how it can be incorporated into the traditional definitions of family.

Many of the couple's motivations and the steps and phases of the process of choosing surrogacy are formed in response to culturally constructed ideas about American kinship (to be discussed in greater detail in Chapter 4), but aside from these shared concerns, a plethora of decisions must be made, attitudes reexamined, social barriers overcome, and ideas about conception, reproduction, and family reformulated. In these respects, a couple's decision to pursue a surrogate remedy to their childlessness is, in the final analysis, a carefully considered and far from unidimensional one. Ultimately, the speed with which a couples' decision to participate in surrogate motherhood will be made can be gauged by studying their relationship to the fertility continuum, specifically, that if they still retain any hope of conception, they will, with a few rare exceptions, continue to reject the idea of surrogacy. Even after they have abandoned all hope of conception and have seriously begun to contemplate adoption, they may continue to reject surrogacy. For those couples who attempt adoption, it is only after they have recognized that it will not provide the solution they seek that they begin to entertain the possibility of surrogate motherhood. As Chapter 4 reveals, the success of the entire surrogacy process is dependent upon the ways in which surrogates, couples, and programs are able to engage and employ the tenets of American kinship ideology to meet their needs.

4

Surrogate Motherhood and
American Kinship

*At the bright center is the individual. And radiating out from him or her
is the family, the essential unit of closeness and of love. For it's the family
that communicates to our children, to the twenty-first century, our
culture, our religious faith, our traditions and history.*

—George Bush, Republican presidential nomination acceptance speech, 1989

*B*EGINNING WITH the earliest theorists such as Lewis Henry Morgan, Emile Durkheim, and Alfred Radcliffe-Brown and continuing with the work of contemporary theorists such as David Schneider, Marilyn Strathern, Jane Collier, Rayna Rapp, and Sylvia Yanagisako, kinship theory has been considered one of the principal areas of study in anthropology. Nevertheless, precise definitions as to what constitutes kinship have been hotly contested throughout the history of the discipline. In view of surrogate motherhood and other medical advances in the area of assisted reproduction, changes in kinship ideology were declared by some to be inevitable,[1] yet in spite of these advances, the central symbols of American kinship ideology have remained unchanged. Assisted reproduction and surrogate motherhood, in particular, introduce numerous questions and issues about the meaning of kinship for participants. As we have seen, programs, surrogates, and couples highlight those aspects of surrogacy that are most consistent with American kinship ideology, deemphasizing those aspects that are not congruent with this ideology. Thus, although the means of achieving relatedness may have changed, the rigorous emphasis on the family and on the biogenetic basis of American kinship remains essentially unchanged.

It can be said, then, that surrogate motherhood is consistent with American kinship ideology in the sense that biogenetic relatedness is achieved (for the father) and that the birth of the child transforms the couple into a family. But although biogenetic relatedness is one of the most important aspects of the surrogate arrangement and is its goal, biogenetic relatedness must be deemphasized during the insemination process and throughout the pregnancy in order to highlight, or place in the foreground, those elements of the relationship that are held to be consonant with American kinship ideology and with "traditional" reproduction. In the interest of achieving these goals, motherhood is reconceptualized as being composed of two separable components: social motherhood and biological motherhood. Social motherhood is, in this configuration, defined as comprising intentionality, choice, and nurturance[2] and is regarded as more important than biological motherhood. This view serves two important functions. First, it deemphasizes the blood tie between the surrogate and the child; and second, it deemphasizes the surrogate's tie to the father vis-à-vis the child. Thus the traditional symbol of unity between the surrogate and the father, created by the child, is circumvented, along with any lingering (if unfounded) connotations of adultery. As we will see, once the child is born and the relationship between the couple and surrogate is effectively terminated, certain elements of the kinship system are permitted to reassert themselves. This can happen only after those kinship elements (e.g., the primacy of the father/child blood tie and the symbolic unity of the couple as it is expressed through or represented by the child) no longer pose a threat to the relationship between the couple and surrogate. As the following analysis will reveal, surrogate motherhood, in spite of its potentially disruptive elements, is being accommodated by the participants under the rubric of preexisting kinship structures and ideology.

Historically there have been three profound shifts in the Western conceptualization of the categories of conception, reproduction, and parenthood. The first shift occurred in response to the separation of intercourse from reproduction through birth control (Snowden, Mitchell, and Snowden 1983); Andrews suggested that this change might have paved the way for surrogacy in the 1980s (1984a:xiii). The second shift occurred in response to the fragmentation of the unity of reproduction wherein it has become possible for pregnancy to occur without necessarily having been "preceded by sexual intercourse" (Snowden, Mitchell, and Snowden 1983:5). The third shift occurred in response to further advances in reproductive medicine wherein the "organic unity of fetus and mother can no longer be assumed" (Martin 1987:20). Not until the emergence of reproductive medicine did the fragmentation of motherhood become a possibility; and now, what was once the "single figure of the mother is dispersed among several potential figures, as the functions of maternal procreation—aspects of her physical parenthood—become dispersed" (Strathern 1991:32).

With the advent of gestational surrogacy, surrogate motherhood, however, not only separates reproduction from sexual intercourse, but it also separates motherhood from pregnancy, creating three discernible categories of motherhood where there was previously only one. These three categories created by surrogacy are (1) the biological mother, the woman who contributes the ovum (the woman whom we have traditionally assumed to be the "real mother"); (2) the gestational mother, the woman who gestates the embryo but bears no genetic relationship to the child; and (3) the social mother, the woman who nurtures the child.

Two of these categories can be readily accounted for in American kinship ideology: The biological mother occupies a position similar to that of a woman who places her child up for adoption, although the intentionality is clearly different in each case. A surrogate intentionally conceives a child for the purpose of surrendering that child to its biological father and his wife; she thus creates a "wanted child," who is, however, wanted by someone other than herself. The social mother is similar to an adoptive mother in that her relationship to the child exists not in nature, but in law alone (Schneider 1968). However, the intentionality of the participants makes social motherhood, in the case of surrogacy, different from adoption in that the child is fathered by the adoptive mother's husband during their current relationship, not in a prior relationship, as in the case of a stepchild.

The gestational mother's position is less clear, for her relationship to the child does not occur strictly either in nature or in law, that is, it is neither "code for conduct" nor "substance" (Schneider 1968), at least as that relationship has tended to be defined. How then is the gestational mother to be accounted for? Should a gestational surrogate's maternal rights be "modeled on the law of paternity, where proof of genetic parentage establishes ... parentage, or ... on the nine month experience of pregnancy as establishing the preponderant interest of ... parentage" (Hull 1990b:152)?

Some theorists have advanced the argument that the definition of biological motherhood might well be expanded to include the entire process of pregnancy because, they argue, the fetus would not be able to develop or survive without the womb provided by the gestational mother. The authors of both the Glover and the Warnock reports are of the opinion that the gestational mother has a "biological link" to the child (Glover 1990; Warnock 1984). It should be noted, however, that the decision to place gestational surrogacy within the realm of "nature," as both the Glover and the Warnock reports do, runs counter to the logic of the motivations expressed by women who choose gestational surrogacy over traditional surrogacy—to carry a child that is "not related" to her—as well as the intentionality of the commissioning couples. It should be added that to call a gestational surrogate, a woman who bears no genetic relationship to the child, the "mother" contradicts the importance of the blood tie as articulated in Euro-American kinship ideology. Gestation, once a biological given, has, in view of the changes wrought by reproductive technologies, become "culturally ambiguous" (Strathern 1992a:27), but whether Euro-American cultural definitions of biogenetic relatedness will be modified by the phenomenon of gestational surrogacy remains unclear. Will those definitions, in the British case, come to emphasize biological relatedness rather than biogenetic relatedness so as to account for the fact that the gestational surrogate provides the physiological/biological environment for the embryo/fetus/child, as the Warnock report has attempted to do? Will the issue be circumvented in the United States through an emphasis on the genetic component of parenthood, characterizing the gestational surrogate as the vessel through which another couple's child is born, as is currently the case among gestational surrogates and commissioning couples?[3]

Both Britain's Warnock Report and the Australian Waller Committee concluded that "when a child is born to a woman following donation of another's egg the woman giving birth should, for all purposes, be regarded in law as the mother of that child" (Shalev 1989:117). For some theorists, the question posed by this decision is why the law should be differentially applied to a gestational surrogate when a sperm donor, for example, bears neither legal rights nor legal duties toward the child and is not regarded as the father of that child (Shalev 1989:117).[4]

The New Jersey Supreme Court's (NJSC) decision concerning the Baby M case illustrates some of the problems inherent not only with surrogate motherhood but with the surrogate contract as well. For example, although the court awarded custody to the father (William Stern), it also awarded the surrogate, the biological mother (Mary Beth Whitehead), visitation rights. That decision relied upon the basic tenets of American kinship, namely, the enduring solidarity created by the blood tie, rather than upon the original intentionality of the parties or on the terms of their contractual agreement.[5] Legal decisions surrounding surrogate motherhood have as a general rule tended to mirror kinship ideology, as the Baby M case demonstrates. The contract was, however, declared "unenforceable" since the court reasoned that a woman could not make a binding pre-birth contract because she would not know how she felt until after the birth. Some legal experts concluded that the decision was a biologically deterministic one, that the "refusal to acknowledge the legal validity of surrogacy agreements implies that women are not competent, by virtue of their biological sex, to act as rational moral agents regarding their reproductive actions" (Shalev 1989:11).

The decision of the NJSC to give the surrogate visitation rights is understood by some to be a reiteration of essentialist ideas about gender: "The biological argument, thus perverted, has been so compelling, so strong, and so oppressive to women for so long, that feminists should invoke it (if at all) only with supreme caution, and with total consciousness of its cultural history, and therefore, of its potential consequences. Otherwise, the danger that the argument may be turned against them is obvious and grave" (Dolgin 1990:103).

Furthermore, it can be reasoned that the law contradicts itself when it states that a sperm donor can legally decide to disavow any moral, legal, or social rights to a fetus before its birth but a surrogate cannot do the same (Shalev 1989). It is important to bear in mind that one of the principal reasons the surrogate solution is chosen by the commissioning couples is precisely that it provides a partial biogenetic remedy (in the case of traditional surrogacy) or a complete biogenetic remedy to childlessness (in the case of gestational surrogacy).

In June 1993, the California Supreme Court upheld the decisions of both the lower court and the court of appeals with respect to the surrogate contract. In *Anna Johnson v. Mark and Crispina Calvert,* Case #SO 23721, the supreme court ruled that gestational surrogacy contracts are enforceable and not at odds with prevailing public policy. Specifically, Justice Edward Penelli wrote: "It is not the role of the judiciary to inhibit the use of reproductive technology when the Legislature has not seen fit to do so. Any such effort would raise serious questions in light of the fundamental nature of the rights of procreation and privacy."

This dispersing, or fragmentation, of motherhood as a by-product of reproductive technologies has resulted in the "claims of one kind of biological mother against other kinds of biological and nonbiological mothers" (Strathern 1991:32). In the California case cited, the gestational surrogate and the commissioning couple both filed custody suits. Under California law, both of the women could, however, claim maternal rights: Johnson, by virtue of being the woman who gave birth to the child; and Calvert, who donated the ovum, because she is the child's genetic mother. In rendering their decision, however, the court in a sense circumvented this issue of relatedness and focused instead upon the intent of the parties as the ultimate and decisive factor in determining parenthood. In addition the court concluded that compensation to the surrogate is understood not as the NJSC ruled—as baby selling or selling the rights to her child—but rather as payment for her services, for gestation and labor, not for relinquishing her parental rights. As we will see, the issue of intent, specifically, the intentionality of the participants, is of

fundamental significance to them. There is little doubt that the California Supreme Court's decision will have far-reaching implications for
commercial surrogate motherhood in the United States.[6]

The fact that the surrogate allows herself to be intentionally inseminated for the purpose of conceiving, bearing, and parting with a child
calls for a reevaluation of biologically deterministic models, which have
tended to inform cultural definitions and expectations about the perceived bond between mother and fetus and mother and child. Surrogate
motherhood thus calls for a reconsideration of the inviolability of the
chain of events between marriage, procreation, and motherhood.[7]

What follows is an analysis of the strategies utilized by both couples
and surrogates to emphasize those aspects of surrogate motherhood
that are most consistent with American kinship ideology, notably, the
importance of family, biogenetic relatedness, and nurturance. I will also
analyze the ways that the couples and surrogates skirt those aspects that
depart from the basic tenets, in particular, how participants in the surrogate mother process have attempted to modify definitions of family, kinship, and relatedness in order to resolve the numerous tensions and am-
biguities created by surrogacy within the context of the American
kinship system. Included for the purposes of comparison is a longitudi-
nal British study, covering the years from 1940 to 1980, of couples choosing donor insemination, or DI (where the semen of a man other than the
husband is used for insemination), a process that poses many of the
same dilemmas experienced by participants in the surrogacy arrangement. DI places the husband, who is not the child's biological father, in
the same structural position as surrogacy places the wife and is thus the
closest available parallel to surrogacy.[8]

Surrogate Motherhood and Donor Insemination

Surrogacy and DI pose several dilemmas for the participants in that
both require that a married couple who would under "traditional" circumstances procreate on their own behalf (within their relationship) go
outside of their marriage and enlist the services of a third party in order
to conceive a child. Both methods are invoked because of the infertility
of one partner. In surrogacy arrangements the couple employs the services of a woman to whom they usually bear no relationship in order to
conceive a child who will be biologically related to the husband. Couples
who choose surrogacy and couples who choose DI offer the same explanation for their choice: to have a child who is genetically related to at
least one member of the couple (their other choices being to remain
childless or to adopt a child who bears no genetic relationship to either
of them). This motivation mirrors the emphasis on the primacy and im-

portance of the blood tie in Euro-American kinship. However, third-party reproduction and the genetic inequity of the arrangement (the fact that only one of them will be genetically linked to the child) require that various strategies be devised to correct for the perceived imbalance in the relationship.

Initially, as we have seen, many husbands view surrogacy as undesirable and express instead a preference for continuing to pursue infertility treatments or adopting a child. They feel that adoption (in which the child is not genetically related to either wife or husband) will allow them to "start out equally." DI wives are similarly aware that their husbands "might have reason to feel excluded and jealous" (Snowden, Mitchell, and Snowden 1983:85). Husbands involved in surrogate arrangements and wives involved in DI are thus cognizant of the inequity of a relationship in which one partner will be considered the "real," that is, the biological, parent whereas the other partner will be considered a parent in law only, not in both nature and law.

DI couples and surrogate couples employ various strategies to remedy these problems. If one considers the widely held belief that a married couple without children "does not quite make a family" (Schneider 1968:33) and the belief that having children is a "natural and normal thing to do" (Snowden, Mitchell, and Snowden 1983:126), it is not, in the final analysis, difficult to understand what motivates infertile couples to stretch the limits of Euro-American kinship in order to have a child. What unites these couples and solidifies their marriage is their quest for a child.[9]

Some researchers have concluded that "couples without children. ... are likely to have unsatisfied needs for giving and receiving affection and for making enduring relationships" (Tizard 1977:2). Thus, even though surrogacy and donor insemination may be regarded as being at symbolic and structural odds with traditional reproduction, the very fact of their childlessness has already made these couples feel "inadequate and stigmatized" (Snowden, Mitchell, and Snowden 1983:125; Miall 1985; Lasker and Borg 1987; Sandelowski and Jones 1986); therefore they are ready to employ nontraditional methods to attain traditional ends. The importance of being able to have children in the lives of these couples is illustrated by the degree of adversity they undergo, first in response to their infertility and childlessness, and later because of their willingness to partake of and grapple with the stigma associated with assisted reproduction.

The definition of a family as two adults with a child or children remains a "powerful normative influence, despite the increasing prevalence of alternative life choices" (Kuchner and Porcino 1988:262). With DI, the stigma is specifically associated with the need to employ an extramarital solution in order to acquire donor semen, which casts doubt upon the husband's "manhood" (Snowden, Mitchell, and Snowden 1983:128): There has long been an association between male infertility and impotence, though the two are not necessarily linked (Humphrey and Humphrey 1988). Sex-role stereotyping, which assigns to males the role of "initiators," thus defining infertile men as "powerless" or passive, and as unable to undertake successfully that which is considered "appropriate masculine behavior" (Snowden, Mitchell, and Snowden 1983:132), exacerbates the situation. The lack of medical knowledge and effective treatment programs (Snowden, Mitchell, and Snowden 1983:121) further contributes to the stigma attaching to male infertility. Although sex-role stereotyping may heighten the stigma associated with male infertility, it may also lessen the stigma associated with female infertility in that the characteristics associated with infertility, such as powerlessness, are more readily considered part of the spectrum of "appropriate feminine behavior" (Snowden, Mitchell, and Snowden 1983:142). This theory is supported in part by the fact that many women with infertile husbands who participate in DI allow others to believe that it is they rather than their husbands who are infertile (Snowden, Mitchell, and Snowden 1983:132). This is a protective strategy to shield men from potential embarrassment or ridicule. Perhaps even more important, it is also a means by which the wife compensates for the fact that the resultant child will be biologically related to her and not to her husband. In addition, when a DI wife feigns infertility, she is aware that any stigma associated with her infertility will be removed once she becomes pregnant, that her infertility can thus be understood as a transient form of infertility, whereas his would not be so understood.

The medical profession as well often routinely shifts the onus of infertility onto the wife, as revealed in an American Medical Association (AMA) statement to the 1979 Ethics Advisory Board to the Department of Health, Education, and Welfare: DI was described as a procedure that "enabled women to bear children and overcome natural impediments to conception and frustration of a basic biological drive" (as quoted in Shalev 1989:107). That statement quite clearly resorts to biologically deterministic and gender-specific ideas, as no mention is made of the fact that DI also allows an infertile man to become a father, albeit a social one. Throughout the history of donor insemination, physicians have paid particular attention to the "psychology of the childless woman," reasoning that a woman's "full psychic role hinged on motherhood, whereas a man's reproductive propensity was secondary to other spheres of social activity" (Shalev 1989:66–67).

For couples who participate in the surrogacy process, the husband's "manhood" is not in question since he is not infertile; it is the wife who bears the brunt of the infertility stigma. It appears that the pain these women experience is related to feelings of inadequacy, loss, and guilt—of not being able to, as several women expressed it, "give my husband a child," which again is understood to result from the cultural significance of children in the Euro-American definition of family. Interestingly enough, the feelings expressed by English men who have been diagnosed as infertile are not dissimilar to the feelings expressed by American women who have been diagnosed as infertile; for example, one infertile man stated that he felt "incomplete" (Snowden, Mitchell, and Snowden 1983:135).

But there is another dimension of infertility that affects women and men differentially not only on a personal level but also on a social and economic one. The director of the Allen program, a psychologist with a practice primarily composed of infertile couples, reported that infertility and the prospect of childlessness affected men and women differentially, with women experiencing a greater degree of psychological difficulty. In one study of couples experiencing infertility, 50 percent of the women and 15 percent of the men viewed their infertility as the most stressful of life experiences (Freeman et al. 1985). The Allen director attributed this difference to the widely held belief that a man's self-image is more closely related to his career, and also that he derives more satisfaction from his career than does a woman. The Allen director viewed this as resulting from biological differences between women and men, namely, the importance of pregnancy and birth in a woman's life cycle. Her theory, like many of the theories that assess the differential impact of infertility on women and men, resorts to biologically deterministic models and tends to give short shrift to the social, cultural, and economic factors that affect the ways in which women and men come to define themselves.

Although there are in fact real differences in the effect that infertility produces on women and men (the subject is beyond the scope of this study), there is no doubt that the importance of children for both DI couples and couples choosing surrogacy can be understood to unite them in a profound way (although the wife's pain is often emphasized, quite likely because it is considered more culturally appropriate to the female role). The following quotations have been excerpted from letters written by couples choosing surrogacy to their state legislature in response to a then-pending bill to criminalize commercial surrogacy:

Dear Legislature:
As the male half of an infertile couple, I can testify to the misery and anguish that not being able to bear a child in the conventional way brings.

In a short letter such as this, it's not possible to demonstrate the pain and suffering that infertility causes. Words can't describe the feelings you have when you see the most important person in your life, your wife, break down and cry at the sight of a pregnant woman. Worse yet, to be awakened from a deep sleep by the crying of your spouse, because she feels that she has failed you by not providing the most essential and basic of human needs—a child. (Husband with an infertile wife, 1989)

Dear Legislature:
As an infertile woman the pain, suffering, and anguish I have suffered over the years has been almost unbearable. Everyone around me has babies, all my friends, all my relatives and I can't have one. Every aspect of life revolves around babies, whether I am watching TV, reading magazines, books, walking down the street; everything and everywhere I am reminded that I cannot do the most natural thing, bear a child. The cruelty of the situation has at times almost destroyed me.

Last year for the very first time I found hope. With an IVF surrogate I could have a biological child of my own. The joy this has brought me is indescribable. With the help of a surrogate I could at last give my husband what he rightfully deserves, a biological baby of our own. (Infertile woman, 1989)

Dear Legislature:
Take a moment and think of the things you value most. For most of us our family comes close to the top of this list. Infertile couples know the emptiness and pain of a life without a family of their own. (Infertile couple, 1989)

Dear Legislature:
Please don't deny us our biological lineage. Surrogate parenting is our only hope to preserve it. We are law-abiding citizens and all we want is the opportunity to have a baby. If we are unable to conceive a biological child, thousands of years of family evolution and lineage will end. It's not fair to deny us this most fundamental and essential need.

Also please don't deny surrogate mothers the opportunity to give the ultimate gift. Life.

Yes, the alternative is adoption. And yes, we will take advantage of this wonderful possibility. It's just that the very core of our existence is tied up in having a biological child. Please don't deny us this chance. (Infertile couple, 1989)

Children, of course, also represent different things to different individuals; they may be viewed as a "public proclamation of sexual maturity," "family continuity," a way to resolve "issues of one's identity in relationship to parents," a way to have "someone to love who will love in return," as providing a "purpose for work and life," or as someone who will care for you later in life (Kuchner and Porcino 1988:262–263). For some couples the need to bear a biological child is related to the desire to perpetuate their "biological lineage"; as we saw, one of these couples stated that without surrogacy "thousands of years of family evolution and lineage will end." The belief that the couple without children does not properly constitute a family is underscored by the statement that "infertile couples know the emptiness and pain of a life without a family of their own." Children are thus symbolically representative of the love and unity of a couple (Schneider 1968), and the quest to have children can be understood as these couples' effort to provide their marriage with the one crucial element that is perceived to be missing.

With DI, the social contradiction stems from the fact that the child has two fathers, and with surrogacy, the child has two mothers. DI fathers resolve this dilemma by "rationally concluding that the role of genitor is unimportant compared with that of the nurturing father" (Snowden, Mitchell, and Snowden 1983:141). These men thus stress the "social reality. ... and minimize the genetic reality" (Snowden, Mitchell, and Snowden 1983:141) and in this way emphasize the importance of nurture over nature. They also receive reinforcement for this position once the child begins (as it undoubtedly will) to exhibit certain mannerisms and characteristics identical with or similar to their own. This phenomenon prompted one—not unrepresentative—father to speculate that perhaps the child was after all his own biological child. As he expressed it, "I keep thinking perhaps he is mine" (Snowden, Mitchell, and Snowden 1983:141). It may in fact be less problematic for DI fathers to conclude that nurture is more important than biology since "whether men like to admit it or not," there "has always been. ... a certain degree of paternal uncertainty" (Caplan 1990:100).

Prior to the emergence of reproductive technologies, the "figure of the mother provided a natural model for the social construction of the 'natural' facts" (Strathern 1991:5). In the past, motherhood was always understood as a unified experience, combining social and biological aspects into one, unlike fatherhood, in which the father acquired a "double identity"; but with the separation of the social and biological elements, motherhood has, in the context of surrogacy, also taken on this double identity (Strathern 1991:4–5). Surrogate motherhood thus produces the "maternal counterpart to the double identity of the father, certain in one mode and uncertain in another" (Strathern 1991:4).

Fathers, Surrogates, and Adoptive Mothers

Other parallels between surrogacy and DI, aside from the fact that both
seek to remedy childlessness, include the fact that both arrangements
transgress the "sexual norms of ... society" in that a "child is being conceived outside the marriage bond and this carries with it connotations
of adultery and illegitimacy" (Snowden, Mitchell, and Snowden
1983:127). IVF candidates often view surrogacy and donor insemination
as problematic and undesirable because both methods introduce a third
party, a "blood tie to a third person and, by implication, extramarital
sex," whereas IVF does not symbolically "separate having children from
sex" (Modell 1989:134). Thus IVF couples are more likely to attempt adoption than to enlist the services of a surrogate or a sperm donor (Modell
1989:134). IVF leaves intact the "conventional experiences of pregnancy,
birth and parenthood" (Modell 1989:134), and participants view IVF as
"natural" in that the "pregnancy and birth [are] themselves natural processes ... comparable to traditional reproduction" (Sandelowski 1991:38).
IVF is understood by the participants as a reproductive technology that
falls safely "within the boundaries of natural conception" (Sandelowski
1991:39). The association of surrogate motherhood with adultery is illustrated by one Brookside program surrogate's comment: "The general
public think I went to bed with the father; people consider this adultery
because of lack of knowledge. The public needs to be educated" (*San Diego Tribune*, 1986).

As discussed in Chapter 3, studies on surrogate motherhood have for
the most part tended to characterize the couples' motivations as fairly
straightforward: to have a child that is biologically related to at least one
member of the couple (Glover 1990). Although genetic relatedness is
clearly one of the primary motivations for couples choosing surrogate
motherhood, it is a simplification to assert this without also acknowl-
edging the extent to which surrogacy contradicts a number of cultural
norms and taking note of the ensuing difficulties encountered by couples, not the least of which is that it involves procreation outside of marriage. Despite the simplicity of the initial motivation of the couple, the
fact that this can only be achieved by employing the services of a woman
other than the husband's wife raises a host of dilemmas. Fathers and
adoptive mothers each develop different strategies to resolve the problems posed by surrogate motherhood. Their disparate concerns stem
not only from the biogenetic relationship the father bears to the child
and the adoptive mother's lack of such a relationship but also from the
differential pressure of having to negotiate the landscape of this novel
terrain. Wives and husbands who pursue a surrogate remedy to their
childlessness must therefore resolve certain of the inherent tensions

that the surrogate arrangement creates; and although they are each faced with different issues, the strategies of both are designed to deemphasize those aspects of the surrogate relationship that are at odds with the basic tenets of American kinship ideology.

For the father, the principal dilemma posed by surrogate motherhood is that a woman other than his wife will be the "mother" of his child. The following quotes by fathers illustrate the not inconsiderable amount of ambiguity created by surrogate motherhood. They also reveal the degree to which the programs' attempts sometimes fall short of their desired goals and objectives, if only temporarily, when those objectives collide with some of the central features of American kinship ideology. For example, Tom, who shared seventeen years of infertility with his wife and who was initially opposed to surrogacy, said:

Yes, the whole thing was at first rather strange. I thought to myself, here she [surrogate] is carrying my baby. Isn't she supposed to be my wife?

Ed, a forty-five-year-old professor who was initially concerned about the exploitation of surrogates by programs and couples, explained:

I felt weird about another woman carrying my child, but as we all got to know one another, it didn't seem weird; it seemed strangely comfortable after a while.

Richard, the software engineer who had wanted to find a surrogate that he and his wife would like as friends, said:

Seeing Jane [the surrogate] in him [his son], it's literally a part of herself she gave, that's fairly profound. I developed an appreciation of the magnitude of what she did and the inappropriateness of approaching this as a business relationship. It didn't seem like such a big thing initially for another woman to carry my baby, a little awkward in not knowing how to relate to her and not wanting to interfere with her relationship with her husband. But after Tommy was born I can see Jane in his appearance and I had a feeling it was a strange thing we did not to have a relationship with Jane. But it's wearing off and I'm not struck so much with [the idea that] I've got a piece of Jane here.

The concern and confusion of husbands are reflected in questions such as Tom's, "Isn't she supposed to be my wife?" Their ambivalence underscores the continued symbolic centrality of sexual intercourse and procreation in American kinship, both of which continue to symbolize unity and love (Schneider 1968). The father's relationship to the surrogate, although it is strictly noncoital, is altered by the fact that it produces what was always the product of a sexual union until the recent past, namely, a child. Feelings of "awkwardness" and very practical concerns over how to relate to both the surrogate and the surrogate's husband stem from the fact that the father/surrogate relationship may be considered a form of adultery by others. In one case, a father, James, when speaking about the surrogate's husband, expressed his confusion in the following manner:

> *I really empathize with Mark [the surrogate's husband]. I really don't understand how he could let his wife have another man's child. I know I couldn't. It's not just her [surrogate] you are affecting.*

Richard expressed a similar feeling:

> *I felt ... a little awkward in not ... wanting to interfere with her relationship with her husband.*

For some, the surrogate mother is understood less as a "substitute mother" than as a "substitute spouse, who carries a child for a man whose wife is infertile" (Robertson 1990:157), and for others the surrogate serves the husband as a "symbolic sexual replacement" (Glover 1990:67). As we have seen, even though the connection between sexual intercourse and reproduction has been severed by technology, the two remain linked.

Although the relationship between the husband and the surrogate is devoid of romantic love and sexual intercourse, it nevertheless produces a child, and therefore that relationship collects those symbolic associations. As one father, Richard, when reflecting upon the surrogate's role, said:

> *I realize now that what Jane gave was a part of herself, that's fairly profound.*

Thus the child serves as a point of connection between the surrogate and the husband in the same way it would normally provide a bridge between the wife and husband. Richard's statement reflects the enduring quality of the blood tie, a relationship that can never be severed in American kinship ideology because blood is "culturally defined as being an objective fact of nature" (Schneider 1968:24). It is therefore impossible for a person to have an ex-blood relative, an ex-mother, ex-father, or ex-sibling (Schneider 1968:24). Besides, of course, the fact that blood is understood as "a shared bodily substance," there is also the "connection between ideas of blood ... and ideas of genes" (Strathern and Franklin

1993:20). Fathers cannot help but acknowledge this connection and comment upon it, and neither can surrogates and adoptive mothers (as we will see).

In addition to concerns about their relationship to the surrogate vis-à-vis the child, fathers are aware that the child produced from their surrogate union is biologically theirs and that their wives bear no such tie. The husband gains his inclusivity in the surrogate arrangement through his biological contribution: He is the genitor and the pater, but it is the surrogate, not his wife, who is the genetrix. As previously discussed, it is not uncommon for husbands to express concern over the possibility that their wives may feel "excluded" from this relationship. Thus surrogacy blurs, obscures, and in some sense redefines normative ideas about spousal relationships and their corresponding boundaries because couples have chosen to seek an extra-conjugal solution to facilitate the conception of their child. On the one hand, the father must grapple with confusion about his relationship to their surrogate, and on the other, the adoptive mother must resolve her feelings of inadequacy connected with being infertile. She must also come to terms with the fact that unlike her husband and her surrogate, she shares no biological relationship to the child.

One of the primary strategies employed by couples and surrogates to address these concerns is to deemphasize the husband's relationship to the surrogate. That is because it is the surrogate/father relationship that raises the specter of adultery, or more accurately of temporary polyandry and temporary polygyny. Couples also downplay the significance of the father's biological link to the child. They focus instead upon the relationship or bond that develops between the adoptive mother and the surrogate mother, and this emphasis is facilitated in several ways. Surrogate and adoptive mother view each other's participation in the process and the ensuing bond that develops between them as central to the process.

As noted earlier, one of the most frequently stated motivations offered by women who are considering becoming surrogates is a desire to help an infertile woman have a child, and the relationship that develops between the surrogate and the adoptive mother in open programs is often very close. Surrogates commonly express what can be described as a woman-focused view, a view that they often elaborate upon in their descriptions of their relationship to the adoptive mothers. For example, one surrogate, Mary, whose adoptive mother gave her a heart-shaped necklace to commemorate the birth of the child, said:

I feel a sisterhood to all women of the world. I am doing this for her, looking to see her holding the baby.

Celeste, who compared herself and other surrogates to "people who want to climb Mt. Everest," said:

The whole miracle of birth would be lost if she [the adoptive mother] wasn't there. If women don't experience birth or their children being born, they would be alienated and would be breeders.

These quotes reveal a strong belief on the part of surrogates that their primary and very crucial task is to provide an infertile women with a child. The adoptive mother and father of the child attempt to resolve the inherent tensions created by surrogacy, in particular, the extent to which it rearranges boundaries, sometimes blurring boundaries between pregnancy and motherhood, genetic relatedness and affectional bonds. Meanwhile, the surrogate's role in achieving these goals is, as we have seen, essential.

From the perspective of both the surrogate and the adoptive mother, it is the surrogate's procreative role and the relationship that develops between surrogate and adoptive mother that make the surrogacy arrangement "special." Women, surrogates reason, would be "alienated" if their role in reproduction and the surrogacy process were viewed as secondary to the procreative role of the father; in such a situation, women would be reduced to "breeders" and motherhood rendered profane. This position mirrors and provides a response to anti-surrogacy theories, which tend to view surrogate motherhood and the other forms of commodification of life as creating a class of breeders. By focusing upon her relationship to the adoptive mother, in particular, to the idea that she is giving the adoptive mother a child, the surrogate shifts the emphasis away from her relationship to the father vis-à-vis the child and from the perception that she will be "giving the baby away." Her relationship with the adoptive mother places the surrogate's actions in a more socially acceptable light. It is interesting to note that this bond reestablishes the unity of the experience of birth by joining or uniting the two woman in their efforts and purpose.

Reproduction is characterized by both surrogates and adoptive mothers as "women's business." An additional reason that both the surrogate and the adoptive mother focus on reproduction as the domain of women is that their relationship serves to deemphasize the technological or impersonal elements of surrogacy while highlighting the human element; it also provides a counterpoint to the belief that surrogate motherhood creates in surrogates a sense of alienation from their own bodies, their own pregnancies, and the children they produce. The symbiotic terms used by both surrogates and adoptive mothers to refer to their relationship are of particular interest. Here again, just as mother-hood is described by surrogates and adoptive mothers as being composed of two roles or parts, social and biological, a sense of self or identity is here represented as also able to be shared. As one adoptive mother, Lucy, a nurse, expressed the relationship:

> *She [the surrogate] represented that part of me that couldn't have a child.*

Celeste, a surrogate, summed up the feeling shared by many surrogates when she stated:

> *She [the adoptive mother] was emotionally pregnant and* I was just physically pregnant. *[Emphasis mine]*

One surrogate described her adoptive mother as being "every bit as pregnant as I was," conveying the sense of shared pregnancy or pregnancy by proxy. Thus pregnancy, like motherhood, is redefined as composed of parts or elements that can be separated and shared by women. When pregnancy and birth are defined as women's business, the father's role is intentionally demoted to a secondary position in the relational triangle. In the interest of assisting this process, the surrogate consistently devalues her own biological contribution and link to the child. In this way, participants focus upon the folk theory of reproduction, which is made possible by the fact that even though in the realm of scientific knowledge, women are acknowledged to be co-creators, "in Europe and America, the knowledge that women are ... co-creators ... has not been encompassed symbolically. Symbols change slowly and the two levels of discourse are hardly ever brought into conjunction" (Delaney 1986:509). In the "dominant folk theory of procreation in the West," paternity in particular has been defined as the "power to create and engender life" (Delaney 1986:510), whereas maternity has come to mean "giving nurturance and giving birth" (Delaney 1986:495). Surrogates therefore emphasize the importance of nurturance and consistently define that aspect of motherhood as a choice that one can either elect to make or elect not to make. The emphasis on nurturance is readily embraced by the surrogate and adoptive mother since "one of the central notions in the modern American construct of the family is that of nurturance" (Collier, Rosaldo, and Yanagisako 1982:34).

One of the most pronounced differences between DI and surrogacy is that DI allows the wife to experience pregnancy while also allowing her husband to be involved in the process from the moment of conception, whereas with surrogacy it is the surrogate who experiences the pregnancy firsthand in that she is "genetically, physically, psychologically and socially involved in the creation and development of the growing child in a way that no male semen donor ever is" (Snowden. Mitchell, and Snowden 1983:17). As Chapter 2 demonstrates, surrogates dismiss or devalue their own biological contribution in order to emphasize the importance of the social, or the nurturant, role played by the adoptive mother. The desire and ability of surrogates and adoptive mothers to separate social motherhood from biological motherhood is understood to be a reworking of the nature/culture dichotomy.

One of the primary strategies employed by the adoptive mother in order to resolve her lack of genetic relatedness to the child is her use of the idea of intentionality. One adoptive mother (Cybil, who is quoted below) described it as conception in the heart, that is, the belief that in the final analysis it was her desire to have a child that brought the surrogate arrangement into being and therefore produced a child. Since the adoptive mother is incapable of giving biological birth, both the adoptive mother and the surrogate focus not on biological relatedness, not on biological birth, and not on the scientific model of women as co-creators, but rather on the idea of intentionality. This position is reinforced by adoptive mothers, as the following quote from Cybil, a full-time mother, reveals:

> Ann is my baby, she was conceived in my heart before she was conceived in Lisa's body.

By saying that the child was "conceived in my heart," the adoptive mother was focusing upon her own mythical conception of the child rather than the genetrix role played by the surrogate, reasoning that her role took precedence over the surrogate's genetrix role since it was her desire for a child that facilitated the surrogate's pregnancy. Motherhood is thus redefined as an important social role in order to avoid the problematic aspect of the surrogate's biogenetic relationship to the child and the adoptive mother's lack of such a link.

The adoptive mother's position is strengthened by the surrogate who dissociates herself from her pregnancy and from the child by echoing her sentiments, for example, "If it wasn't for this couple, I wouldn't be pregnant," or "It's their baby," or "She was every bit as pregnant as I was." By focusing on the mythical conception or on the amount of love they are able to bestow upon the child, adoptive mothers are able to view their participation in the process as essential. The words of an adoptive mother, Susan, illustrate this belief that the child was created by love:

> Someday my unborn child will know that he or she was created from the very special love of three people.

This idea of intentionality or "choice" is of great importance to surrogates, whose use of the term suggests that they may have been influenced by feminist arguments that a woman has the right to choose what to do with her body, in particular, to make her own decisions with respect to sexual relations, birth control, or abortion. In any case, surrogates believe that motherhood is composed of two separable components: the biological process, conception, pregnancy, and delivery; and the social process, intentionality, love, and nurturance. They reason that a woman can choose to nurture, that is, to accept the role of social mother, or can reject that role. The surrogate's reasons for articulating this are twofold: This emphasis on social mothering helps the adoptive mother in that it allows her to fully experience her mythical conception and her pseudo-pregnancy; and it benefits the surrogate by eliminating any suggestion of illegitimacy and adultery and in this way normalizes the situation from her perspective as well. When we consider that the surrogate is conceiving a child for another couple, outside of her own marriage, we can see that a surrogate's efforts to deny that the child is hers cast her actions in a less stigmatizing light for herself, her husband, and her family. In addition, the surrogate is being paid by the couple to forfeit the child; it would be at odds with the goal of making the experience a positive and fulfilling one for the couple if she were to call attention to her biological relationship to the child or to emphasize her bond with the father. The decision on the part of the surrogate to intentionally conceive a child that she will not mother is, in American culture, anathema to cultural definitions of motherhood. However, by focusing on nurturance as a choice, surrogates and adoptive mothers highlight one of the most acceptable and central cultural embodiments of motherhood and thus shift the focus away from the anomalous quality of the surrogate's actions, her decision to "give her baby away." Surrogates go to great lengths to define nurturance and to highlight its importance, as illustrated by their pronouncements about the specialness of the children they are creating.[10]

The bond that develops between the surrogate and the adoptive mother is necessary for two reasons: It merges the adoptive mother and surrogate into one in order to maintain the unity of experience (or erase boundaries), and it also establishes and maintains boundaries as needed between the surrogate and the father. The majority of surrogates are married (85 percent), as are the majority of couples who engage the services of a surrogate (98 percent). Thus, if the surrogate were to focus her affections and attention on the father rather than the wife, thereby forming a primary attachment and bond with him, she would threaten not only her own marriage but also the couple's marriage. The surrogate therefore focuses upon the adoptive mother and the adoptive mother focuses upon the surrogate in order to avert this potential problem by anticipating and circumventing it. What surrogates, couples, and programs attempt to create is a new sense of order and appropriate relations and boundaries by directing their attention to the sanctity of motherhood as illustrated by the surrogate and adoptive mother bond. Celeste, a surrogate, expressed this idea of shared motherhood and the special relational bond it creates:

> *Mother's Day is going to be special to both of us, we are kind of like sisters.*

The way in which surrogates and adoptive mothers interact can also be seen as an extension of women's roles as the sustainers of social connections, since traditionally "women ... maintain the primary bonds with relatives" (Farber 1971:74; Di Leonardi 1987).

Once the adoptive mother and surrogate have bonded with each other, forming an emotional attachment, two things are accomplished. First, the focus of the relational triangle is shifted away from the surrogate and the father and onto the adoptive mother's new role as someone who is experiencing what I call a "pseudo-pregnancy." This pseudo-pregnancy also allows the adoptive mother to begin to bond with the child while it is in utero. The idea of a pseudo-pregnancy is reinforced by her attendance at doctor's appointments, obstetrical exams, checkups, birthing classes, and related appointments. (It should be noted that although the pseudo-pregnancy usually remains just that, a role-playing imaginary construct, it can lead to difficulties such as those described in the case of the adoptive mother who was simulating her own pregnancy, with plans to allow others to believe that the child was her own biological child.) The pseudo-pregnancy of the adoptive mother thus affords her access into the dyad between her husband and the surrogate not only by transforming the dyad into a triad but also by designating the adoptive mother as the central player.

Although the adoptive mother's pseudo-pregnancy and emotional conception of the child results in many personal rewards for her, it also serves to obscure any lingering connotations of adultery and illegitimacy. Besides fulfilling the adoptive mother's needs to feel included in the triad, the pseudo-pregnancy provides her husband an opportunity to return his focus to his wife's role (as wife and mother). This minimizes for him the confusion created by the fact that the surrogate is carrying his child and is literally "the mother of his child." The child, of course, remains a symbol of unity, a reminder of the husband's and surrogate's noncoital, yet reproductive, union.

The adoptive mother's entry into the dyad through emotionality and role-playing serves to normalize the relationship and to neutralize any remaining ambivalence created by the surrogacy arrangement. Her role thus mitigates the confusion or fear that her husband may be experiencing. It also serves to lessen the centrality and importance of his biological contribution and his biological link to their surrogate vis-à-vis the child. When Cybil, an adoptive mother, said, for example, "Ann is my baby, she was conceived in my heart before she was conceived in Lisa's [the surrogate's] body," she was reiterating and emphasizing the importance of the child's emotional conception. Without that conception (or desire for a child), there would in fact be no child: thus the emphasis placed upon its being a "wanted child." In this sense, the husband's role is a biological/genetic one and the adoptive mother's role is an emotional one. Although I do not intend to suggest that there is no emotional attachment on the father's part, it should be noted that his emotionality originates in and is predicated upon his biological role and contribution. Just as the adoptive mother views the child as the product of her emotional conception, the surrogate focuses upon the adoptive mother's desire for the child so that although the adoptive mother's husband may have facilitated the creation of the child, his role is reduced to that of a secondary figure, a situation that is less threatening and more comfortable for all parties concerned.

All the participants in the surrogate motherhood arrangement de-emphasize the importance of biological relatedness as it pertains to women and emphasize motherhood as nurturance so that the adoptive mother's inability to give birth, or her inability to become a genetrix, to become both wife and mother, is made to seem insignificant. The adoptive mother's situation is reformulated so that she is not only a wife in that she has a sexual relationship with her husband but she is also, through surrogacy, a mother because her desire for a child brought that child into existence and because she nurtures the child.

One case in which programs were unsuccessful in their attempts to restructure the bonds between participants offers an illustration of the sometimes tenuous nature of the surrogacy triad and the importance of maintaining the appropriate boundaries within it. One of the fathers interviewed said that he developed a closer relationship to their surrogate than did his wife.

In this case, the fact that the father believed he was closer than his wife to their surrogate (though it should be noted his wife thought that she was closer to their surrogate) reveals what can occur when the adoptive mother is not firmly established as a central figure. During the course of the interview, Bruce, a thirty-eight-year-old real-estate broker, who considered surrogacy his "salvation," said:

I would be prepared to pay her [surrogate] another fee so that she would not have a child for someone else. It's something so special, to do it for one couple, and if she did it for another couple, she would be too much of a baby machine.

He then added:

You [interviewer] didn't ask me, but I wouldn't do it with another surrogate.

Bruce's description of his relationship to his surrogate could be characterized as spouselike in that he alluded to issues of fidelity and commitment. His willingness to pay his surrogate not to have a child for another infertile couple suggests that if she were to do so, he would consider her action a form of betrayal similar to adultery. The fact that Bruce would not wish to have a child with another surrogate implies a pledge of fidelity of the kind involved in a marriage vow, a pledge that he would like to take and have his surrogate take as well and for which he would be willing to remunerate her. He also appeared to suggest that his surrogate's reputation was somehow connected to his own when he said that if she were to have another child for a different couple, she would become "too much of a baby machine." Although surrogacy does in fact separate sexual intercourse from conception and pregnancy from motherhood, there remains, as Bruce's remarks suggest, the biological tie established between the father and the surrogate through the birth of the child.

For some adoptive mothers, however, the importance of the blood tie, with all of its attendant symbolic meanings, cannot be completely resolved through the mythic conception (pseudo-pregnancy) or through the reassuring knowledge that the child will know only the adoptive mother as its mother. One adoptive mother, Melissa, who was initially apprehensive, or "scared," about surrogacy and who had undergone four unsuccessful in vitro attempts, stated the problem in this way:

I think of him [child] as Joe's side of the family. I wish he had some traits of my family. I'll always feel that way.

The fact that Melissa is not able to see herself in the child although she is able to identify her husband's and his family's genetic "traits" in the child intensifies her feeling of exclusion and reminds her that she does not have a biogenetic tie to the child, that her relationship exists solely in law and not in both nature and in law, as it does for her husband. Thus, in spite of the emphasis placed by programs, couples, and surrogates on nurturance, the primacy of the blood relationship in American culture and the idea that it creates a "state of almost mystical commonality and identity" (Schneider 1968:25) remains a forceful influence.

Another adoptive mother, Karen, the executive who went to the library to research surrogacy, expressed her feelings this way:

There are times when I see my husband with him and I'm a little sad because they are carbon copies and I know he can't see me in him.

Although the motivation to pursue a surrogate solution to childlessness is always determined to an extent by the desire to attain biogenetic relatedness, in the final analysis, the attainment of that biogenetic link "simultaneously promotes the severance of that link for other individuals" (Overall 1987:150), most notably for the adoptive mother (and, with DI, for the adoptive father). The lingering and resurgent importance of that biogenetic link once the child has been born is illustrated by the following quote by Susan, an adoptive mother:

There are times, many times, I think who is this child? I still have moments, I flash on Betty [the surrogate], she is a significant part of Chris's [the child's] life.

Such statements reflect the belief that it is impossible for a blood relative, in this case, the surrogate, to become an ex-mother, in spite of the efforts of the programs to facilitate the demise of that relationship, and to alter the couple's and surrogate's perceptions about what relatedness means.

The ideal of having a child who is biologically related to both the wife and the husband, which can be fully realized with gestational surrogacy, cannot be achieved with traditional surrogacy. It is theorized that when continued advances in IVF technology are translated into higher success rates, more couples (if physiologically capable) will select gestational surrogacy for the simple reason that it most closely approximates traditional reproduction without introducing any of the potentially sensitive problems that traditional surrogacy raises. In gestational surrogacy most of the elements of American kinship remain intact: IVF transforms the wife into the genetrix and the husband into the genitor and provides a child who is biologically related to both wife and husband and is thus a symbol of the couple's love and marriage bond.[11] Gestational surrogacy is similar to Insemination by Husband (IH) in that it does not challenge the underlying tenets of the biogenetic basis of American kinship ideology. The tendency of couples pursuing IVF to "incorporate conceptive technology within the boundaries of natural conception" (Sandelowski 1991:39) is accomplished by focusing not upon fertilization (which occurs in a petri dish and represents a departure from traditional reproduction) but rather upon the genetic and gestational components of IVF

(Sandelowski 1991:38), which are consistent with traditional reproduction. As might have been expected, couples choosing gestational surrogacy emphasize their roles as genetrix and genitor; when asked if they consider the child theirs, they emphatically respond, "She *is* ours!"

Thus far, egg banks have been used primarily by women whose infertility is related to their inability to produce a viable ovum but who are nonetheless able to sustain a pregnancy (see Appendix J). In 1991, I theorized that with the proliferation of "egg banks," some couples after initially considering traditional surrogacy would prefer to select an anonymous egg donor, not in the interest of equalizing the relationship between the husband and wife per se, but rather because it weakens the surrogate's claim to the child (Ragoné 1991), and as of 1994, directors report that this is occurring.

Because of the emphasis these couples place on having a child who is biologically related to at least one of them, it was initially perplexing to learn that less than 2 percent of couples choose to have a paternity test performed on the child once it has been born (an option offered to all couples). According to the contract (see Appendix B, Section XIII), the couple is not required to accept the child until a paternity test is performed—if requested—to verify that the child is in fact the husband's child. This degree of confidence is surprising in view of the fact that some paternal doubt is always present. Insemination (see Appendix K) is most often conducted in a physician's office, but some programs permit home insemination, which makes the process more susceptible to error, at least from a symbolic point of view, in that the formal setting and structure provided by the presence of a physician is removed. Additionally, in more practical terms, both the use of frozen semen and the practice of shipping fresh semen when the surrogate and father are separated by geographical distance introduce the possibility of mix-ups. Another and perhaps more important factor that introduces doubt is the possibility that the surrogate did not abstain from intercourse with her husband, as agreed upon in the contract. In one case, a paternity test was performed when a disabled child was born to the surrogate and a dispute arose over the discontinuation of life-sustaining treatments. The surrogate's husband was determined to be the father of the child, a material breach of the contract. Although errors such as these are not unheard of in the surrogate industry, they do not for the most part appear to cause undue concern for the couples. When asked about paternity testing, wives frequently respond in this fashion, "We knew she was ours from the minute we saw her," or "We decided that it really didn't matter; he was ours no matter what."

These statements, even though they may initially appear to contradict the stated purpose of pursuing a partial biogenetic solution to childlessness, can upon further study be understood to fulfill two important functions. From the wife's perspective, an element of doubt as to the child's paternity introduces a variable that equalizes the issue of relatedness. The husband, as we have seen, is aware that he has a decisive advantage over his wife as evident in the frequently expressed initial preference for adoption or continued infertility treatments; thus a slight element of doubt about the child's paternity redresses the imbalance from his perspective as well. However, biogenetic relatedness remains a preoccupation with most couples, as seen in instances where a couple desires to have a second surrogate child: The norm is to reengage the services of the original surrogate if she is willing. The primary reason offered for this preference is that the child will have a full sibling, rather than the half-sibling that would be produced if another surrogate were selected. Surrogates frequently discuss their hopes that their couple will decide to have a second child so that they can give the child "a brother or sister." The surrogate's rationale in these cases is the same as that of the couple, to provide the family with genetic continuity. It should be noted that there are many more surrogates willing to have a second child for their couple than there are couples interested in having a second child. Most couples cite either age or financial constraints as obstacles to having a second child.

Because surrogacy is a relatively new phenomenon and little studied, its effects on children and the family are not known. There are, however, more extensive data on donor insemination and its effects upon the children produced thereby. Because of the close parallels between DI and surrogacy, some of these data may shed light on the future of surrogate children and their parents with respect to their personal relationships. Since a great deal of secrecy continues to surround the issue of DI, it is not surprising that according to the studies done on this subject, the majority of DI participants have not told their children about their origins (Snowden, Mitchell, and Snowden 1983). But in cases in which they have been told, DI children appeared to be "enjoying life and happy to be alive," knowing that they "owed their existence to AID [artificial insemination by donor]. They were pleased to feel that their parents had wanted a child so badly and that they were that child which fulfilled their parent's wishes" (Snowden, Mitchell, and Snowden 1983:98).

Furthermore, it was found that when DI children were informed of the circumstances of their origins, that knowledge, rather than damaging their relationship to their parents, appeared to enhance it (Snowden, Mitchell, and Snowden 1983:123). Nor was the experience of being told of their origins found to be "particularly traumatic" (Snowden, Mitchell, and Snowden 1983:123). The reasons for this appear to be that, unlike adopted children, who must come to terms with having been "abandoned by their natural mother ... an AID child is above all else, a wanted child and has no experience of rejection" (Snowden, Mitchell, and Snowden 1983:123).

Whether the same experience will hold true for surrogate children is presently unknown, although surrogate children share the experience of being "wanted" children and may therefore share in the positive feelings of DI children. However, unlike the surrogate child, the DI child has a biological mother who is also its social mother; whereas the surrogate child might be perceived as having lost her/his biological mother.

Although almost all of the couples who choose surrogacy and enroll in open programs anticipate informing their child of its origins, couples who select closed programs may not be so forthcoming. Studies on adopted children reveal that "adoptees have a healthy curiosity about their origins and a need for a full personal history in order to complete their sense of self" (Humphrey and Humphrey 1988:111). It has been shown that secrecy, in the case of DI, "whilst ostensibly being maintained for the sake of the child, is closely bound up with the concept of stigma" (Snowden, Mitchell, and Snowden 1983:121) and is "reminiscent of the practice followed by adoptive parents" (when parents do not tell a traditionally adopted child that he/she has been adopted) about which it has been concluded that "emotional energy spent on denial and concealment is better expended in facing and resolving the inherent problems" (Snowden, Mitchell, and Snowden 1983:147).

The authors of the DI study concluded that parents should be assisted with information about "how best to set about the practical task of telling their children in practical terms" (Snowden, Mitchell, and Snowden 1983:123) of their origins. In the open programs both couples and surrogates avail themselves of what is commonly referred to as the "broken tummy" theory to explain to their children their birth origins. Surrogates explain to their children that they are having a child for their couple because the adoptive mother's "tummy is broken" and that the baby belongs not to the surrogate and her family but to the couple.[12] In turn, the couple is instructed to tell their child that its mother's tummy is broken and that that is why a surrogate had to give birth to him or her. Within the open surrogate programs, the broken tummy story has gained overwhelming acceptance by industry personnel, adoptive couples, and surrogates alike. Fifteen out of the seventeen individuals interviewed, or about 88 percent, planned to use (or did use) this explanation. Parents involved in the surrogacy process frequently express concern about the proper age at which to tell their children because although they have been advised by open programs to share this information, no specific guidelines accompany the suggestion.

When Tom, one of the fathers I interviewed, for example, told me that he thought it might be best to let his son believe that he had been adopted until he had reached adulthood, his wife, who had overheard that part of the conversation, promptly poked her head into the room to say: "Absolutely not. He will be told the truth from the beginning." Some couples are very forthcoming, telling all their friends and even acquaintances of their surrogacy plans, whereas others tell primarily family members, allowing neighbors and acquaintances to believe that the child is adopted. Almost 65 percent, or eleven, of the couples interviewed from the open programs intended to tell their child of its origins before she/he reached adulthood. For these couples, the point at issue is the appropriate time at which to tell the child. Many couples expressed the belief that the moment the child expresses curiosity about the subject is the proper time to introduce the subject.

Couples are in the position of having to invent, almost independently, their own methods of informing the child about her/his origins. The strategy of one adoptive mother, a member of the staff at the Brookside program, whose surrogate was her own biological sister, is a good example. In telling her child about her origins, she combined the words "mother" and "aunt" to create the term "mattie," the kinship term her daughter now uses for the woman who is both her biological mother and her aunt. In addition to creating origin stories and new kinship terms, couples often create symbolic rituals or invent new ways to honor their relationship to their surrogate, such as the previously mentioned joint celebration of Mother's Day. For example, when Betty, the surrogate whose own father offered to pay her not to become a surrogate, told her couple, Susan and Ken, about the ritual she "created" after her own son's birth, in which she buried the placenta in her yard and then planted a fruit tree on that site, they decided to reenact the ritual with "Chris's [surrogate child's] placenta," planting a second fruit tree in Betty's yard to commemorate the event. Another couple named their child after their surrogate, thereby incorporating her name into their family history. Another surrogate, Carolyn, who described surrogacy as the "ultimate way to give," was invited to participate as a birth coach for her adoptive mother, when the adoptive mother herself became pregnant (through the use of GIFT). As Carolyn explained the sense of equal exchange and shared experience:

I was her coach; I was there for the C-section and I took the movies this time!

In summary, assisted reproductive techniques such as surrogacy, which are designed to redress the problem of infertility and resulting childlessness, do introduce numerous structural and symbolic questions as well as more practical issues such as the proper time to inform a child of her or his origins. On the simplest level, surrogacy assists the infertile by helping them to overcome their childlessness; however, as we have seen, it also introduces potential problems, for example, by providing a biogenetic link for only one parent and excluding the other parent.

From the couple's perspective, surrogacy is conceptualized not as a radical departure from tradition but as an attempt to achieve a traditional and acceptable end: to have a child who is biologically related to at least one of them, in this case, the father. This idea is consistent with the emphasis on the primacy of the blood tie in American kinship ideology and the importance of family. Thus, although biogenetic relatedness is the initial motivation for, and the ultimate goal of, surrogacy and the facet of surrogacy that makes it consistent with the biogenetic basis of American kinship ideology, such relatedness must be deemphasized, even devalued, by all the participants in order to make surrogacy consistent with American cultural values about appropriate relations between wives and husbands.

I have attempted to illustrate that surrogates' stated motivations for choosing surrogate motherhood represent but one aspect of a whole complex of motivations; thus although surrogates clearly do, as they say, enjoy being pregnant, take pleasure in being able to help an infertile couple start a family of their own, and value the remuneration they receive, there are other equally, if not more, compelling reasons motivating this unique group of women to become surrogate mothers. In addition to broadening the understanding of the motivations of the couples who choose to pursue a surrogate solution, I hope to have illuminated the complexity of their deliberative process and eventual accommodation of surrogacy as an aspect of their lives.

As we have seen, surrogates as a group tend to highlight only those aspects of surrogacy that are consistent with traditional reproduction. They emphasize, for example, the importance of family, motherhood, and nurturance. Like the couples, they deemphasize those aspects of the surrogate relationship that represent a departure from traditionally held beliefs surrounding motherhood, reproduction, and the family. Interspersed, however, with surrogates' assertions that surrogate motherhood is merely an extension of their conventional female roles as mothers are frequent interjections about the unique, exciting, and special nature of what they are doing.

It is not surprising, in view of their socialization, their life experiences, and their somewhat limited choices, that surrogates claim that it is their love of children, pregnancy, and family and a desire to help others that motivate them to become surrogates. To do otherwise would be to acknowledge that there may be inconsistencies within and areas of conflict between their traditional female roles as wives, mothers, and home-makers and their newfound public personae as surrogate mothers.

In conclusion, it can be said that all the participants involved in the surrogacy process wish to attain traditional ends and are therefore willing to set aside their reservations about the means by which parenthood is attained. Cloaking surrogacy in tradition, they attempt to circumvent some of the thornier issues raised by the surrogacy process, and in this way, programs and participants pick and choose among American cultural values about family, parenthood, and reproduction, now choosing biological relatedness, now nurture, as it suits their needs.

APPENDIX A

Couple's Biographical Sketch for Surrogate Mother

Adam and June

Adam is 45, June is 46.

Adam and I met in 1979 while we were both working at the _____. Adam had just been transferred from his hometown and was working for _____. I had been transferred from a company in Boston to _____ in 1978. Adam was walking down the stairs, and when I saw him for the first time, I nearly fell—up the stairs. We have been together since July of 1979 and were married in February of 1982—ten years.

We live in _____.

Although we met when we both had careers in the _____ business. Adam is now an attorney and I am a homemaker and stay at home mother of Emily, who will be 3 in January, 1993. I also help run a support group, the Association of Parents Through Surrogacy, which I do from my home. We both feel that in spite of the other things we do, the most important job we have is being a parent. That is also our favorite job.

We are both Protestant.

Our fertility problem is due to me being a DES child—my eggs were fine, but my uterus was unable to hold a pregnancy. We spent years and every available surgery and solution trying to have a child.

Adam is very tall, with a quiet, gentle way about him. He was raised in Kansas on farms and loves the country and animals. He has an older and a younger sister and comes from a very large extended family as his father was one of ten children, and his mother was one of four. They all live mainly in Kansas—Adam being lured away by the _____ business. He was a marine and fought in Vietnam. Adam is solid and honest and real, and is still one of the nicest people I have ever met.

Adam is the kind of man who you just know will take care of everything. He is patient and kind and smart. Adam is also one of the most loving fathers I have ever imagined. He adores our daughter, Emily, and she him. When he comes home at night and she runs to him, he lights up from the inside out.

I, June, come from a long line of Bostonians. I grew up outside of Boston. I really had a happy childhood. I have an outgoing, energetic personality, and have great passion for the things that are important to me—such as Adam, my family and friends, and my determination to be a mother. I come from a family of five children, and was blessed with a fabulous mother. Being a mother was really the only job I ever wanted. Adam and I are a good match—he is tall with brown hair

139

and blue eyes, I am short with blonde hair and green eyes. More importantly, we are a good balance of personalities—Adam is calm and reserved—so that I don't have to be.

Our main enjoyment is our daughter and the time we spend together as a family. We go to the park, to the ponyrides, to the beach to fly a kite. We go to New Hampshire for a vacation in the summer where I spent summers growing up. We spend the vacation with my family there on Lake _____. We also go to Adam's family in Kansas for vacation, again so that we can spend time with his family. We also love to read, listen to music, dance, and we love our two dogs. I love to cook, so we eat well. After years of only being able to dream about having children, we are very aware of the joy our daughter brings to us.

We have chosen to work with a surrogate because it gave us a genetic link to our children. Our daughter was born by a surrogate, and it was a very positive experience with a fabulous outcome—Emily! We believe very passionately in surrogacy as a wonderful solution to our infertility. We very much want to know the birth mother of our child and are very committed to surrogacy as a way of creating a family.

We live in a modest home with a yard and two dogs in a neighborhood with nice children. Physically our home is the colors that we love, and is full of antiques and other oddities from my family. (I like being surrounded by things that belonged to people that I loved.) We eat our meals together—frequently at Emily's child size table in the kitchen—(Adam gets a big chair.) We love to have friends for dinner—either eating outside or at my grandmother's dining room table. We like friends, good food, conversation and lots of laughter and candlelight. We have strong values and know that the most important thing we can ever pass on to our children is the love and strength of a family.

Both of us come from large, close families, so we will have those relationships to share. Even though we don't live near our families, we speak to them weekly. Emily is very attached to her aunts and uncles and grandparents, in spite of the miles. We also have many old friends who have been friends all of our lives, and they are like family as well. Living so far away from where we grew up, we have very purposely developed friendships over the years that would feel like family to us.

We have one daughter, Emily, who will be 3 in January, 1993. We have always wanted her to have a sister or brother because we don't want her to be an only child. We know how important it will be later in her life to have a sibling. Having lost my mother 11 years ago, I know how important it is to my sisters and brothers that we have each other.

We hope to have an open, honest, and friendly relationship with our surrogate. We are supportive and open people and would want a caring and happy relationship. We maintain contact on a regular basis with our surrogate, Elizabeth, and have been to visit her in the midwest within the year. We think of her and her family as very special friends who will always be in our lives. It is important to us that our children know the truth about their special beginnings, and that the door always be open to them to know more if they wish. I would hope that our surrogates and our children will always be as proud of what we accomplished as we are.

Contract

The following is a sample contract. It is not intended to be used in a surrogacy arrangement or in any other assisted reproduction arrangement. The author strongly recommends that anyone considering entering into any such arrangement utilize their own counsel. Anyone utilizing this contract in violation of the above proviso is doing so in violation of copyright law and shall be prosecuted to the fullest extent of the law.

THIS AGREEMENT is made by and between (hereinafter referred to as "Surrogate") and her husband, if any (hereinafter referred to as "Husband"), and (hereinafter referred to as "Natural Father"), and his wife (hereinafter referred to as "Adopting Mother"). "The Program," as mentioned herein, refers to the ————, which represents the Natural Father and Adopting Mother, in helping them select a Surrogate, in administration of this Agreement, and in designating appropriate professionals, whether medical, psychological, legal or otherwise, when called for herein.

Recitals

THIS AGREEMENT is made with reference to the following facts:

(1) The Natural Father and Adopting Mother (hereinafter referred to also as "Prospective Parents" are a married couple, living together as man and wife, both over the age of eighteen (18) years, who are desirous of entering into the following Agreement: The Natural Father desires to have a child or children biologically related to him, and the Adopting Mother desires to take into their home and adopting the child or children as her own which is/are biologically related to her husband. The Adopting Mother warrants she is either incapable of conceiving or carrying a pregnancy to term or has been advised by a physician that a pregnancy would be medically dangerous to herself or any child she may conceive. The couple further warrants that all representations, either oral or written, made to the Program, any professional herein, or to the surrogate and her husband, if any, are true.

(2) The Surrogate and her Husband, if any, is/are over the age of eighteen (18) years and are desirous of entering into the following Agreement. The Surrogate and her husband, if any, warrant that all representations, either oral or written, made to the Program, any professional herein or to the Prospective Parents, are true.

(3) The Surrogate and her Husband, if any, does not desire to have a parental relationship with any child born pursuant to this Agreement. Further, she/they believe the Child is morally that of the Prospective Parents.

(4) The parties desire to maintain confidentialities between themselves, one to another, and between themselves and the public.

(5) SURROGATE PARENTING is a new and unsettled area of the law, and for that reason, no warranties have been or can be made as to the ultimate cost, liability or obligation of the parties which may result from judicial process as a result of the conduct contemplated herein. The parties understand and acknowledge that the following State Penal Code Sections exist: Penal Code Section 181 which prohibits involuntary servitude; Penal Code Section 182 which prohibits conspiracy to commit a crime; Penal Code Section 273 which makes it a misdemeanor to pay or receive money or anything of value in return for the consent to an adoption by a parent of his/her child; and Civil Code Section 224(p) which prohibits advertising for adoption without a valid license. The parties further understand that these Penal Codes have never been applied to Surrogate Parenting.

(6) WHILE THE UNDERSIGNED ARE ENTERING INTO THIS AGREEMENT WITH THE INTENTION OF BEING FULLY BOUND BY ITS TERMS, EACH HAVE BEEN INFORMED BY THEIR ATTORNEY THAT THIS CONTRACT IN WHOLE OR IN PART MAY BE DECLARED VOID AS AGAINST PUBLIC POLICY BY THE STATE COURTS OR HELD UNENFORCEABLE IN WHOLE OR IN PART BY SAID COURT, THAT PORTION WHICH IS UNENFORCEABLE IS SEVERABLE. FURTHER, NO ASPECT OF THIS CONTRACT MAY BE ENFORCED IF SUCH ENFORCEMENT VIOLATES ANY NON WAIVABLE CIVIL OR CONSTITUTIONAL RIGHT OF ANY PARTY TO THIS CONTRACT.

(7) IT IS EXPRESSLY UNDERSTOOD THAT THIS CONTRACT IN NO WAY CONSTITUTES PAYMENT FOR A CHILD OR RELINQUISHMENT OF A CHILD, OR CONSENT TO ADOPTION.

IN ADDITION, THE PARENTAGE AND/OR PARENTAL RIGHTS AND OBLICATIONS REGARDING CHILDREN BORN PURSUANT TO THIS TYPE OF AGREEMENT REMAINS UNSETTLED IN _____ AT THIS TIME.

The parties understand that the Prospective Parents have spent many years, suffered much pain and agony to bring a child into their family and are now relying greatly on the Surrogate and her Husband, if any, for a child. It is also understood by the parties that grave, severe and intense emotional stress, humiliation and mental anguish may occur to either party as a result of a material breach by the other party, and that the breaching party may be held liable for intentional infliction of emotional distress.

NOW, THEREFORE, in consideration of the mutual promises contained herein and with the intentions of being legally bound hereby, the parties agree as follows:

I

THE FOLLOWING PROVISIONS ARE SUBJECT TO A COURT OF COMPETENT JURISDICTION TO DETERMINE THE BEST INTERESTS OF THE CHILD BORN PURSUANT TO THIS AGREEMENT.

The Prospective Parents are entering into a written contractual agreement with the Surrogate and her Husband, if any, whereby the Surrogate shall be artifically inseminated by the Natural Father so that the Surrogate may bear a child biologically related to the Natural Father, taken to the home of the Prospective Parents, and subsequently adopted by the Adopting Mother as her child. The birth of the child shall take place in _____, unless otherwise agreed upon. UNLESS THERE HAS BEEN A MATERIAL, INCURABLE BREACH ON THE PART OF THE SURROGATE AND HER HUSBAND, IF ANY, THE PROSPECTIVE PARENTS SHALL TAKE IMMEDIATE, FULL AND ABSOLUTE CUSTODY OF THE CHILD/CHILDREN UPON BIRTH, NOTWITHSTANDING ANY CONGENITAL, PHYSICAL OR MENTAL ABNORMALITY OF THE CHILD/CHILDREN. THE SURROGATE AND HER HUSBAND, IF ANY, SHALL NOT BE HELD LIABLE FOR SUPPORT, CUSTODY OR ANY OTHER LIABILITY WHATSOEVER RELATING TO THE CHILD/CHILDREN BORN PURSUANT TO THIS AGREEMENT.

II

"Child," as referred to in this Agreement, shall include all children born simultaneously pursuant to the insemination as defined in the terms and provisions of this Agreement, provided the parentage of the Child is determined pursuant to the terms of this Agreement.

III

The Prospective Parents assume the legal and parental responsibilities for any Child as defined herein which may possess congenital abnormality or defects, and the parties to this Agreement acknowledge that they have been advised and are aware of the risk of such abnormalities and/or defects.

IV

The Surrogate and her Husband, if any, based on her/their information and belief, represent that she is capable of conceiving, carrying, and bearing healthy, normal children, and further warrants she has produced at least one healthy child. The surrogate and her husband, if any, agrees that she/they will not attempt to form a parent-child relationship with any Child she may bear pursuant to the provisions of this Agreement and shall freely and readily, within a reasonable time, terminate all parental rights to said Child pursuant to this Agreement in order to aid the Adopting Mother in legalizing her relationship to the Child, and in order to aid the Prospective Parents in the formation and/or continuance of their parent-child relationship with the Child. The Surrogate, and her husband, if any, shall immediately give full custody of the Child to the Prospective Parents upon the birth of the Child.

V

All parties hereby agree to undergo psychological evaluation by a psychologist and/or psychotherapist designated by the Program or its agent. The Prospective Parents shall pay for the cost of said psychological review and/or evaluation. All parties shall sign prior to her/their psychological evaluation a medical release form authorizing the Program to secure the release of this psychological evaluation and/or screening. All parties agree to undergo any psychological counseling and/or therapy designated by said psychologist/psychotherapist prior to or during the pregnancy and while this Agreement is in effect.

VI

Prior to insemination, the Surrogate shall undergo a physical examination under the direction of and to the extent determined in the sole discretion of a physician designated by the Program to determine whether her physical health and well-being are satisfactory. The Surrogate and the Natural Father shall undergo testing for venereal diseases (including AIDS) in order to protect the health of the Surrogate and the Child. If the Surrogate is married or cohabiting with a man, both the Surrogate and her husband or cohabitant shall undergo venereal diseases testing (including AIDS) as described herein. The Surrogate and the Prospective Parents agree to undergo any medical testing that the above mentioned physician deems necessary while this Agreement is in effect.

VII

It is the responsibility of each party to this contract to facilitate procedural aspects of the adoption such as obtaining birth certificates, marriage and divorce certificates or other documentation requested by the Program or any party's attorney.

VIII

In the event that the contemplated pregnancy has not occurred within a reasonable time (this is contemplated to be six to twelve cycles of inseminations) in the opinion of the inseminating physician, this Agreement shall terminate by written notice to the Surrogate and/or her Husband, if any. Such notice is to be given by the inseminating physician, the Program or any party herein.

IX

During the term of this Agreement, the parties agree to immediately inform the Program in writing of any material change in their circumstances which may reasonably affect this Agreement. These changes include, but are not limited to, change of address, illness or death of a party, loss of employment, changes in insurance coverage, exposure to communicable illness.

X

The Surrogate agrees to and shall declare that she did not have any sexual intercourse from the time of the signing of the contract and *preceding* that time at least one cycle (one period) until the pregnancy has been confirmed in writing by the inseminating physician. The Surrogate further agrees to and shall declare that she did not engage in any activity in which the possibility of semen, other than that utilized by the above-mentioned inseminating physician, was introduced into her body such that the possibility of a pregnancy other than that contemplated by this Agreement may have occurred. This paragraph is hereby waived in its entirety upon proof of sterility of Surrogate's husband, only as to sexual intercourse between the Surrogate and her husband.

XI

The Surrogate further agrees to adhere to all medical instructions given to her by the inseminating physician, as well as her independent obstetrician. The Surrogate agrees not to smoke cigarettes, drink alcoholic beverages, use any illegal drugs, non-prescription medication or prescribed medication without consent from the above physicians.

The Surrogate agrees to follow a prenatal medical examination schedule as prescribed by her independent obstetrician, as well as adhere to all requirements regarding the taking of medicine and vitamins prescribed by her treating obstetrician and/or the inseminating physician. The Surrogate further agrees to submit to any medical test or procedure deemed necessary or advisable by her obstetrician and/or the inseminating physician including, but not limited to, amniocentesis. Except as otherwise stated in this paragraph, failure to conform to all or any of the provisions of this paragraph shall constitute a breach of the Agreement by the Surrogate.

XII

The Surrogate agrees that she will not abort the Child once conceived except if, in the opinion of the inseminating physician or her independent obstetrician, such action is necessary for the physical health of the Surrogate, or if the Child has been determined by either physician to be physiologically abnormal and an abortion is advisable. In the event of either of these two contingencies, the Surrogate agrees to submit to said abortion. Any decision to abort is to be made by the Prospective Parents, except in a medical emergency where the Prospective Parents are unavailable or cannot reasonably be contacted. In the event of a miscarriage or abortion as described herein, no funds paid by the Prospective Parents to the Surrogate shall be returned. If such an event occurs, the Agreement shall be deemed terminated with no further liability by any party other than the Prospective Parents still remaining liable for such costs incurred to date by the Surrogate pursuant to the terms of this paragraph. However, in the event the parties choose to resume artificial insemination after an abortion or miscarriage, this contract shall remain in full force and effect and the termination is deemed waived. ALL PARTIES UNDERSTAND THAT A PREGNANT WOMAN HAS THE ABSOLUTE CONSTITUTIONAL RIGHT TO ABORT OR NOT ABORT ANY FETUS SHE IS CARRYING. ANY PROMISE TO THE CONTRARY IS UNENFORCEABLE.

XIII

Subsequent to the birth of the Child, the Surrogate, the Natural Father and the Child shall submit, if requested, to an H.L.A. test at the expense of the Prospective Parents.

The Natural Father's being excluded by the H.L.A. test shall constitute an incurable material breach on the part of the Surrogate.

XIV

The Surrogate and her Husband, if any, agree to submit to the Program proper documentation that the Surrogate has incurred or will incur the following kinds of expenses, for which the Program shall arrange prompt payment from Prospective Parents' trust funds, if necessary; Obstetrical, Nursing, Hospital and Maternity care, pharmaceutical, and pediatrics. Payments for expenses not yet incurred by the Surrogate shall only be made when advance payment is necessary. The Surrogate and her Husband, if any, agree to submit all bills as described above to applicable insurance carriers prior to submission for payment to the Program. The Surrogate's insurance is deemed PRIMARY INSURANCE. The couple shall only be responsible for those medical payments not paid by the Surrogate's medical insurance.

XV

The Surrogate and her Husband, if any, warrant that she/they are aware of medical risks including death, which may result from the conduct contemplated by this Agreement and including, but not limited to, risks involved in medical examinations, artificial insemination, conception, pregnancy, childbirth and postpartem complications. Said risks have been explained to the Surrogate and her Husband, if any, by a physician. The Surrogate and her Husband, if any, agree to assume all of the above-stated risks and to release the Prospective Parents, the Program, their agents and employees, including the professionals and others contemplated and/or involved in any aspect of this Agreement from any legal liability except professional malpractice (malfeasance, negligence).

XVI

The Prospective Parents, the Program, or any professionals designated herein, shall not be responsible for any lost wages of the Surrogate and her Husband, if any, child-care expenses of the Surrogate and her Husband, if any, transportation expenses incurred by the Surrogate and her Husband, if any, or any other expenses resulting from the performance of this Agreement unless specifically enumerated herein. The consideration paid the Surrogate is intended to compensate her for unforeseen and unanticipated expenses such as travel, child care, lost wages, discomfort, pain and inconvenience by the Surrogate, her Husband (if any) and her family.

XVII

In recognition of the Prospective Parents' obligation to support this Child and pay for the Surrogate's services, the Prospective Parents agree to pay as indicated in Exhibit "A" attached hereto and incorporated herein by reference. The Surrogate shall receive full payment for her services notwithstanding whether the child is born alive or with congenital, physical or mental abnormality.

XVIII

The Prospective Parents shall pay the costs of a term life insurance policy on the Surrogate's life having a face value as designated in Exhibit "A" payable to the named beneficiary designated by the Surrogate and her Husband, if any. Said policy shall be bought upon confirmation of conception by the inseminating physician and shall remain in effect for two months subsequent to the birth of the Child or longer as is reasonable if medical complications develop. The named beneficiaries under this policy must include the Surrogate's Husband, if any, and children, if any, whether in trust or otherwise. The premiums on said policy shall be deposited into and paid through the trust account of the Program.

XIX

Surrogate and/or her Husband, if any, shall maintain her/their existing medical insurance plan during the entire term of this Agreement. If Surrogate does not have medical maternity insurance covering catastrophic illness and major hospitalization, Prospective Parents shall obtain the same for Surrogate at their expense. Coverage under said insurance shall commence prior to the artificial insemination and continue in force until two months after delivery of the Child or longer as is reasonable if medical complications develop. In no event shall the Prospective Parents be responsible for such medical insurance for longer than three years. The Program shall immediately be informed of any and all notices received by or that come to the attention of the Surrogate and/or her Husband, if any, or any party regarding said insurance coverage, but not limited to cancellation notices, past payment due notices, and changes in coverage (amendments). The Program is the administrator of this Agreement. It does not guarantee payment or performance in any manner by any party or professional retained to aid in the performance of or in contemplation of entering into this Agreement.

XX

The entire amount anticipated by this Agreement shall be placed in the trust account of the Program prior to the commencement of artificial insemination of the Surrogate.

XXI

The Surrogate and her Husband, if any, agree that she/they will not seek to view or contact the Child after the Child's hospital stay nor will the Surrogate and her Husband, if any, seek to view or meet with the Prospective Parents or their families, unless waived by the Prospective Parents.

XXII

The parties agree that they will not provide or allow to provide any information to the public, news media, or any other individual regarding their involvement in surrogate parenting or the involvement of any other party in surrogate parenting or the identity of any party herein without written permission of the other party. The parties understand that confidentiality as described herein does not contemplate speaking with friends, relatives and acquaintances about their own involvement in the Surrogate Program. Such conversations are allowed and do not constitute a breach of confidentiality, provided that the identity of the other party is not disclosed.

XXIII

In the event of the death of the Natural Father prior to the birth of the Child, all of the rights and obligations of the Surrogate and her Husband, if any, shall be of equal force and effect notwithstanding such event. The Child shall be placed in the custody of the Adopting Mother pursuant to this Agreement. The Surrogate and her Husband, if any, and the Adopting Mother shall go forth under the terms of this Contract and agree to effectuate all of the terms contained herein and allow the adoption of the child by the Adopting Mother.

In the event of the death of the Adopting Mother prior to the birth of the Child, all rights and obligations of the Surrogate and her Husband, if any, shall be of equal force and effect notwithstanding such event. All items contained herein shall remain in effect as are consistent with the intentions of the terms of this Agreement, and the Surrogate and her Husband, if any, shall still relinquish all parental rights to the Child in favor of the Natural Father. The Prospective Parents shall make suitable arrangements for the care and custody of the child should both the Natural Father and Adopting Mother die.

XXIV

Since the Child is the genetic product of the Natural Father and the Surrogate, it may in the future become necessary to obtain information of a medical nature from a party to this Agreement. Therefore, the parties agree to inform the Program or its designated agents of any change of current address in perpetuity. If medical information must be obtained from any party, such party agrees to furnish such information.

XXV

The Parties warrant that she/they have consulted independent legal counsel and have been advised regarding the terms, conditions, rights, duties, and liabilities, arising under the conduct contemplated by this Agreement. The Prospective Parents shall reimburse the Surrogate and her Husband, if any, to the extent specified in Exhibit "A" for said independent legal counsel.

XXVI

In the event that any party materially violates any of the provisions contained herein without legal excuse, such violation shall constitute a material breach, and in addition to all other remedies available at law or equity, this Agreement may be terminated forthwith at the option of the aggrieved party without further liability on the part of the nonbreaching party. In the event that the Prospective Parents terminate this Agreement pursuant to the provisions contained herein, the Prospective Parents shall be under no obligation to pay any monies to the Surrogate or her Husband, if any, or reimburse any of her/their expenses incurred. In addition, the Surrogate and her Husband, if any, must reimburse the Prospective Parents for all sums expended pursuant to this Agreement, plus interest at the máximum allowable rate at the time the breach was discovered. In the event the Prospective Parents materially breach the contract without legal excuse, the Surrogate shall still receive all funds due her under the contract.

As a precondition to any violation constituting a breach, the party committing the violation shall be given written notice of such alleged violation, within a reasonable time after discovery, and shall have a reasonable opportunity to cure the alleged violation, if possible.

Subject to cure, a breach by the Prospective Parents shall constitute a breach by both, and a breach by either the Surrogate or her Husband, if any, shall constitute a breach by both.

Any violation of an express warranty contained herein shall constitute a material breach. The continued performance of an aggrieved party following a material breach shall not constitute a waiver, and all rights accruing or retained by the aggrieved party shall remain in full force and effect. In the event a material breach is subject to cure, and said cure is effectuated, the confirmed performance of an aggrieved party shall constitute a waiver.

XXVII

In the event of a material breach for which the Prospective Parents terminate this Agreement, all funds remaining in the trust account of the Program deposited by the Prospective Parents in excess of those sums necessary for payment of expenses already incurred shall be returned to the Prospective Parents forthwith upon their demand. Prior to returning said funds, the Program shall give ten (10) days written notice to the Surrogate and her Husband, if any.

XXVIII

The parties agree that if conflicting claims are made by the parties upon the Program for payment from trust funds, the Program may at its discretion interplead said funds into the Court of appropriate jurisdiction.

XXIX

The Prospective Parents and Surrogate and her Husband, if any, recognize and acknowledge that the Program shall act as agent for the Prospective Parents in all matters pertaining to this Agreement in order to maintain confidentiality and to expedite administration of this Agreement. It is understood that while the Program may act as agent, it is not party to this Agreement.

XXX

Notwithstanding the agency created in the paragraph next above, no agency, independent contractor, partnership, employment or joint venture is created or intended to be created between the parties herein.

XXXI

The parties warrant that all information contained in the various applications and written Medical History Questionnaire provided the Program in connection with this Agreement is true and correct. The parties further warrant that they have not knowingly omitted any material information relating to questions contained in the various applications and Medical History Questionnaire.

XXXII

The parties expressly understand and agree that neither the Program, the psychologist/psychotherapist, the Attorney, agents or employees of same, nor the professionals whose services are contemplated under this Agreement guarantee or warrant the following: (1) That the Surrogate will in fact conceive a Child after insemination with the semen of the Natural Father; (2) that the Child if conceived will be a physically and mentally healthy child free of birth or congenital defects; or (3) that the Surrogate and her Husband, if any, will comply with the terms and provisions of this Agreement; and (4) that the Prospective Parents will comply with the terms of this Agreement.

XXXIII

This Agreement shall be amended only by a written agreement signed by all the parties.

XXXIV

LIMITATION OF REMEDIES: In order to maintain the confidentiality contemplated herein: In the event litigation arises out of this Agreement, the parties, their legal counsel, their heirs and representatives agree to make all efforts to maintain such confidentiality as is intended by this Agreement as to the general public and as to each other, including, but not limited to, requesting that Court records be sealed, requesting the Court to invoke gag orders, requesting the Court in its procedures and in the conducting of hearings to maintain confidential the identity of the parties.

XXXV

This Agreement may be executed in two or more counterparts each of which shall be an original but all of which shall constitute one and the same instrument. The original of the respective counterparts shall be maintained by the Program for the benefit of all parties.

XXXVI

This Agreement sets forth the entire agreement between the parties. All agreements, covenants, representations and warranties, expressed and implied, oral and written, of the parties are contained herein. No other agreements, covenants, representations, nor warranties, expressed or implied, oral or written, have been made by any party to the other(s) with respect of this Contract. All prior and contemporaneous conversations, negotiations, possible and alleged agreements, representations, covenants and warranties with respect to this Contract are waived, merged and superseded. This is an integrated Agreement.

XXXVII

No provision of this Agreement is to be interpreted for or against any party because that party or that party's legal representative or agent drafted the provisions.

XXXVIII

In the event any of the provisions, whether sentences or entire paragraphs, of this Agreement are deemed to be invalid or unenforceable, the same shall be deemed severable from the remainder of this Agreement and shall not cause the invalidity or unenforceability of the remainder of this Agreement. If such provision shall be deemed invalid due to its scope or breadth such provision shall be deemed valid to the extent of the scope or breadth permitted by law.

XXXIX

Each party acknowledges that it fully understands the Agreement and its legal effect in that it is signing the same freely and voluntarily and that no party has any reason to believe that the other parties did not freely and voluntarily execute this Agreement.

XL

This Agreement has been drafted and executed in ———, and shall be governed by, construed and enforced in accordance with the laws of the State.

_____
SURROGATE

DATE_____

_____
SURROGATE'S HUSBAND, IF ANY

DATE_____

_____
NATURAL FATHER

DATE_____

_____
ADOPTING MOTHER

DATE_____

Exhibit "A"

A. PAYMENT SCHEDULE PURSUANT TO PARAGRAPH XVIII: The Surrogate shall be paid as follows: The total of $10,000.00.**

1. One Thousand Dollars ($1,000.00) upon confirmation of pregnancy.
2. Two Thousand Dollars ($2,000.00) at the end of the first trimester.
3. Two Thousand Dollars ($2,000.00) at the end of the second trimester.
4. One Thousand Dollars ($1,000.00) one (1) week after the birth of the child.

5. Four Thousand Dollars ($4,000.00) six (6) weeks after the birth of the child. The Program shall withhold sums from the Surrogate Mother's final payment until all advances, insurance Explanation of Benefits, and final expenses are resolved.

6. In the event the Surrogate fails to conceive after six (6) cycles of inseminations, she shall receive Five Hundred Dollars ($500.00) upon termination of the Agreement.

**Attendance at group support meetings is mandatory. The Surrogate fee shall be reduced by $100.00 for EACH monthly group support meeting which is missed by the Surrogate. Reductions shall be subtracted from the next scheduled fee payment.

To avoid disputes as to whether an absence is justifiable, or not, TWO absences will be allowed, without reduction of fee.

B. INSURANCE SCHEDULE AND PAYMENTS PURSUANT TO PARAGRAPH XIX AS FOLLOWS:

1. Life insurance to be obtained on the Surrogate's life with a face value of Two Hundred Thousand Dollars ($200,000.00), the beneficiary to be her children and husband, if any.

2. Medical insurance currently held by Surrogate to be kept in full force and effect during the term of this Agreement. Surrogate is to file (present a claim) all medical bills, hospital bills, prescriptions and other expenses covered by the medical insurance with the insurance company. Said claims are to be filed within ten (10) days after receipt of medical or other billing or expense. All monies not paid by the insurance company will be paid by the Adopting Couple pursuant to this Agreement. Any reimbursement payments and copies of all Benefit Explanation Letters received by the Surrogate from the insurance company for medical expenses incurred will be forwarded to this office for reimbursement to the Adopting Couple.

C. ADDITIONAL TERMS:

1. Maternity clothing allowance of (maximum) Five Hundred Dollars ($500.00) will be paid after the first trimester.

2. Travel, babysitting and miscellaneous allowance of approximately One Hundred Twenty-five Dollars ($125.00) per month commencing from the signing of this Agreement to confirmation of pregnancy and approximately One Hundred Twenty-five Dollars ($125.00) per month after confirmation of pregnancy to the delivery, pursuant to written informal statement from Surrogate. Surrogate and husband, if any, acknowledge that it is her responsibility to submit an itemized statement for payment of monthly expense allowances (transportation, etc.) and that payment will not be paid without receipt thereof. The statement should

include the date and expense incurred, the nature of the expense and the amount (for example: 10/12/84 trip to doctor—10 miles—$2.00, etc.).

3. The Prospective Parents shall be responsible for Surrogate's payment of $250.00 plus expenses for independent legal counsel.

4. The Surrogate, and her husband, if any, agree that the Prospective Parents are privy to psychological and medical information relating to the Surrogate's and her husband, if any, mental and physical health and any other pertinent information relating specifically to this surrogacy arrangement.

THE PROGRAM IS NOT GIVING ANY OF THE PARTIES LEGAL ADVICE ON TAXATION OR IM-MIGRATION. THE PARTIES SHOULD CONSULT INDEPENDENT COUNSEL REGARDING TAX MATTERS OR IMMIGRATION MATTERS THAT MAY ARISE.

IT IS THE RESPONSIBILITY OF ANY PARTY RECEIVING PAYMENT OR OTHER BENEFITS PURSUANT TO THIS AGREEMENT TO REPORT RECEIPT OF SAID PAYMENTS OR BENEFITS TO THE PROPER TAXING AUTHORITIES, STATE, FEDERAL, OR OTHERWISE.

_____   _____
SURROGATE   SURROGATE'S HUSBAND (IF ANY)

_____   _____
NATURAL FATHER   ADOPTING MOTHER

Phone Intake Form and
Letter to Prospective Surrogate

DATE: _____

TELEPHONE INQUIRY _____ WRITTEN INQUIRY _____

TAKEN BY _____

(AGE 21–36) _____

NAME _____

ADDRESS _____

CITY _____ STATE _____ ZIP CODE _____

TELEPHONE NO. _____ (h) _____ (w)

WHERE DID YOU HEAR ABOUT US: _____

_____

NUMBER OF CHILDREN: _____ AGES OF CHILDREN: _____

(CIRCLE ONE) MARRIED SINGLE DIVORCED SEPARATED WIDOWED

SELF SUPPORTIVE: _____ SMOKER _____ NON-SMOKER ____

COMMENTS: _____

_____

_____

_____

_____

_____

_____

_____

_____

_____

DATE INFO PACK SENT OUT: _____

April 20, 1989

Dear Ms. _____,

Thank you for your interest in exploring the surrogate experience. Helping a childless couple become a family is perhaps the ultimate gift. We commend you for your consideration of surrogacy—it is an expression of the caring and giving nature of humanity that is so welcome in today's society.

Enclosed you will find several articles which we hope you find of interest. You will also find an application to become a surrogate mother in our program. If you'd like to know more about surrogacy, please complete the application and return it to us.

When we have received your application, we will review it and then contact you for an interview. During this appointment you will be meeting with the Center's staff. If you are married or in a committed relationship, we request that your husband or significant other attend this first meeting.

The purpose of this initial meeting is to answer all of your questions and to help you decide if being a surrogate mother is right for you. No commitment on either side is made at this time.

Please take the time to complete the enclosed application and don't forget to enclose photos of you and your family. If you don't have photos handy, please send in your application without them and forward them later. Again, thank you for your inquiry, and we look forward to hearing from you.

Sincerely yours,

Administrator
encls.

Detailed Application Form
for Surrogate Mothers

SURROGATE MOTHER INFORMATION SHEET
(CONFIDENTIAL)

Note: This is a confidential record and will be kept in this office.
Information contained here will not be released to any person except when
authorized by you.

DATE: 6-10-91

Please attach a recent
photograph of yourself and
your children here.

PERSONAL INFORMATION:

NAME: Anne Marie

AGE: 26   DATE OF BIRTH: 1-2-65   SOCIAL SECURITY NUMBER _____

MAIDEN LAST NAME, IF DIFFERENT: _____

PRESENT ADDRESS: _____

PHONE: (HOME) _____   (WORK)( ) N/A

SPOUSE: Jay   AGE: 28   DATE OF BIRTH: 6-26-62

IN CASE OF EMERGENCY NOTIFY: Jay

U.S. CITIZEN: YES ✓ NO ___ ETHNIC BACKGROUND: Cauc - Am. Indian

HEIGHT: 5'4"   WEIGHT: 115   EYE COLOR: Hazel   HAIR: Brown

(CIRCLE ONE) (MARRIED)   SINGLE   DIVORCED   SEPARATED   WIDOWED

NUMBER OF CHILDREN: 2   MALES: 1   AGES: 3½

FEMALES: 1   AGES: 7 mo.

RELIGIOUS BACKGROUND: Baptized Catholic - but not practicing it.

EMPLOYMENT INFORMATION:

	EMPLOYER	LOCATION	POSITION	DATES EMPLOYED
1.	N/A			
2.				
3.				

YOUR CURRENT INCOME: _____

HUSBAND'S PRESENT EMPLOYER: _____

HUSBAND'S POSITION: Route-Sales

HUSBAND'S CURRENT INCOME: 27,000.00 Annual

HUSBAND'S: SOCIAL SECURITY NO. _____ DRIVERS LICENSE _____

HOW MANY PERSONS DO YOU SUPPORT, INCLUDING YOURSELF?: _____

GENERAL QUESTIONS:

WHERE DID YOU LEARN ABOUT OUR ORGANIZATION?: (I've been a Surrogate w/ you before.) Originally saw ad on T.V. interview in 1988, then answered ad in paper, not knowing They were one in the same.

IF A NEWSPAPER, WHICH ONE?: _____

BRIEFLY EXPLAIN YOUR UNDERSTANDING ABOUT HOW THE SURROGATE MOTHER PROGRAM WORKS:

An infertile couple who can't conceive either because she doesn't produce eggs (AI) or doesn't have a functioning uterus (IVF)

WHY DO YOU WANT TO BECOME A SURROGATE MOTHER?: The self satisfaction of being able to help a couple become a family. I know a few couples who are unable to have their own children, and I've done it before and it was a wonderful experience.

HEALTH INFORMATION:

GENERAL HEALTH CONDITION: Good _____

DO YOU HAVE ANY MEDICAL PROBLEMS? YES___ NO ✓ IF YES, PLEASE EXPLAIN:

_____
_____
_____
_____
_____
_____

PREGNANCIES:

	PRESENT MARRIAGE	PREVIOUS MARRIAGE
NUMBER OF PREGNANCIES:	4	
NUMBER OF ABORTIONS:	—	
NUMBER OF CHILDREN BORN ALIVE:	3	
STILLBIRTHS:	—	
CAESAREAN BIRTHS:	1	
MISCARRIAGES:	1	
COMPLICATIONS (YES OR NO):	NO - Premature labor	
MONTHS TRYING TO CONCEIVE:	9	

ARE YOU PRESENTLY USING BIRTH CONTROL? YES ✓ NO___ IF YES, GIVE CURRENT METHOD:

Condoms, foam _____

HOW LONG HAVE YOU USED THIS PARTICULAR FORM OF BIRTH CONTROL?: 7 mos. _____

ANY COMPLICATIONS?: No _____

DO YOU SMOKE?: YES___ NO ✓ IF YES, HOW MUCH? _____

DO YOU USE ALCOHOLIC BEVERAGES?: YES ✓ NO___ IF YES, HOW OFTEN?

(NUMBER OF TIMES PER DAY, WEEK ETC.): 1-2 per mo.

BLOOD TYPE: O ___ RH FACTOR: POSITIVE ✓ ___ NEGATIVE _____

HEALTH INSURANCE: YES ✓ NO___ MATERNITY COVERAGE: YES ✓ NO___

    HEALTH INSURANCE COMPANY: _____

    POLICY NUMBER: _____

    IF GROUP INSURANCE, NAME OF GROUP: _____

_____

WHAT REASSURANCE CAN WE GIVE THE COUPLE ADOPTING YOUR CHILD THAT YOU WILL NOT CHANGE
YOUR MIND?:
I couldnt do that to the couple knowing how desperately they have tried to have their own, plus the fact that I've done it before without a problem.

WHAT KIND OF SUPPORT DO YOU EXPECT FOR BEING A SURROGATE FROM THE FOLLOWING PEOPLE IN
YOUR LIFE?

PARENTS?: _my mother has no problem with it, she was a great support the first time I did it. my father doesnt approve of it at all. (parents are divorced)_

HUSBAND/BOYFRIEND?: _Husband backs me up 100%, says its my decision, its my body._

FRIENDS/CO-WORKERS?: _friends think its a great thing, but most of them say they wouldnt be able to do it._

DO YOU OWN AND DRIVE A CAR? YES ✓ NO___
DO YOU HAVE AUTOMOBILE INSURANCE? YES ✓ NO___
DO YOU HAVE A VALID DRIVER'S LICENSE? YES ✓ NO___

IF YES, GIVE ISSUING STATE AND NUMBER:_____

NO LEGAL EXPENSES WILL BE CHARGED TO SURROGATE OR HUSBAND, IF ANY. FURTHERMORE, IF YOU
ARE NOT ACCEPTED INTO THE PROGRAM, ANY MILEAGE OR BABYSITTING EXPENSES FOR THE INITIAL
CONSULTATION ARE THE RESPONSIBILITY OF THE SURROGATE AND/OR HUSBAND.

I/We declare that I/we understand the above-captioned statement.

DATED: _6-10-91_   _Anne Marie_
                                         APPLICANT

                                         _____
                                         HUSBAND, IF ANY

SURROGATE MOTHER INFORMATION SHEET NO. 2
(CONFIDENTIAL)

Note: This is a confidential record and will be kept in this office.
Information contained here will not be released to any person except
when authorized by you.

DATE: June 15, 1991

PERSONAL INFORMATION:

NAME: Anne Marie

PLEASE GIVE THE DATE AND PLACE OF EACH MARRIAGE AND/OR DIVORCE: _____
Jan. 4 1986   Las Vegas, Nevada

EDUCATION:

GRAMMAR SCHOOL: _____ GRADE COMPLETED: 6

HIGH SCHOOL: _____ GRADE COMPLETED: 12

COLLEGE: _____ HOURS COMPLETED: 1/2 semester

SUBJECTS OF SPECIAL STUDY OR RESEARCH: _____

ACTIVITIES (Civic, Athletic, etc.): _____

HEALTH INFORMATION:

DATE OF LAST PHYSICAL EXAM: May 29, 1991 DOCTOR: Dale

PAP SMEAR: YES ✓ NO___ DATE: May 29, 1991 RESULT: _____

PAST MEDICAL PROBLEMS:
PLEASE LIST PROBLEM, DATE OF ILLNESS/INJURY, AND RESOLUTION.
Ruptured ovarian cyst 1991 - surgery.
Ruptured ectopic pregnancy 1986 partial removal of fallopian tube.

MEDICATIONS YOU TAKE REGULARLY:
Anaprox DS   REASON: Menstrual cramps
_____ REASON: _____
_____ REASON: _____

IS YOUR DIET WELL BALANCED? YES ✓ NO_____

DO YOU SLEEP WELL? YES ✓ NO_____

DO YOU EXERCISE? YES ✓ NO_____ TYPE OF EXERCISE: Walking, some weights
                                                  Cycling

FAMILY HISTORY:

ANY FAMILY GENETIC PROBLEMS? _No_____

LIST EACH FAMILY MEMBER: IF LIVING   IF DECEASED
                             AGE   HEALTH   AGE AT DEATH   CAUSE

GRANDFATHER	72	fair (maternal)		
GRANDMOTHER	72	fair (paternal)		
GRANDFATHER			45	accident
GRANDMOTHER			70	heart trouble
FATHER	49	good		
MOTHER	5_	good		
SIBLINGS	30	fair (brother)	30	suicide
HUSBAND	34	good		
CHILDREN	3	good		
	7 mos	good		

HAS ANY BLOOD RELATION EVER HAD:
                                                        HOW ARE YOU RELATED?

CANCER	YES____	NO ✓	
TUBERCULOSIS	YES____	NO ✓	
DIABETES	YES ✓	NO____	maternal grandmother, mother
HEART TROUBLE	YES ✓	NO____	'' ''
HIGH BLOOD PRESSURE	YES ✓	NO____	'' '' + father
STROKE	YES ✓	NO____	
EPILEPSY	YES____	NO ✓	'' ''
INSANITY	YES____	NO ✓	
SUICIDE	YES ✓	NO____	brother
ALCOHOLISM	YES ✓	NO____	mother, brother
HYPERACTIVITY	YES____	NO ✓	

HAVE YOU HAD PSYCHOLOGICAL COUNSELING IN THE PAST? YES____ NO ✓
IF YES, PLEASE DESCRIBE THE CIRCUMSTANCES, DATES AND THE EXTENT:_____
_____

MARITAL HISTORY:

                              THIS MARRIAGE   PRIOR MARRIAGE

YEARS MARRIED	5 yrs		N/A
BIRTH CONTROL USED	YES ✓ NO____		YES____ NO____
TYPE OF BIRTH CONTROL	pill + condoms, foam		
YEARS USED	4½ yrs		
MONTHS TRYING TO CONCEIVE	9 months		

GENERAL QUESTION:

WOULD YOU BE WILLING TO HAVE YOUR PREGNANCY TERMINATED (A THERAPEUTIC
ABORTION) IF THERE IS EVIDENCE THAT THE CHILD WILL BE BORN WITH SERIOUS BIRTH
DEFECTS? yes
_____

ADDITIONAL PERSONAL HISTORY:

PLEASE EXPLAIN ALL "YES" ANSWERS ON A SEPARATE SHEET OF PAPER.

HAVE EITHER YOU OR YOUR HUSBAND EVER:

>   BEEN IN BANKRUPTCY?   YES____   NO ✓
>   BEEN IN A MENTAL HOSPITAL?   YES____ NO ✓
>   HAD PSYCHOTHERAPY?   YES____   NO ✓
>   BEEN ARRESTED (PLEASE INCLUDE DRUNK DRIVING ARRESTS)? YES___ NO ✓
>   BEEN TURNED DOWN BY AN ADOTPION AGENCY?   YES___   NO ✓
>   PLACED A CHILD FOR ADOPTION?   YES____   NO ✓
>   IF MARRIED, FILED FOR DIVORCE, DISSOLUTION, LEGAL SEPARATION OR
>   ANNULMENT OF THIS MARRIAGE?   YES____ NO ✓
>   PAST DUE ON ANY COURT ORDERED INSTALLMENT OF CHILD SUPPORT? YES__ NO ✓
>   HAVE ANY LEGAL CASES OR CLAIMS PENDING AT THE PRESENT TIME? YES__ NO ✓

AUTHORIZATION AND RELEASE

I authorize investigations of all statements contained in this application. I
understand that misrepresentations or omission of facts called for is cause
for rejection as a Surrogate Mother. Further, I understand that signing this
form is not an acceptance, but a preliminary information form.

I further authorize release of the information (medical and other information)
contained in this application to the   agents, and
employees, including physicians and psychotherapists, and prospective parents.

Dated: June 15, 1991   Anne Marie
                                        APPLICANT

                                        _____
                                        HUSBAND, IF ANY

Biographical Sketches
of Potential Surrogates

Jennifer

Background

Jennifer is a 23 year old. She lives in ———.

Jennifer is a single parent with one son. Her son, ———, is three years old. Jennifer works as a secretary for ——— and coaches a girl's basketball team.

Jennifer was raised by her biological mother in the area until she was adopted at the age of nine along with her brother, who is two years younger. She describes her adoptive parents as providing a good home. She describes her childhood years as being centered around her brother and that sibling relationship.

Both adopted parents are remarried at this time and Jennifer has a large extended family that is close and seen often. Jennifer's pregnancy history is uncomplicated. She had a C-section. She describes her pregnancy as being "very easy."

Why a Surrogate?

Jennifer reports following all the literature on surrogacy and considering it for quite some time. She admires her adopted parents for waiting for their adopted children and their ability to love her and her brother. Her parents' experience has helped Jennifer understand the world of infertility. She feels the more positive one contributes to the world, the more positive life becomes.

Another reason Jennifer is interested in being a surrogate is her own positive parenting experience. She loves kids and would like to help another couple who really want children to achieve that goal.

Consideration

Jennifer is a very verbal, open person who shares a lot of her life. She is up-front with her emotions and handles them naturally. It seems that her background has taught her to be very adaptable and flexible. Jennifer describes herself as a "survivor with lack of patience for laziness."

Jennifer has a good support system of people around her who are positive about surrogacy. Although there are no studies to prove what kind of woman makes a good surrogate, it appears that Jennifer will be a fine participant in the program.

Shelly and Matthew

March 1989

Shelly and Matthew have been together four years. They have two children, a boy 2 1/2 years old and a girl 13 months. Shelly is 26 years old. Matthew is 41. They have recently moved to —— from ——.

Shelly's pregnancies have been unremarkable. She describes her pregnancies as "easy and comfortable." Both children were delivered naturally. Matthew has had a vasectomy. They have medical and maternity insurance.

Shelly has had several friends who are infertile. She feels an identification with those couples and would like to help someone in their situation achieve the goal of parenting. Furthermore, Shelly had mild endometriosis prior to conceiving. Though now apparently cured, she and Matthew have a heightened sympathy for the infertile. Although not directly stated, the idea of the adventure in doing something this unusual is also appealing to Shelly.

Shelly and Matthew prefer to work with a couple who do not smoke and are educated and professional. They would also prefer to have a couple who will be involved where possible during the pregnancy. After the birth, Shelly would like to definitely hear from them during the child's first year to assure her that "they are settled and fine" and to offer any child-care advice if need be. This couple is clearly committed to being good parents to their own children, and consequently feel a "moral obligation" to make sure that the prospective couple are good parents.

Shelly is a very bright and articulate person. She and Matthew are both educated and professional. They appear to have a stable relationship that has been nurtured with enthusiasm.

They describe themselves as "good parents, who feel morally obligated to make sure this child goes to good parents." Shelly and Matthew appear to be mature and responsible people. It appears that they will be fine participants in the program.

Surrogate Mother's
Biographical Sketch for Couple

Jay and Anne Marie

Anne Marie is 26, Jay is 29.

OUR RELATIONSHIP: We met through a mutual friend, moved in together 2 weeks after our first date, and married 6 months later. We've been married for 5 1/2 years.

WHERE WE LIVE: _____, California.

CHILDREN & BIRTH EXPERIENCES: Two children; Zachary 3 1/2 years and Tess 7 months. My first pregnancy ended after 5 weeks due to a tubal pregnancy. I started premature labor with Zachary at 35 weeks, was given medication to stop the labor but the medication didn't help and I continued to contract but after a few days my contractions stopped and I continued my pregnancy to term. Zachary was born 1 day early. My second pregnancy was a surrogate baby. I went into premature labor at 27 weeks and was hospitalized for 9 days. I was on medication to stop the labor for the 9 days and the rest of my pregnancy. I was taken off work and told to stay off my feet as much as possible, at 35 weeks, my OB-GYN allowed me to go back to work part time. After one day of work, I went into labor and gave birth to a beautiful 5 lb. 3 oz. girl. She was very healthy and only had to stay at the hospital 4 days to get her weight up a little. (By the way, Zachary was 8 lbs. 12 oz.) My third pregnancy was my little girl. The pregnancy went well, except I started contracting at 5 months. My OB put me on oral medication which pretty much took care of the situation. After a few weeks on the medication, my contractions had been under control so I didn't have to take it any more. At 36 weeks I went into labor which was too far progressed and had my beautiful daughter. She was 5 lbs. 15 oz. She was perfectly healthy and we went home from the hospital the next day. (Zachary was a c-section and the other two were vaginal.) My OB says because of me working and on my feet a lot, that's probably why I had early contractions and labors. I am now an at home mom and don't plan on going back to work for a long while. I feel now that I'm at home and not pressed to do anything physical, I'm more relaxed and I don't think I would have a problem with a pregnancy this time around.

OUR DESCRIPTION: I am 5'4" and a lot of people have said I look like Susan St. James or Ali McGraw. (I personally don't see the resemblance!) Jay is 5'11 1/2" (I just say he's 6 foot). A lot of people think he looks like Jay Leno and he HATES that! We are both very outgoing and open minded, we are not drinkers or drug users, and we are both pretty active physically. Jay much more than I, he loves biking and hiking. We enjoy camping but haven't done it in awhile because of the kids. At least I haven't done it, but Jay has gone a couple of times with the guys. Jay does all our cooking and is very health conscious.

OUR CHILDREN: Zachary is 3 1/2 and very energetic and physical, obviously he gets it from his father, Tess is 7 months and a very good baby. I feel our family is complete, we've been blessed with one of each gender and I don't think I can handle any more! Zachary is in preschool now three days a week and that gives me time alone with Tess. We like taking the kids to the park quite often and I try to take them both for a walk in the afternoon every day.

FAMILY: Both our immediate family is small. My parents are divorced. My mother lives in Arizona and my father lives in California. Both are remarried and have been for 10 years. I have an older brother in AZ, but we don't get along too well, never have. Jay's mother lives in _____, his father passed on when he was 3. He has an older brother that lives in Texas and they are quite close. Most of Jay's family live out of state and mine are in CA and AZ.

OUR RELIGIOUS BELIEFS: Both Jay and myself are not religious people. My father's side of the family was raised Catholic, my mother's side really had no religious upbringing. I believe there is some "Great Spirit" watching over us and helps us make the right decisions in life's endeavors. We believe in ourselves to make the right decisions and we don't steal, kill etc.

WHY WE CHOSE TO BE A SURROGATE: We both know people who cannot have their own children physically and feel this is truly an ultimate gift to be able to give the gift of life to a couple who so desperately wants a family.

I have chosen to be a surrogate again because the first time was so very fulfilling. It was a wonderful feeling to see the joy and happiness I brought to the couple when their baby was born. We have kept in contact with letters and pictures and I was able to see the baby once since her birth. They are very happy with their little girl and don't plan on having anymore children because they think they are too old to have another. My contact with the parents will be strictly up to the couple once the baby is born, but during pregnancy I would like to be very close emotionally because I want the couple to experience everything there is with their baby and progress of the pregnancy. If we live close to each other, that would be ultimate because the couple could go to doctor's appts., feel their baby move, kick etc. if they so choose. And being close also means they will be sure be able to make the birth. That's very important to me that the couple be there for the birth.

The Importance of Genetic Screening

Genetic screening for carriers of certain inherited disorders provides important information for couples who are planning a pregnancy. It is estimated that all individuals are "carriers" of between five to ten recessive genes. A carrier has one normal gene and one abnormal gene for a specific disorder in each of his or her cells. Sometimes this situation is called carrying a trait. Generally, a carrier of a recessive gene does not have the symptoms of that inherited disease because the normal gene covers up the abnormal gene, there is a one in four chance that any child they have will inherit the recessive gene from both parents and have a severe form of the disease. This disease state occurs when there is no normal gene to cover up the abnormal recessive gene.

Screening for carriers of genetic traits is an important component in matching couples with a surrogate when using artificial insemination (AI), as well as important for couples who will be using *in vitro* fertilization (IVF). Screening is recommended for individuals from certain ethnic groups where the incidence of specific genetic diseases are higher than found in the general population.

Genetic screening is particularly important for American Blacks who have a higher risk of being carriers of sickle cell trait, Ashkenazi Jews who have an increased risk of carrying the Tay Sachs gene, and individuals of Mediterranean or Southeast Asian descent who have a higher chance of being carriers of Thalassemia. A common misconception is that genetic screening is not necessary unless there is a family history of that genetic disease in the individual's family. This is incorrect, and in fact, in the majority of cases where an individual is identified as being a carrier of a recessive disease, there is no relative with that disease. That is because being a carrier of a genetic disease does not imply any reproductive disadvantage. It is only when two carriers each contribute the abnormal gene in the egg and sperm that affected offspring will be born. Usually, there is no known prior history of the disease in either side of the family and thus, genetic screening for all individuals in high risk population groups is the only way to identify carriers.

Some common questions about genetic screening are answered below:

Q: *Does genetic screening test for any inherited disorder?*

A: No. Genetic screening is performed for a specific disease and tests for the presence of one copy of an abnormal gene. Genetic screening is only available for certain inherited disorders. The need for genetic screening is usually determined by an individual's ethnic background.

Q: *Should I be screened even if I know that there has never been a family member with a genetic disease?*

A: Yes. It is important to remember that carriers are usually detected when there is no known prior history of the disease on either side of the family. In fact, very few carriers have a family member with a genetic disease. Therefore, carrier screening should be considered by all individuals within those populations with an increased incidence of a specific genetic disease.

Q: *My husband and I are considering IVF. He is Jewish, and I am Christian. Is Tay Sachs screening recommended even though only one of us is Jewish?*

A: Yes, your husband should be screened for Tay Sachs prior to embarking on a pregnancy. We know that anyone, regardless of ethnic background can be a carrier of any recessive disease. If your husband is a non-carrier, you do not need to proceed with screening.

Q: *Do I need to be screened with each pregnancy?*

A: No. Carrier status does not change within an individual. We are either carriers or non-carriers from before the time we are born, and carrier screening need not be repeated with a second pregnancy.

Q: *If I am a carrier, and my husband is a non-carrier of a genetic disease, do we have an increased risk to have an affected baby?*

A: No. Both the mother and the father need to be carriers of the same trait in order to increase the risk for an affected offspring.

Q: *If my husband and I are both carriers of the same trait, is IVF still an option for us?*

A: Yes, IVF followed by prenatal diagnosis would still be an option for couples who strongly prefer IVF over AI. However, the couple should be aware that if they are both carriers, there is a one in four chance that the fetus will be affected with the disease. Prenatal diagnosis is available using chorionic villus sampling (CVS) or amniocentesis in the first or second trimester of pregnancy for couples who are willing to take this risk.

Q: *How common is it to be a carrier of these genetic traits?*

A: Carriers within defined ethnic groups are relatively common. About one in twenty-seven Ashkenazi Jews is a Tay Sachs carrier. Among American Blacks, the frequency of carrying the trait for sickle cell is about one in twelve. The frequency of carrying the gene for Thalassemia in Greeks, Italians, Chinese and South Asians is between one in twenty-five and one in thirty individuals.

Genetic screening to determine carrier status is recommended prior to pregnancy in order to obtain as much information about the potential genetic risks well in advance. This allows the couples to be matched with surrogates in such a way as to minimize the risk for a baby with genetic disease. Alternatively, IVF couples will be more informed about their potential risks for a baby with a genetic disease, which may influence their decision regarding AI versus IVF.

Prospective Parent's Medical Genetics Questionnaire

Name _____ Age _____ Birth Date _____ Sex __

Address _____ Zip _____

Occupation _____ Home Phone _____

Spouse's name _____ Work Phone _____

Family History

1. What is your ethnic background? _____

2. Please check yes or no for the following questions

	Yes	No
a) Do you have any Jewish ancestry?		
b) Do you have any French Canadian ancestry?		
c) Do you have any South East Asian Ancestry?		
d) Do you have any Mediterranean (i.e., Italian, Greek) ancestry?		
e) Do you have any Black ancestry?		
f) Are you aware of any family history of the following disorders:		
Down Syndrome		
Cystic Fibrosis		
Tay Sachs		
Sickle Cell Anemia		
Thalassemia		
Dwarfism		
Muscular Dystrophy		
Hemophilia		

3. How many times have you (or a partner) been pregnant? _____
4. How many biological children do you have? _____ Boys

_____ Girls

Please describe any history of health problems in your children.

_____

_____

5. Are your parents living? _____ mother
_____ father

If not, what was the cause of their death? _____
Please describe any history of health problems in your parents.
    mother _____
    father _____

6.   How many miscarriages have you (or a partner) had? _____
    At what stage of pregnancy did these occur? _____

7.   Have you ever had HIV (AIDS) testing? _____
    If yes, when was this done? _____
    What were the results? _____

8.   Have you had any serious medical illnesses? _____
    If yes, please explain _____
    _____

9.   Have you ever had surgery? _____
    If yes, please explain _____
    _____

10.   Have you ever been hospitalized? _____
    If yes, please explain _____
    _____

11.   Do you take any medications on a regular basis? _____
    If yes, please explain _____
    _____

12.   Do you smoke tobacco? _____

13.   Do you have high blood pressure? _____

14.   The following questions apply to your children, siblings, parents, grand-
    parents, aunts, uncles, and cousins. Please check the appropriate box if
    any of these family members have had a history of any of the following
    medical problems.

	You	Your children	Your brothers/ sisters	Your parents	Your aunts/ uncles	Your cousins
a) a genetic (inherited) condition						
b) mental retardation						
c) a birth defect						
d) a congenital disorder						
e) a physical handicap						
f) seizures						
g) mental illness (e.g., depression, schizophrenia)						

h) an unusual dermatologic disorder						
i) a stillbirth or childhood death						
j) congenital heart defect						
k) alcoholism						
l) drug or other substance abuse						
m) neurologic disorders						
n) death before age 50						

Have any family members had any of the following conditions diagnosed before age 45?

	You	Your children	Your brothers/ sisters	Your parents	Your aunts/ uncles	Your cousins
Cancer						
Heart Disease						
Diabetes						
Tumors						
Respiratory Problems						
Kidney Disorder						
Skeletal Problems						

Phone Intake Form for Prospective Parents

DATE: _____

AI: _____ IVF: _____ ER: _____ LEGAL: _____

TELEPHONE INQUIRY _____ WRITTEN INQUIRY _____

TAKEN BY _____

NAME _____

ADDRESS _____

CITY _____ STATE _____ ZIP CODE _____

TELEPHONE NO. _____ (h) _____ (W)

REFERRED BY? _____ _____

MARRIED FOR _____YRS   AGES: HUSBAND _____ WIFE _____

_____

COMMENTS: _____

_____

_____

_____

_____

_____

_____

_____

_____

_____

DATE INFO SENT: _____

APPENDIX I

Prospective Parents Questionnaire

CONFIDENTIAL PRESPECTIVE PARENTS QUESTIONNAIRE

DATE OF CONSULTATION: _4/23/87_

NAME

(HUSBAND):____ADAM____JOHN_____ _____
     (LAST)   (FIRST)   (MIDDLE)   SOCIAL SECURITY #

(WIFE):____JUNE____WESTON_____ _____
     (LAST)   (FIRST)   (MIDDLE)   SOCIAL SECURITY #

ADDRESS: _____

_____ HOME PHONE _____

IN CASE OF EMERGENCY NOTIFY:___ _____

_____ PHONE NO. _____

BUSINESS: (HUSBAND)   (WIFE)

                  _____   _____

ADDRESS: _____   _____

                  _____   _____

PHONE: _____   _____

GENERAL DESCRIPTION: (HUSBAND)   (WIFE)

	(HUSBAND)	(WIFE)
DO YOU SMOKE?	YES ___ NO ✓	YES ___ NO ✓
HAIR:	BROWN	BLONDE
COMPLEX:	FAIR	FAIR
EYES:	BLUE	GREEN
HEIGHT:	6'4"	5'2½"
WEIGHT:	190	120
AGE:	39	40
BIRTHPLACE:	HOLTON, KANSAS	BOSTON MASS.
DATE OF BIRTH:	9-30-47	9-1-46
NAT'L ANCESTRY:	SCOTTISH IRISH GERMAN	ENGLISH
RELIGION:	PROTESTANT	PROTESTANT
HOBBIES:	SPORTS	COOKING TRYING TO HAVE A CHILD
OCCUPATION:	LAW	ADM ASS'T - FILM
HEALTH:	EXCELLENT	EXCELLENT
BLOOD TYPE:		A
DATE OF MARRIAGE:	2-27-82	married 5 years.
PLACE OF MARRIAGE:	MALIBU, CA.	

3/87   QUEST

177

EDUCATION: (HUSBAND)   (WIFE)

HIGH SCHOOL: _____   _____

COLLEGE: _____   _____

YEARS COMPLETED: 4   5

DEGREES & DATE: HS 1965   HS 1964

FINANCIAL SUMMARY: (HUSBAND)   (WIFE)

AVERAGE ANNUAL INCOME: ~~$15,000~~ 35,500 42,000   ~~$27,000~~ 0

LIFE INSURANCE: _____   _____

REAL ESTATE EQUITY: $75,000   _____

AGGREGATE SAVINGS &
SECURITIES: _____   _____

NET WORTH: _____   _____

TYPE OF DWELLING: OWN ✓ RENT_____   MONTHLY PAYMENT/RENT: $707
APPROX. MARKET VALUE: $140,000   EQUITY: $75,000

OTHER CHILDREN: (HUSBAND)   NONE   (WIFE)
    NAME   AGE   NAME   AGE
_____   _____
_____   _____
_____   _____

PRIOR MARRIAGES: (HUSBAND)   (WIFE)

SPOUSES NAME: _____   _____

MARRIAGE
(DATE & PLACE) DEC, 1978   JUNE, 1969

TERMINATED
(DATE & PLACE) 1979   1972

NO. OF CHILDREN: 0   0

PERSONAL HISTORY: (CIRLE ONE)

HAVE EITHER OF YOU:
    FILED FOR BANKRUPTCY? YES (NO)
    HAD PSYCHOTHERAPY? YES (NO)
    BEEN IN A MENTAL HOSPITAL? YES (NO)
    BEEN ARRESTED (EXCEPT MINOR TRAFFIC OFFENSES)? YES (NO)
    FILED FOR DIVORCE, DISSOLUTION, LEGAL SEPARATION OR ANNULMENT
    OF THIS MARRIAGE? YES (NO)
    ARE YOU PAST DUE ON ANY COURT ORDERED INSTALLMENT OF CHILD
    SUPPORT? YES (NO)

PERSONAL HISTORY (CON'D):

PLEASE DESCRIBE INFERFILITY PROBLEM BELOW:

WIFE 'DES' BABY - CONGENITAL DEFORMITIES WHICH HAVE
BEEN CORRECTED SURGICALLY TO NO AVAIL. HAVE TRIED
ALL AVENUES.

HUSBAND FINE.

PLEASE LIST ANY HEALTH PROBLEMS AND/OR GENETIC PROBLEMS IN YOUR
FAMILY. PLEASE INCLUDE ANY MEDICATION YOU ARE CURRENTLY TAKING.

NONE

MEDICAL INFORMATION:

INSURED: _____

COMPANY: _____ POLICY NO. _____

HAVE YOU HAD A SPERM ANALYSIS? YES ✓ NO_____ A FREEZE TEST? YES
NO ✓ IF YES, PLEASE GIVE THE RESULTS: SPERM ANALYSIS FINE
_____

REFERRED BY: WRONG number -

I DECLARE THAT THE ABOVE IS TRUE AND CORRECT.

DATED: 4/28/87   Adam J.
                                  HUSBAND
                                  June W.
                                  WIFE

*NOTE:
    Please read and sign the attached Authorization to Receive or
    Release Medical, Psychological, and Other Information.

- 3 -

AUTHORIZATION TO RECEIVE OR RELEASE MEDICAL

PSYCHOLOGICAL AND OTHER INFORMATION

     I/We hereby authorize you to permit the

         their representatives, designees, agents, or the bearer
of this document to examine and/or copy by photostat, or in any
other manner, all records of history, examination, diagnosis,
treatment, x-rays, prognosis, and any other information, including
charges for services rendered relating to all the care rendered
to _____.

     This authorization is valid until my/our written notice of
withdrawal is received by   and
I/we agree that a photocopy of this authorization is as valid as the
original.

     I/We, the undersigned, Clients, have read this authorization
and acknowledge that I/we, the client(s), or a person authorized by
me/us, will receive a copy of this authorization upon request.

Dated:___4/23/87_____   ___Adam J._____
                                   HUSBAND

                                   ___June W._____
                                   WIFE

- 4 -

Egg Donor Program

The Process

The Program is pleased to be able to offer an egg donor program. It enables another sector of the infertile community to take advantage of advances in the new reproductive technologies.

Who Can Benefit from an Egg Donor Program?

The Program offers the first organized, comprehensive egg donor program. This enables women who can carry a pregnancy but cannot produce eggs (or whose eggs carry a genetic defect) to conceive through the in vitro fertilization process (IVF) and bear a child. It also provides fertile women with a new opportunity to help childless couples build their families.

Why an Egg Donor Program?

In the past, egg donor programs have relied on IVF patients (who are infertile to begin with) to donate excess eggs to infertile couples on a random basis. There has never been a program such as ours in which egg donors were specifically solicited, screened and matched with prospective recipients. In addition, all legal, psychological and administrative functions are coordinated by the program.

How Does It Work?

Our experience with surrogate mothers enables us to find and screen potential egg donors who will then undergo non-surgical transvaginal aspiration of their eggs for donation to infertile couples. The women who donate eggs have basically the same psychological profile as our surrogate mothers. Their ages range from 21 through 34, they are in excellent health, and are responsible, empathic women.

In addition to undergoing a mandatory, comprehensive medical and psychological screening program, the Egg Donors also receive fertility drug therapy to increase the number of eggs produced. All Egg Donors and Prospective Parents are matched by our psychologist so that the parties are comfortable and fully informed.

A Professional Team

Infertility Specialists

The Program works in conjunction with recognized infertility specialists who utilize the newest and most advanced reproductive technologies available. All

181

parties are medically screened and evaluated for participation in the Egg Donor program and must undergo thorough Social Disease Testing, including AIDS.

Psychological Counseling

Psychologist for the Program, Dr. ———, is specifically trained and nationally recognized for her work in the field of adoption and surrogacy. Both Egg Donors and Prospective Parents are required to undergo psychological evaluation and counseling. Egg Donors meet with other Egg Donors and the psychologist for periodic, mandatory support group meetings. Elective group support sessions for the Prospective Couple are also available throughout the program.

Legal Expertise

Attorney ——— is a recognized authority, law professor, international lecturer, author and practitioner in the field of Alternative Reproduction Law. He negotiates and drafts all contractual agreements. Egg Donor and Prospective Parents contract with each other much the same as in our traditional surrogate mother program, insuring that the requisite safeguards and procedural guidelines are in place. All parties must be represented by independent legal counsel.

Administrative Staff

Our administrative staff coordinates between Egg Donor, Prospective Parents, doctors, psychologists, laboratories, hospitals and attorneys. The administrative staff also manages the trust funds, obtains all necessary legal documents, monitors all aspects of the program, including disbursement of all expenses on behalf of the Prospective Parents, and furnishes a full accounting to all parties.

What the Egg Donor Contract Does

1. Establishes financial responsibility on the part of the Prospective Parents and guarantees that funds are placed in a trust account to cover all anticipated expenses.
2. Declares the Prospective Parents are financially, legally and custodially responsible for the child no matter what.
3. Provides that all parties must have legal and medical informed consent (all parties must be represented by counsel).
4. Provides that social disease testing (including AIDS) is done on all parties. Provides that the Egg Donor be medically examined and declared medically appropriate for the program.
5. Provides all parties with current status of the law (e.g. ownership of embryos, disposition of embryos, and legal definition of parentage).
6. Establishes specific responsibilities of each party so as to minimize misunderstandings later on.
7. Establishes that records be kept on all parties in the event information on a party is later needed for legal or medical reasons.
8. Provides a legal and psychological framework so all aspects of this process are thought out, considered and pondered by everyone prior to entering into this agreement.

9. Outlines confidentiality concerns and provides for privacy for all parties.
10. Addresses the issue of contact between all parties in the future.

Approximate Costs

The total cost to a couple participating in our Egg Donor Program is approximately Seventeen Thousand Dollars ($17,000.00), depending on what medical insurance will reimburse, and is broken down as follows:

Program's Professional Fees

The Program charges a fee of Six Thousand Dollars ($6,000.00) to match a couple with an appropriate Egg Donor. This fee represents all advertising and professional costs in finding a suitable candidate, psychological screening and counseling, matching her with a couple, negotiating the contract and administration of all the legal, psychological and medical procedures. Included in these fees are funds which are spent for research, public education and lobbying efforts directed at keeping open and expanding the options of infertile couples.

Donor Fees

In addition to the above professional fees to the Program, the donor receives the sum of One Thousand Five Hundred Dollars ($1,500.00) as her payment for the actual egg retrieval procedure, fertility drug treatment, and an ultrasound monitoring she will undergo, plus an additional Five Hundred Dollars ($500.00) in miscellaneous expenses such as travel, babysitting, etc.

Medical Expenses

These costs are estimates only. Please check directly with the physician who will be performing the procedure. Some of these costs may be reduced by medical insurance. Medical fees for the egg recipient including full screening and one (1) cycle hormonal evaluation. The cost is approximately Four Thousand Dollars ($4,000.00).

We estimate that the medical costs involving the Egg Donor herself to be approximately Five Thousand Dollars ($5,000.00). This should include the medical screening, the cost of fertility drugs and the medical procedure to remove the donor's eggs (through transvaginal aspiration).

Miscellaneous Costs

There is an additional cost of approximately Two Hundred Dollars ($200.00) for payment to the Egg Donor's attorney. It is our policy that all Egg Donors entering our program must be represented by counsel when signing the contract. It is critical that the Egg Donor have full legal and medical informed consent.

Egg Recipient Instructions
History of Egg Donation

In the past five years, the use of in vitro fertilized donor eggs has been widely applied, with resulting births in many countries including Australia, England, Israel, and the United States.

There have been two major advances in reproductive technology that make the use of donor eggs a viable option for women who would not otherwise be able to have a child. The first advance has been the introduction of ultrasound guided transvaginal (non-surgical) recovery of donor eggs. This is an outpatient procedure requiring only local anesthesia and sedation; laparoscopy and general anesthesia are not required. The second advance is the success in cryopreservation (freezing) of in vitro fertilized embryos. In our program, donor and recipient's cycles are synchronized to insure transfer of fresh ova and thus optimize the chance of a conception. However, if more eggs are retrieved and fertilized than necessary, extra ova can be frozen for use in later cycles, thus making the entire procedure more cost effective.

Participant

The Prospective Parents must be married and either unable to conceive a child or have genetically defective eggs. The wife must have a uterus and no medical contraindication to pregnancy or to labor and delivery of such a pregnancy. The donor eggs are needed either to replace her own (if they are defective), or if she cannot produce her own. The Recipient woman may require donor eggs for medical reasons including the following:

1. She has premature ovarian failure (P.O.F.), due to surgical castration, chemo or radiation therapy, or simply unexplained causes.
2. She carries an X-linked or autosomal dominant genetic disorder for which there is no prenatal diagnostic testing.
3. She has a history of recurrent (three or more) early pregnancy loss secondary to a chromosomal defect (translocation, deletion).
4. She has a history of repeated (more than three) attempts at in vitro fertilization with suboptimal ovarian stimulation in terms of egg yield or embryo development, or failure of pregnancy after the transfer of numerous apparently healthy embryos.

Psychological Evaluation

The Recipient and her spouse will meet with a clinical psychologist to insure their understanding of the process, to discuss their needs in terms of a suitable egg donor, and to address any questions they might have.

Legal Process

Prospective Parents and Egg Donor each meet with an attorney to discuss the contractual agreement into which they both enter. This contract defines all parties' rights and responsibilities, as well as the legal status and disposition of the embryos. No adoption is required as the legal mother of the child is the woman who gives birth to it, regardless of its genetic makeup.

The Medical Procedure

The Recipient will initially undergo a medical evaluation and consultation by the treating physician. The husband will have a semen analysis and culture to assess the fertilizing capacity of his sperm (if he has not previously done so within the last six months). The physician will explain the process in detail, as well as all risks involved, so that the Prospective Parents have full, informed medical consent.

For Ovum Substitution (Recipient has her own ovaries): The Recipient has her own menstrual cycles, which are synchronized (by means of fertility drugs) with the Egg Donor's cycles so that the embryos are ready for transfer when the Recipient's uterus is hormonally receptive. The Recipient's cycle is monitored by daily measurement of hormones (blood tests) and ovarian follicular ultrasounds beginning on day 3–4 until ovulation mid-cycle. Ovulation is confirmed by ultrasound. Embryos are then transfered into either the Recipient's uterus (IVF) or fallopian tubes (GIFT) if possible. The timing of the transfer is based on Recipient's day of ovulation and stage of embryo development. Recipient may receive additional hormonal support after the transfer of up to four fresh embryos. Twelve or more days after the transfer, Recipient will take a pregnancy test and if it is positive, she will have additional blood tests to measure pregnancy hormone levels until a pregnancy is confirmed by ultrasound.

Evaluation of Egg Donor (Typical time is two months)

I. Initial Interview of Candidate and Spouse (if any)

Clinical interview with licensed psychologist with a specialty in adoption and surrogacy to cover history, motivations, intelligence, personality and other variables.

Meeting with attorney to cover informed consent, contract, liability, legalities, finances.

II. Mandatory Attendance to Group Counseling

Counseling sessions led by staff psychologist. Candidates will meet with other Egg Donors for several hours prior to acceptance. Thereafter, periodic support group meetings will be held.

III. Psychological Testing

Minnesota Multiphasic Personality Inventory given and analyzed. Results compared to national data and to specific egg donor/surrogate population. (If any personality traits are more than 2 standard deviations above the norm or if pathology is exhibited the candidate is rejected.)

IV. Medical Screening

The candidate is evaluated by the treating infertility specialist. A typical exam includes general medical history, pregnancy and fertility history, gynecological exam, full social disease testing (including AIDS), hormonal testing, and informed consent concerns.

V. Continual Psychological Assessment

Counseling will be provided throughout evaluation and egg retrieval process, via telephone, face-to-face meetings and support group meetings.

VI. Legal Consultation

Prior to beginning medical procedures Egg Donor and spouse must review the contract with an independent counsel.

Handling of Semen Specimen and Insemination Instructions

Instructions for Semen Collection and Shipping (Please read entire instruction sheet <u>before</u> you need to ship)

Enclosed with these instructions you will find several plastic vials for storage and shipping of your semen specimen. Save all the packaging in which these arrived, as you will re-use it for insulation and shipping of your specimen. If you have not already received it, you will soon receive via Federal Express a box of ten vials of a refrigeration medium called Test Yolk Buffer. This will enable you to collect a semen specimen and ship it overnight for a next-day insemination without freezing the sample. Freezing causes about a 50% reduction in the count (number of sperm) and motility (how well the sperm move). Using the Test Yolk Buffer medium not only eliminates damage done by freezing but actually improves the overall quality of the specimen. It's as if you are doing a fresh insemination. Below you will find instructions on how to use the Test Yolk Buffer medium and how to ship your semen specimen for next-day or even same-day inseminations. (Even though the Test Yolk Buffer will arrive with its own instructions, ignore them. They do not apply to this type of application.)

Semen Collection

1. Upon receipt of the Test Yolk Buffer medium, place immediately in your freezer until you need to use it.

2. Your surrogate mom or someone at the Program will call you and let you know that the ovulation test kit has indicated that your surrogate has had an LH surge and her ovu-stick has turned blue. This means she will probably ovulate in the next day or two.

3. Upon receiving this call, take out a vial of the medium stored in your freezer and bring up to room temperature. You may run it under lukewarm water to speed up the process. DO NOT heat it above room temperature (37°C).

4. Collect the semen sample by masturbation into a sterile container (boil a glass jar for 20 minutes), ideally, following a two-to-three-day abstinence period. If this is not possible (you have ejaculated the day before you got the call) collect the sample anyway. It is still viable for inseminations. However, do not abstain <u>more</u> than 5 days, as motility decreases. Avoid hot baths, hot tubs or tight clothing as this also is detrimental to sperm.

5. Allow semen to liquefy at room temperature for 30 minutes. Then combine the sperm sample with equal parts of the Test Yolk Buffer medium (which is now also room temperature) in the plastic vial provided. You can simply eyeball the proportions. Mix well by gently shaking and make sure cap is on securely. Tape the cap on with adhesive tape, as the vibrations from transporting the specimen can loosen even the most securely tightened cap. Label the vial clearly with your name, date, time of collection, and days since last emission. If you are mailing it within twelve hours, re-package it exactly as you received it. This will insure its safe arrival.

It is now ready for shipping or mailing. If you are not shipping the sample within 12 hours, store it in your refrigerator. Sudden changes in temperature reduce the motility of the sperm, so if you put it in the refrigerator for storage, make sure you protect (insulate) it by standing it first in a glass of room-temperature water and place the entire glass with the tube in the refrigerator. This allows the temperature of the sperm sample to lower slowly.

Shipping Instructions

There are several ways to ship your semen specimen. Keep in mind that your un-frozen sample will maintain maximum viability for only 48 hours after collection. It is not necessary to refrigerate the sample for shipping. We have experimented and found that there is no difference in count or motility between refrigerated and non-refrigerated samples. In fact, when combined with the Test Yolk Buffer, semen can remain unrefrigerated for up to two days without damage to the sample. This is because the buffer contains an antibiotic which inhibits bacteria growth.

The Quickest Way

The quickest way to send the sample is by an airline that has same-day service. Depending on where you live, you could produce a sample in the morning and your surrogate mom could have it for an afternoon insemination. This would involve calling the airline for its schedules, going down to the airport to book your specimen on a flight, calling your surrogate mom with the time of arrival so she can go down to the airport on the receiving end and pick it up. Obviously, if your surrogate does not live close enough to an airport to make this convenient for her, this method of shipping will not work for you.

The Easiest Way

If you cannot ship your specimen the same day or if it is inconvenient for your surrogate mom to pick it up at the airport, ship it Federal Express or Airborne Express to the inseminating physician's office. Enclosed you will find his name, address and telephone number, as well as storage and processing instructions for the inseminating physician which you should include with the semen specimen when you ship it. Call Federal or Airborne and find out when the last flight of the day is scheduled. This will probably be in the evening sometime between 5 and 11 P.M. in order for it to be received by 10:30 A.M. the next morning. Produce the sample as close to shipping time as is possible. You should call the inseminating physician's office to notify them of its arrival the next morning. Tell them <u>not</u> to store the sample in the freezer. In fact, if they are using it for an insemination later that day, tell them not to even refrigerate it, as this will reduce the motility. This specimen is good for one or two fresh inseminations only. Usually the inseminating physician likes to do at least two or three inseminations during your surrogate mom's fertile period. This means that you should always have frozen semen banked at the doctor's office, even if you are doing a "fresh" insemination.

Weekend Shipping

If, heaven forbid, you find you must inseminate on a Sunday or Monday, you will discover that none of the overnight courier services will ship or deliver on Sunday. Most, however, will ship on Saturday for an extra charge (about $10.), but this does you little good for a Sunday insemination as it cannot be delivered until Monday. However, it probably won't even be good for a Monday insemination, as by this time, it will be over 48 hours old and contaminated by bacteria. If you are industrious and want to send it refrigerated (<u>not</u> frozen), pack it in a box with blue ice (that stuff that goes in coolers etc.) and hopefully it will be good for a Monday insemination if you want to send it on Saturday. (Make sure you mark a Saturday pick-up in the appropriate box on the airbill, and make sure that the place you deposit your package <u>has</u> a Saturday pick-up.)

The <u>best</u> way to ship your specimen for a Sunday or Monday insemination is to use American Airlines "same day, door-to-door small package service," which costs about $75. You must take it down to the airlines, and they will ship it directly to your surrogate mom's <u>home address</u> (make sure you <u>have it</u>), and she will take it with her to the insemination. Notify her of the approximate time of its delivery and tell her to store it in a cool place, but not to refrigerate. Call the airlines for their flight schedules, then go down to the airport at least <u>one hour</u> before the flight is scheduled to depart, with your specimen well-packaged (insulated but not refrigerated) in a shoe-box-sized package. Just take it to the ticket counter and book it on the desired flight.

Even though these instructions may seem complicated, once you do it there's nothing to it! Please do not hesitate to call this office if you have any questions; ask to speak to the Coordinator at ———. Good luck with your next insemination!

YOUR PHYSICIAN'S ADDRESS AND PHONE NUMBER

_____

_____

_____

PHONE: _____   ATTN: _____

Please remember to label your vial clearly (you can use tape or the enclosed labels) and include the enclosed PHYSICIAN'S INSTRUCTIONS.

Physicians' Instructions for Handling of Semen Specimen

In the enclosed package you will find a labeled semen specimen which has been mixed with equal parts of a refrigeration medium called Test Yolk Buffer. Please note time and date of collection.

This specimen has been sent overnight delivery, so it probably was produced 12–48 hours previously. It was sent insulated, but unrefrigerated. We have found that because of the antibiotic in the Test Yolk Buffer, this sample maintains maximum viability for 48 hours, after which it should be refrigerated. (Do not freeze.) If you refrigerate, insulate the sample from shock by standing in a glass of room-temperature water before placing in refrigerator. It should cool down slowly. Hopefully, the specimen will be used for insemination within 48 hours so refrigeration becomes unnecessary, as we find cooling it decreases the motility.

The specimen can be used as is, in a cervical cap or sponge, for insemination. (Obviously, its normal count is decreased by 50% as it is mixed in equal parts with the Test Yolk Buffer.) Or, if necessary, it can be manipulated as if it were a fresh sample. For example, it can be washed, or you can do a swim-up for interuterine insemination, or it can be processed for sex selection. Studies have shown a significant increase in the ability of human sperm to penetrate zona-free hamster eggs after 24–48 hours of storage in the Test Yolk Buffer.

If you have further questions, please do not hesitate to call the Coordinator at the Program, ———. Good luck with the insemination and if possible, call and let me know how the sample looked. This is a new use for the Test Yolk Buffer Medium, and any data you can give me would be appreciated. So far, semen specimens shipped this way have looked great, and we have achieved several pregnancies using this method. I would be happy to share my information with you. Thanks.

Insemination Instructions

Now that you have been matched, the process of trying to achieve a pregnancy begins. This is an exciting time, filled with hopes and expectations—everybody involved wants this baby to be conceived in the quickest time possible. The following is a guide to facilitate the insemination process.

Perhaps a preface to this guide should be a reminder that fertility and achieving a pregnancy is still not an exact science; there are so many unknown factors influencing fertility that even with all the advances in reproductive technology, conception remains as much an art as a science. Fertility is not an all or nothing proposition—it's a matter of degree. Factors such as age, stress and timing can affect how fertile any two people are in a given cycle. Unknown factors such as antibodies, antigens, and the "chemistry" between two individuals can also affect conception. Studies show that semen from a fertile, anonymous sperm donor will repeatedly fail to impregnate two different, fertile women, yet will immediately produce conception in a third woman.

Nobody is more interested in achieving this pregnancy than you. After three years of having no control over your fertility, you now have the opportunity to greatly influence how quickly you achieve a pregnancy. Despite the mysteries of fertility, there <u>are</u> factors which you <u>can</u> control. The Program encourages both the infertile couple and the surrogate mother to take direct responsibility for their inseminations. The Program will be glad to assist. However, third-party involvement often results in more confusion than help. Direct contact with one another, the inseminating doctor and/or the fertility laboratory will result in well-timed, successful inseminations. This means:

1. All parties should have the phone numbers and names of key people necessary to reach:

    a. each other: _____

    b. the inseminating doctor: _____

    c. the fertility laboratory if the sample is processed
    or to be delivered there: _____

    d. if you are using frozen semen, the sperm bank
    where it was deposited: _____

    e. The Program: _____

    f. Psychologist's home phone: _____

    g. Coordinator's home phone: _____

2. The surrogate mom <u>and</u> the couple should both keep track of her cycles on a calendar. When the surrogate starts her cycle, <u>she should call her couple and let them know</u>. That is DAY ONE (1) of her cycle. (In a normal, 28-day cycle, the surrogate will most likely ovulate around day 14. This means you should inseminate on day 13 and 14.) This allows them both to determine ahead of time when they think she may be ovulating, and gives everybody time to plan, especially if those days might fall on a weekend. If the couple doesn't hear from their surrogate, they should call her. You should both have a very clear idea of when she will ovulate.

3. Depending on the average length of her cycle, the surrogate mom should begin using her ovulation predictor kit (ovustick, ovuquick—you can get one here at the Program), at least three days before she usually ovulates. Once she begins using it, she should use it once a day, but NOT BEFORE 11 A.M. IN THE MORNING! This is because the body <u>always</u> releases LH (lutenizing hormone) between 1 and 3 A.M. at night and it takes 9–10 hours for it to show up in your urine, which is what makes the stick (dot) turn blue in your ovulation predictor kit. You will ovulate approximately 24–37 hours after the stick first indicates an LH surge (turns blue). IDEALLY, YOU SHOULD INSEMINATE ON THE DAY THE STICK TURNS BLUE AND THE DAY AFTER. This may not be possible if you are not local and are shipping test yolk buffer for fresh inseminations. In this case, you should take an educated guess based on the surrogate mom's past cycles and pre-arrange a day to ship the semen and do the insemination. If it turns out to be too early, you can always ship another sample.

4. It is the <u>surrogate's</u> responsibility a.) to make sure she has an adequate supply of ovusticks; b.) to call her couple when she <u>starts her cycle</u> and when her <u>ovusticks change color</u>; c.) to make her own insemination appointments, notify her couple of the times and dates, and show up on time. She should call the Pro-

gram for necessary names and phone numbers if she has not already done so, or if she has any questions.

5. It is the couple's responsibility a.) to make sure that if they are using frozen semen, they have an adequate supply for that month's inseminations (call the sperm bank where you made your deposits); b.) if they are using test yolk buffer for fresh semen shipping, to call the Coordinator at the Program when they need more buffer, vials, packaging, etc. (they should call before they need to use it, as it takes at least two days to ship it); c.) if they want to know how the sample looked in terms of quality or how accurate the timing of the insemination was, to feel free to personally call the inseminating physician and/or the fertility laboratory where the sample was processed. The couple should call the Program for all necessary names and phone numbers if they have not already done so. If couples do not hear from their surrogate mom regarding insemination dates and times, call her!

6. Both surrogate and couple should call the Coordinator at the Program with information about the start of a cycle, dates of insemination, quality and timing of insemination if you have spoken with the doctor—any relevant or important information, such as if you are using fertility drugs, sonograms or temperature charts to aid in inseminations. The Coordinator keeps detailed records on each couple and their surrogate mom, and updating her each cycle will be in your own best interest—that way we all can be more aggressive and effective in timing inseminations and achieving a pregnancy.

7. Studies have shown that it takes an average of 4.9 months to achieve a pregnancy in a normal fertile woman with donor insemination, assuming correct timing of the inseminations. If you do not achieve a pregnancy after at least six months of WELL-TIMED inseminations, feel free to confer with the doctor, or the Program as to what other steps might be taken. Above all, do not blame yourselves or each other if a conception does not result in any given cycle. Stress does not improve fertility! GOOD LUCK!!!

Notes

Introduction

1. That is the case in which a couple, William and Elizabeth Stern, contracted with a surrogate, Mary Beth Whitehead, because Mrs. Stern suffered from multiple sclerosis, a condition that a pregnancy could have exacerbated. Once the child was born, Whitehead refused to relinquish the child to the Sterns, and in 1987 William Stern, the biological father, brought suit against Mary Beth Whitehead in order to enforce the terms of the surrogate contract.

2. See Rapp (1978:279) for a historical perspective on the idea of the demise of the American family.

3. At that time, it was not unusual for individuals posing as potential surrogates to attempt to infiltrate programs in order to report their findings to anti-surrogacy organizations.

4. All the programs I contacted, except for one, agreed to participate.

5. Surrogate mother programs are located throughout the United States, and commissioning couples travel to the United States from all over the world.

6. Some directors expressed disappointment that I had elected to use pseudonyms rather than program names, hoping that a favorable assessment of their program under its real name would serve to increase its client base. Many surrogates also let me know that they were willing to have their real names printed.

7. The Frick program is perhaps best known for having accepted Mary Beth Whitehead as a surrogate and subsequently matching her with the Sterns (father and adoptive mother) in what has come to be known as the Baby M case, the most publicized dispute to date between a surrogate and a couple over the custody of a child conceived by a surrogate mother.

8. Although most of the data for this study have been derived from open programs, I have also spoken with administrative assistants from closed programs and ex-surrogates and couples who interviewed at closed programs.

9. It should be noted that since this director is engaged in a full-time law practice and has numerous outside interests and commitments, the number of surrogate mother contracts she arranges does not exceed more than two per year; thus the data would not have appreciably altered my findings.

10. I find Strathern's statement that a woman who "acts on behalf of another's motherhood is a surrogate mother" very useful here. As such, surrogates are understood as those who assist "real" mothers "overcome a particular impairment" (Strathern 1992b:9), a definition shared by participants in the surrogacy process.

11. See, for example, the Andrews article entitled "The Stork Market: The Law of the New Reproductive Technologies" (1984b). See also Delaney's use of the term

"soft" (1986:508) to explain procreation to children, and her explication of the persistence of the folk theory of reproduction.

12. See also Figure 1.1 for the use of the stork image in surrogate mother program advertising.

Chapter 1

1. In 1988 there were ten established surrogate mother programs in the United States; at present (1994), two of the programs are no longer in business and a third program is located in a state where legislation to ban commercial surrogacy took effect 1 July 1993.

2. When surrogacy was in its infancy, in the late 1970s and early 1980s, the ban on payment in adoption procedures influenced opinions about payment for surrogacy. Surrogates did not receive remuneration, and surrogacy at that time tended to involve "surrogates having babies for middle-class and blue-collar couples" (Andrews 1992:48). Once programs began to offer payment, however, the service became available for the most part only to those who could afford it, usually upper-income couples, and the majority of couples remain largely upper-middle-class people, whereas the majority of surrogates are working-class women.

3. Pseudonyms (for people and programs) are used in the text, notes, and appendixes to protect the confidentiality of the participants.

4. In Parker's study, the average is twenty-five (Parker 1983).

5. To my knowledge, none of the open programs (Wick, Allen, or Brookside) will arrange a closed contract, and couples desirous of closed contracts are turned away, although this practice appears to have been permitted in the past.

6. Program directors frequently give presentations at RESOLVE meetings.

7. In 1992, she did hire an assistant (an ex-surrogate who works full-time).

8. Since couples informed me that they chose a program like the Wick because it seemed more personal than programs like the Brookside, it is possible that some directors of the smaller programs emphasize this idea so as to attract couples and surrogates who desire a more personal or homelike atmosphere: in fact, the director of the Wick program maintains her office in her home.

9. As of 1994, the Wick program now pays $15,000.

10. This ad, "Give the Gift of Life," was created after newspapers refused to run ads with the phrase "Surrogate Mother Wanted" in them. As of 1994, these newspapers' policies are no longer effect, and they will now publish such ads.

11. ZIFT has, as of this writing in 1994, fallen into disuse since it has been ascertained that it does not significantly increase the chances for a successful implantation/pregnancy/birth.

12. Open programs tend to prefer surrogates who are within commuting distance of their programs so that they can attend support-group meetings and so that directors/psychologists can maintain closer contact with them than would be possible if the surrogates resided out of state. Closed programs are less concerned with recruiting local surrogates since there is minimal personal interaction. They are also able to recruit surrogates from all over the United States, which makes the waiting period for couples shorter.

13. The Allen director provided me a packet of newspaper articles that profiled her program; the next several quotes have been excerpted from those articles and are illustrative of the type of material programs collect and then share with their prospective couples and surrogates.

14. This is, of course, not expected of couples who reside abroad.

Chapter 2

1. Terms such as "single mother" illustrate the extent to which the stigma of illegitimacy has lost some of its impact; terms such as "working mother" are no longer viewed as contradictions (Rapp 1987), since such terms, like surrogate motherhood, also reconcile the domestic and public split.

2. In 1992, I observed an intake interview with a potential surrogate, her husband, and the staff psychologist at the Brookside program. When asked why she had decided to become a surrogate, the surrogate replied, "The Deirdre Hall article in *People* magazine pushed me over the edge." Deirdre Hall is a soap opera star who, when a tabloid threatened to tell her story, was forced to publicly acknowledge that she had engaged in a contract to have a surrogate bear a child for her.

3. Parker's study revealed that the test scores of surrogate mothers were "within one standard deviation of normal" (Parker 1983:117–118).

4. The current practice is to have surrogates and couples write their own biographical statements rather than have the program psychologist write them.

5. There have been, to my knowledge, at least one Asian surrogate and three Jewish surrogates. With the increase in the rate of gestational surrogacy, there has been a commensurate increase in the number of Hispanic American, Asian American, and African American surrogates; this trend may need to be addressed with respect to concerns about exploitation.

6. Surrogates did not rank their reasons in order of importance.

7. The issue of remuneration is a complicated one; however, it is important to note that surrogates in open programs receive from their couples what might be referred to as benefits or perks, specifically, they are taken out to lunch, dinner, carnivals, and so forth, and it is very common that after the birth the couple give their surrogate another gift, most often in the form of an expensive piece of jewelry or a vacation.

8. In Britain, surrogates, who do not receive compensation, that is, who participate in noncommercial arrangements, are also understood to be giving to their couples the "Gift of Life" (Cannell 1990:677).

9. This formulation of the surrogate child as a gift is, of course, not unique to surrogacy; see, for example, the use of "Gift of Life" as an advertisement for both blood and organ donation. Cross-culturally, the literature on gift giving is fairly extensive, see for example, Fruzzetti's *The Gift of a Virgin: Women, Marriage, and Ritual in a Bengali Society* (1987).

10. For further discussion on the issue of remuneration, see Wolfram 1989.

11. When women's incomes are considered supplemental to men's incomes, industry is provided with a convenient justification for paying women wages that are substantially lower than those of men (Margolis 1984:196). In the United States, family patterns (in which women continue to be the primary caretakers of chil-

dren) determine the type of work in which women are employed. This pattern can be seen in retail sales, known for its poor wages and able to accommodate aspects of a woman's life cycle such as motherhood by providing part-time work (see Benson 1984:119).

12. Follow-up field visits to the Brookside program (in 1992 and 1994) revealed that the rate of gestational surrogacy had increased from less than 5 percent in 1988–1990 to close to 50 percent in 1992, with a success rate of approximately 25 percent, a meteoric rise in the number of couples pursuing gestational surrogacy (as of 1994 the success rate has increased to 28 percent). The Wick director also stated that 50 percent of surrogacy arrangements are now gestational. Clearly, the success rate of IVF may be responsible, at least in part, for this rapid increase in gestational surrogacy, but the question as to why gestational surrogates are willing to incur greater physical risks will require further study.

13. With the many advances in cryopreservation that have occurred since my original research took place, there is less hesitancy on the part of infertility specialists to freeze embryos; but in order to increase the odds of successful implantation and pregnancy, physicians routinely implant more than two embryos.

14. As a recent California Supreme Court decision concerning gestational surrogacy has revealed, intentionality may prove to be the crux of the matter in legal issues.

15. Franks' conclusion that surrogates "appeared to be feminine women with slightly increased energy levels and social extroversion tendencies" (Franks 1981:1379) may explain why surrogates wish to prolong the surrogate experience.

Chapter 3

1. Images such as these are also said to be common in organizations such as Concerned United Birthparents (CUB), a group of individuals who are searching for the biological children that they placed with an agency for adoption. Many of them view adoptive couples as self-serving and privileged, motivated not by the desire to love and care for a child but by a desire for ownership and image (Modell 1986:654).

2. Tentatively, I would suggest that wives' feelings of inadequacy appear to be exacerbated by the fact that they are older than their husbands and by their belief that their inability to bear a child is not "fair" to their husbands.

3. During an interview between a prospective couple and the director of the Brookside program, the couple (who were U.S. citizens residing in a Latin American country) said that they had rejected adoption in their host country because they believed that adoption there often involved black market baby selling, which they found unacceptable.

4. Couples frequently report having read about surrogacy in one of Lori Andrews's two books on reproductive technologies, *New Conceptions: A Consumer's Guide to the Newest Infertility Treatments* (1984a), or *Between Strangers: Surrogate Mothers, Expectant Fathers and Brave New Babies* (1989).

5. Many surrogates told me that they were first motivated to contact surrogate mother programs and become a surrogate in order to rectify what they perceived to be the wrong committed by Mary Beth Whitehead when she refused to relinquish Melissa (Baby M) to the Sterns in the Baby M case.

6. Robertson referred to couples in closed programs as "non-interactive" as compared to the more "interactive" couples who choose open programs.

7. Since this director did not permit me to contact her couples, this conclusion was drawn through inference from the information provided to me by her surrogates.

8. In the past, some of the open programs apparently displayed more tolerance for couples who were ambivalent concerning contact with their surrogate, and couples were permitted to contact their surrogates through the programs, as David and his wife initially did, but all the open programs I studied claimed not to permit this flexibility. I was told that this practice was not permitted at the Brookside, Wick, and Allen programs, and I did not find any evidence to the contrary. David and his wife were discussing an earlier arrangement.

Chapter 4

1. See, for example, Chris Shore's conclusion that "our most basic assumptions about parenthood, procreation, conception, and the family are about to undergo a radical transformation" (Shore 1992:301).

2. See, for example, the ways in which nurturance is understood to be on the one hand a "source of moral authority for female action" and on the other hand a way of confining women to the "unappreciated tasks of caring for dependent people" (Ginsburg 1987:627).

3. As part of this definitional matrix, it seems likely that a restriction or ban on commercial surrogacy will produce differences in definition.

4. In terms of the time and biological processes invested, sperm donation and pregnancy cannot be equated; however, the issue of an individual's right to decide how and in what way she or he chooses to use her or his reproductive resources is an area of commonality between the two.

5. The fact that Mary Beth Whitehead sought custody of the child may have been an indication that she had preexisting marital difficulties.

6. I want to expressly thank William Handel for sharing with me his interpretation of this recent decision and for keeping me apprised of this and other legal decisions.

7. The "dominant procreation story" in the United States is one in which "pregnancy necessarily results in childbirth and motherhood, preferably within marriage" (Ginsburg 1987:623).

8. Clearly there are differences between the United States and Britain that inform the responses to surrogate motherhood, illustrated by the British ban on commercial surrogacy, but I believe that the shared importance of the blood tie unites American and British couples who are pursuing surrogate motherhood. I also found the motivation of British couples pursuing DI and American couples pursuing surrogate motherhood strikingly similar and worthy of comparison, as are the ways in which they attempt to reconcile the lack of a biogenetic tie for one of the partners.

9. In Britain, for example, the idea of children as "strengthening the infertile couple" would, as the Warnock report concluded, be undermined if a surrogate were to want custody of the child (Cannell 1990:674).

10. As revealed in both pro-choice and pro-life narratives, nurturance is "em-

braced" and viewed as "both natural to women and the basis of their cultural authority" (Ginsburg 1987:629).

11. In 1988–1990, when the bulk of this research was conducted, gestational surrogacy constituted less than 5 percent of the Brookside program's arrangements. As I indicated in Chapter 2, Note 9, the rate had increased to 50 percent by the time I revisited the program in 1992 and again in 1994 and was also reported to be 50 percent at the Wick program. Although I had predicted an increase in the rates of gestational surrogacy in 1989 (see Ragoné 1991), I did not anticipate an increase of this magnitude in such a short period of time. This change is deserving of further study.

12. Although surrogates (both traditional and IVF) deny or minimize their biological connection to the child, all the traditional surrogates interviewed (who had their own children) had told or planned to tell their children that the surrogate child was their half-sibling.

References

Abu-Lughod, Lila. 1986. *Veiled Sentiments: Honor and Poetry in a Bedouin Society.* Berkeley: University of California Press.

Alexander, P. 1988. "Memorandum on Surrogate/Contract Birth Mothering," 27 April.

Andrews, Lori. 1984a. *New Conceptions: A Consumer's Guide to the Newest Infertility Treatments.* New York: Ballantine.

_____. 1984b. "The Stork Market: The Law of the New Reproductive Technologies." *American Bar Association Journal* 70:50–56.

_____. 1989. *Between Strangers: Surrogate Mothers, Expectant Fathers and Brave New Babies.* New York: Harper and Row.

_____. 1992. "Surrogacy Wars." *California Lawyer* 12(10):43–50, 106.

Barker-Benfield, G. J. 1977. "Sexual Surgery in Late Nineteenth Century America." In *Seizing Our Bodies,* ed. C. Dreifus. New York: Vintage Books.

Barnes, J. 1973. "Genetrix: Genitor: Nature: Culture?" In *The Character of Kinship,* ed. J. Goody. Cambridge: Cambridge University Press.

Benson, S. 1984. "Women in Retail Sales Work: The Continuing Dilemma of Service." In *My Troubles Are Going to Have Trouble with Me,* ed. K. Sacks and D. Remy. New Brunswick, N.J.: Rutgers University Press.

Birke, Lynda, and Wendy Faulkner. 1980. "Introduction." In *Brighton Women and Science Group,* ed. Brighton Women and Science Group. London: Virago Press.

Birns, Beverly, and Niza ben-Ner. 1987. "Psychoanalysis Constructs Motherhood." In *The Different Faces of Motherhood,* ed. B. Birns and D. Hay. New York: Plenum Press.

Blank, Robert. 1990. *Regulating Reproduction.* New York: Columbia University Press.

Bonnicksen, Andrea. 1989. *In Vitro Fertilization: Building Policy from Laboratory to Legislation.* New York: Columbia University Press.

Bott, Elizabeth. 1957. *Family and Social Network.* London: Tavistock.

_____. 1975. "Urban Families: Conjugal Roles and Social Networks." In *City Ways: A Selective Reader in Urban Anthropology,* ed. J.Friedle and N. Chrisman. New York: Crowell Company.

Cannell, Fanella. 1990. "Concepts of Parenthood: The Warnock Report, The Gillick Debate and Modern Myths." *American Ethnologist* 17(4):667–686.

Caplan, Arthur. 1990. "The Ethics of In Vitro Fertilization." In *Ethical Issues in the New Reproductive Technologies,* ed. R. Hall. Belmont, Calif.: Wadsworth Publishing.

Chadwick, Ruth. 1987. "Having Children: Introduction." In *Ethics, Reproduction and Genetic Control,* ed. R. Chadwick. London: Croom Helm.

Chafe, William. 1977. *Women and Equality: Changing Patterns in American Culture*. New York: Oxford University Press.

Chesler, Phyllis. 1988. *Sacred Bond: The Legacy of Baby M*. New York: Random House.

Chodorow, Nancy. 1974. "Family Structure and Feminine Personality." In *Woman, Culture and Society*, ed. M. Rosaldo and L. Lamphere. Stanford, Calif.: Stanford University Press.

———. 1978. *The Reproduction of Mothering*. Berkeley: University of California Press.

Chodorow, Nancy, and Susan Contratto. 1982. "The Fantasy of the Perfect Mother." In *Rethinking the Family*, ed. B. Thorne and M. Yalom. New York: Longman.

Collier, Jane, Michelle Rosaldo, and Sylvia Yanagisako. 1982. "Is There a Family?" In *Rethinking the Family*, ed. B. Thorne and M. Yalom. New York: Longman.

Collier, Jane, and Sylvia Yanagisako. 1987a. "Introduction." In *Gender and Kinship: Essays Toward a Unified Analysis*, ed. J. Collier and S. Yanagisako. Stanford, Calif.: Stanford University Press.

———. 1987b. "Toward a Unified Analysis of Gender and Kinship." In *Gender and Kinship: Essays Toward a Unified Analysis*, ed. J. Collier and S. Yanagisako. Stanford, Calif.: Stanford University Press.

Comaroff, Jean. 1987. "Sui Genderis: Feminism, Kinship Theory and Structural Domains." In *Gender and Kinship: Essays Toward a Unified Analysis*, ed. J. Collier and S. Yanagisako. Stanford, Calif.: Stanford University Press.

Comaroff, John, and Jean Comaroff. 1992. *Ethnography and the Historical Imagination*. Boulder: Westview Press.

Corea, Gena. 1984. "Egg Snatchers." In *Test-Tube Women*, ed. R Arditti, R. Klein, and S. Minden. London: Pandora Press.

———. 1985. *The Mother Machine*. New York: Harper and Row.

———. 1987. "The Reproductive Brothel." In *Man-Made Women*, ed. G. Corea et al. Indianapolis: Indiana University Press.

Cott, Nancy. 1977. *The Bonds of Womanhood*. New Haven: Yale University Press.

Davis, Angela. 1986. "Racism, Birth Control and Reproductive Rights." In *All American Women*, ed. J. Cole. New York: Free Press.

Davis-Floyd, Robbie. 1988. "Birth as an American Rite of Passage." In *Childbirth in America*, ed. K. Michaelson. Westport, Conn.: Bergin and Garvey Publishers.

Delaney, Carol. 1986. "The Meaning of Paternity and the Virgin Birth Debate." *Man* 24(3):497–513.

———. 1991. *The Seed and the Soil*. Berkeley: University of California Press.

Deutsch, Francine. 1983. *Child Services: On Behalf of Children*. Monterey, Calif.: Brooks-Cole.

Di Leonardi, M. 1987. "The Female World of Cards and Holidays: Women, Families and the Work of Kinship." *Signs* 12(3):440–453.

Dolgin, Janet. 1990. "Status and Contract in Feminist Legal Theory of the Family: A Reply to Bartlett." *Women's Rights Law Reporter* 12(2):103–113.

———. 1993. "Just a Gene: Judicial Assumptions About Parenthood." *UCLA Law Review* 40(3):637–694.

Dorris, Michael. 1989. *The Broken Cord: A Family's Ongoing Struggle with Fetal Alcohol Syndrome*. New York: Harper and Row.

Dreifus, Claudia. 1977. "Introduction." In *Seizing Our Bodies*, ed. C. Dreifus. New York: Vintage Books.

Dworkin, Andrea. 1978. *Right-Wing Women*. New York: Perigee Books.

Easton, Barbara. 1979. "Feminism and the Contemporary Family." In *A Heritage of Her Own*, ed. H. Pleck and N. Cott. New York: Simon and Schuster.

Ehrenreich, Barbara, and Deidre English. 1973. *Complaints and Disorders: The Sexual Politics of Sickness*. New York: Feminist Press.

_____. 1977. "Complaints and Disorders: The Sexual Politics of Sickness." In *Seizing Our Bodies*, ed. C. Dreifus. New York: Vintage Books.

_____. 1979. *Witches, Midwives and Nurses: A History of Women Healers*. New York: Feminist Press.

Elshtain, Jean. 1981. *Public Men, Private Woman: Woman in Social and Political Thought*. Princeton: Princeton University Press.

Farber, Bernard. 1971. *Kinship and Class: A Midwestern Study*. New York: Basic Books.

Ferree, M. 1984. "Sacrifice, Satisfaction and Social Change: Employment and the Family." In *My Troubles Are Going to Have Trouble with Me*, ed. D. Remy and K. Sacks. New Brunswick, N.J.: Rutgers University Press.

Franklin, Sarah. forthcoming. *Contested Conceptions: A Cultural Account of Assisted Reproduction*. London: Routledge.

Franks, Darrell. 1981. "Psychiatric Evaluation of Women in a Surrogate Mother Program." *American Journal of Psychiatry* 138(10):1378–1379.

Freeman, Ellen, et al. 1985. "Psychological Evaluation and Support in a Program of In Vitro Fertilization and Embryo Transfer." *Fertility and Sterility* 43(1):48–53.

Fruzzetti, Lina. 1987. *The Gift of a Virgin: Women, Marriage, and Ritual in a Bengali Society*. New Brunswick, N.J.: Rutgers University Press.

Ginsburg, Faye. 1987. "Procreation Stories: Reproduction, Nurturance and Procreation in Life Narratives of Abortion Activists." *American Ethnologist* 14(4):623–636.

_____. 1988. *Contested Lives: The Abortion Debate in an American Community*. Berkeley: University of California Press.

Glover, Jonathan. 1990. *Ethics of New Reproductive Technologies: The Glover Report to the European Commission*. DeKalb: Northern Illinois University Press.

Goffman, Erving. 1963. *Stigma: Notes on the Management of Spoiled Identity*. Englewood Cliffs, N.J.: Prentice-Hall.

Gullestad, Marianne. 1992. *The Art of Social Relations*. Oslo: Scandinavian Press.

Hanafin, Hilary. 1984. "Surrogate Mothers: An Exploratory Study." Doctoral dissertation. California School of Professional Psychology, Los Angeles.

Hare, R. M. 1987. "In Vitro Fertilisation and the Warnock Report." In *Ethics, Reproduction and Genetic Control*, ed. R. Chadwick. London: Virago Press.

Harris, B. 1979. "Careers, Conflict and Children: The Legacy of the Cult of Domesticity." In *Career and Motherhood*, ed. A. Richard and B. Harris. New York: Human Sciences Press.

Hay, Dale, and Jo Ellen Vespo. 1988. "Social Learning Perspective on the Development of Mother-Child Relationships." In *The Different Faces of Motherhood*, ed. B. Birns and D. Hay. New York: Plenum Press.

Heyl, B. 1988. "Commercial Contracts and Human Connectedness." *Society* 25(3):11–16.

Hubbard, Ruth. 1990. *The Politics of Women's Biology.* New Brunswick, N.J.: Rutgers University Press.

Hull, Richard. 1990a. "Artificial Insemination." In *Ethical Issues in the New Reproductive Technologies,* ed. R. Hull. Belmont, Calif.: Wadsworth Publishers.

———. 1990b. Gestational Surrogacy and Surrogate Motherhood." In *Ethical Issues in the New Reproductive Technologies,* ed. R. Hull. Belmont, Calif.: Wadsworth Publishers.

Humphrey, Michael, and Heather Humphrey. 1988. *Families with a Difference: Varieties of Surrogate Parenthood.* London: Routledge & Kegan Paul.

Kadushin, A. 1980. *Child Welfare Services.* New York: Macmillan.

Katz-Rothman, Barbara. 1982. *In Labor: Women and Power in the Birthplace.* New York: Norton and Company.

———. 1984. "The Meaning of Choice in Reproductive Technology." In *Test-Tube Women,* ed. R. Arditti et al. London: Pandora Press.

———. 1988. "Cheap Labor, Sex, Class, Race and Surrogacy." *Society* 25(3):21–22.

Kessler-Harris, Alice. 1979. "Where Are the Organized Women Workers?" In *A Heritage of Her Own,* ed. N. Cott and H. Pleck. New York: Simon and Schuster.

———. 1982. *Out to Work.* New York: Oxford University Press.

Kuchner, Jean, and Jane Porcino. 1988. "Delayed Motherhood." In *The Different Faces of Motherhood,* ed. B. Birns and D. Hay. New York: Plenum Press.

Lamphere, Louise. 1987. "Feminism and Anthropology: The Struggle to Reshape Our Thinking About Gender." In *The Impact of Feminist Research on the Academy,* ed. C. Farnham. Bloomington: Indiana University Press.

Lasker, Judith, and Borg, Susan. 1987. *In Search of Parenthood: Coping with Infertility and High-Tech Conception.* Boston: Beacon Press.

Levi-Strauss, Claude. 1969. *The Elementary Structures of Kinship.* London: Eyre and Spottiswoode.

Luker, Kristin. 1984. *Abortion and the Politics of Motherhood.* Berkeley: University of California Press.

MacCormack, Carol. 1980. "Nature, Culture and Gender, A Critique." In *Nature, Culture and Gender,* ed. C. MacCormack and M. Strathern. Cambridge: Cambridge University Press.

McCartney, Kathleen, and Deborah Phillips. 1988. "Motherhood and Childcare." In *The Different Faces of Motherhood,* ed. B. Birns and D. Hay. New York: Plenum Press.

Malinowski, Bronislaw. 1932. *The Sexual Life of Savages in Northwestern Melanesia.* London: Routledge & Kegan Paul.

Margolis, Maxine. 1984. *Mothers and Such.* Berkeley: University of California Press.

Martin, Emily. 1987. *The Woman in the Body: A Cultural Analysis of Reproduction.* Boston: Beacon Press.

Miall, Charlene. 1985. "Perceptions of Informal Sanctioning and the Stigma of Involuntary Childlessness." *Deviant Behavior* 6:383–403.

Michaelson, Karen. 1988. "Childbirth in America: A Brief History and Contemporary Issues." In *Childbirth in America,* ed. K. Michaelson. Westport, Conn.: Bergin and Garvey Publishers.

Modell, Judith. 1986. "In Search: The Purported Biological Basis of Parenthood." *American Ethnologist* 13(4):646–661.

———. 1989. "Last Chance Babies: Interpretations of Parenthood in an In Vitro Fertilization Program." *Medical Anthropology Quarterly* 3:124–138.

Neuhaus, Robert. 1988. "Renting Women, Buying Babies and Class Struggles." *Society* 25(3):8–10.

New York State Task Force. 1988. *Surrogate Parenting: Analysis and Recommendations for Public Policy.* New York: N.Y. State Task Force on Life and Law.

Ortner, Sherry. 1974. "Is Female to Male as Nature Is to Culture?" In *Women, Culture and Society*, ed. M. Rosaldo and L. Lamphere. Stanford, Calif.: Stanford University Press.

OTA (Office of Technology Assessment). 1988. *Infertility: Medical and Social Choices.* Washington, D.C.: Government Printing Office.

Overall, Christine. 1987. *Ethics and Human Reproduction: A Feminist Analysis.* Boston: Allen and Unwin.

Parker, Philip. 1982. "Surrogate Motherhood: The Interaction of Litigation, Legislation and Psychiatry." *International Journal of Law* 5:35–37.

———. 1983. "Motivation of Surrogate Mothers: Initial Findings." *American Journal of Psychiatry* 140:117–119.

Petchesky, Rosalind. 1984. "Reproductive Freedom: Beyond a Woman's Right to Choose." In *Women, Sex and Sexuality*, ed. C. Stimpson and E. Person. Chicago: University of Chicago Press.

Pfeffer, Naomi, and Anne Woollett. 1983. *The Experience of Infertility.* London: Virago Press.

Pleck, H., and N. Cott. 1979. *A Heritage of Her Own.* New York: Simon and Schuster.

Quinn, Naomi. 1977. "Anthropological Studies on Women's Status." *Annual Review of Anthropology* 6:181–225.

Radcliffe-Brown, Alfred. 1950. "Introduction." In *African Systems of Kinship and Marriage*, ed. A. Radcliffe-Brown and D. Forde. Oxford: Oxford University Press.

Ragoné, Helena. 1991. "Surrogate Motherhood in America." Ph.D. dissertation. Brown University, Providence, R.I.

Rapp, Rayna. 1978. "Family and Class in Contemporary America: Notes Toward an Understanding of Ideology." *Science and Society* 42(3):278–300.

———. 1982. "Family and Class in Contemporary America." In *Rethinking the Family*, ed. B.Thorn and M. Yalom. New York: Longman.

———. 1987. "Toward a Nuclear Freeze? The Gender Politics of Euro-American Kinship Analysis." In *Gender and Kinship: Essays Toward a Unified Analysis*, ed. J. Collier and S. Yanagisako. Stanford, Calif.: Stanford University Press.

———. 1990. "Constructing Amniocentesis: Maternal and Medical Discourses." In *Uncertain Terms: Negotiating Gender in American Culture.* ed. Faye Ginsburg and Anna Lowenhaupt Tsing. Boston: Beacon Press.

Reame, Nancy, and Philip Parker. 1990. "Surrogate Pregnancy: Clinical Features of Forty-Four Cases." *American Journal of Obstetrical Gynecology* 162:1220–1225.

Reiter, Rayna. 1975. "Men and Women in the South of France: Public and Private Domains." In *Toward an Anthropology of Women*, ed. R. Reiter. New York: Monthly Review Press.

Resnick, Rita. 1989. "Surrogate Mother Relationships: Early Attachment and Child Relinquishment." Doctoral dissertation. Fielding Institute, Santa Barbara, Calif.

Robertson, John. 1990. "Surrogate Mothers, Not So Novel After All." In *Ethical Issues in the New Reproductive Technologies*, ed. R. Hull. Belmont, Calif.: Wadsworth Publishers.

Rosaldo, Michelle. 1974. "Woman, Culture and Society: A Theoretical Overview." In *Woman, Culture and Society*, ed. M. Rosaldo and L. Lamphere. Stanford, Calif.: Stanford University Press.

Rubin, Gayle. 1975. "The Traffic in Woman: Notes on the Political Economy of Sex." In *Toward an Anthropology of Women*, ed. R. Reiter. New York: Monthly Review Press.

Rubin, Lillian. 1976. *Worlds of Pain: Life in the Working Class Family*. New York: Basic Books.

Rule, Ann. 1988. *Small Sacrifices*. New York: Dutton.

Sacks, Karen. 1974. "Engels Revisited: Women, the Organization of Production and Private Property." In *Woman, Culture and Society*, ed. M. Rosaldo and L. Lamphere. Stanford, Calif.: Stanford University Press.

_____. 1984. "Generations of Working-Class Families." In *My Troubles Are Going to Have Trouble with Me*, ed. D. Remy and K. Sacks. New Brunswick, N.J.: Rutgers University Press.

Sandelowski, Margarete. 1991. "Compelled to Try: The Never-Enough Quality of Conceptive Technology." *Medical Anthropology Quarterly* 5(1):29–47.

Sandelowski, Margarete, and Linda Jones. 1986. "Social Exchanges of Infertile Women." *Issues in Mental Health Nursing* 8:173–189.

San Diego Tribune. 1986. "Surrogate Mothers: Not All Regret or Renege on the Delicate Pact." December 26.

San Diego Union. 1982. "Pregnancy by Proxy." Section D, "Currents." August 1.

Schneider, David. 1968. *American Kinship: A Cultural Account*. Englewood Cliffs, N.J.: Prentice-Hall.

_____. 1972. "What Is Kinship All About?" In *Kinship Studies in the Morgan Centennial Year*, ed. P. Reining. Washington, D.C.: Anthropological Society.

_____. 1976. "Notes Toward a Theory of Culture." In *Meaning in Anthropology*, ed. K. Basso and H. Selby. Albuquerque: University of New Mexico Press.

_____. 1979. "Kinship, Community and Locality in American Culture." In *Kin and Communities in Families in America*, ed. Smithsonian Institute. Washington, D.C.: Smithsonian Institute Press.

_____. 1984. *A Critique of the Study of Kinship*. Ann Arbor: University of Michigan Press.

Schneider, David, and George Homans. 1971. "Kinship Terminology and the American Kinship System." In *Readings in Kinship and Social Structure*, ed. N. Graburn. San Francisco: Harper and Row.

Schneider, David, and Raymond Smith. 1973. *Class Differences and Sex Roles in American Kinship and Family Structure*. Englewood Cliffs, N.J.: Prentice-Hall.

Shalev, Carmel. 1989. *Birth Power: The Case for Surrogacy*. New Haven: Yale University Press.

Shore, Chris. 1992. "Virgin Births and Sterile Debates: Anthropology and the New Reproductive Technologies." *Current Anthropology* 33(3):295–314.

Simmel, Georg. 1978. *The Philosophy of Money.* London: Routledge and Kegan Paul.

Singer, Peter, and Deanne Wells. 1985. *Making Babies: The New Science of Ethics and Conception.* New York: Macmillan.

Smart, Carol. 1990. "There Is of Course the Distinction Dictated by Nature: Law and the Problem of Paternity." In *Ethical Issues in the New Reproductive Technologies*, ed. R. Hull. Belmont, Calif.: Wadsworth Publishers.

Snowden, R., G. Mitchell, and E. Snowden. 1983. *Artificial Reproduction: A Social Investigation.* London: Allen and Unwin.

Society for Assisted Reproductive Technology and the American Fertility Society. 1993. "Assisted Reproductive Technology in the United States and Canada: 1991 Results from the Society for Assisted Reproductive Technology Generated from the American Fertility Society Registry." *Fertility and Sterility* 59 (5):956–962.

Stangel, John. 1979. *The New Fertility and Conception.* New York: Plume Books.

Steadman, Jennifer, and Gillian McClosky. 1987. "The Prospect of Surrogate Mothering and Clinical Concerns." *Canadian Journal of Psychiatry* 32:545–550.

Sternglanz, Sarah, and Alison Nash. 1988. "Ethnological Contributions to the Study of Human Motherhood." In *The Different Faces of Motherhood*, ed. B. Birns and D. Hay. New York: Plenum Press.

Strathern, Marilyn. 1980. "No Nature, No Culture: The Hagen Case." In *Nature, Culture and Gender*, ed. C. MacCormack and M. Strathern. Cambridge: Cambridge University Press.

———. 1984. "Domesticity and the Denigration of Women." In *Rethinking Woman's Roles: Perspectives from the Pacific*, ed. D. O'Brien and S. Tiffany. Berkeley: University of California Press.

———. 1991. "The Pursuit of Certainty: Investigating Kinship in the Late Twentieth Century." Paper presented at the American Anthropology Association Meeting, Chicago, Illinois.

———. 1992a. *Reproducing the Future.* New York: Routledge.

———. 1992b. "Surrogates and Substitutes: New Practices for Old?" In *The Politics of Modernity*, ed. J. Good and I. Velody. Durham, UK: Centre for the History of Human Sciences [manuscript in press].

Strathern, Marilyn, and Sarah Franklin. 1993. "Kinship and the New Genetic Technologies: An Assessment of Existing Anthropological Research." A Report compiled for the Commission of the European Communities Medical Research Division (DG-XII) Human Genome Analysis Programme.

Tiffany, Sharon. 1982. *Women, Work and Motherhood.* Englewood Cliffs, N.J.: Prentice-Hall.

Tizard, Barbara. 1977. *Adoption: A Second Chance.* New York: Free Press.

Warnock, Mary. 1984. *The Warnock Report: Report of the Committee of Inquiry into Human Fertilisation and Embryology.* London: Her Majesty's Stationary Office.

Winslade, William. 1981. "Surrogate Mothers: Private Right or Public Wrong." *Journal of Medical Ethics* 7:153–154.

Wolf, Margery. 1972. *Women and the Family in Rural Taiwan.* Stanford, Calif.: Stanford University Press.

Wolfram, Sybil. 1989. "Surrogacy in the United Kingdom." In *New Approaches to Human Reproduction,* ed. L. Whiteford and M. Poland. Boulder: Westview Press.

Yanagisako, Sylvia. 1979. "Family and Household: The Analysis of Domestic Groups." *Annual Review of Anthropology* 8:161–205.

———. 1987. "Mixed Metaphors: Native and Anthropological Models of Gender and Kinship Domains." In *Gender and Kinship: Essays Toward a Unified Analysis,* ed. J. Collier and S. Yanagisako. Stanford, Calif.: Stanford University Press.

Zelizer, Vivian. 1985. *Pricing the Priceless Child.* New York: Basic Books.

———. 1988. "From Baby Farms to Baby M." *Society* 25(3):23–28.

About the Book and Author

Surrogate Motherhood: Conception in the Heart is a compelling account written with analytical clarity and remarkable compassion. Helena Ragoné has given long overdue humanity and voice to the actual participants in the surrogate motherhood experience—a heretofore inaccessible population—and the results are fascinating. Anyone interested in fertility, parenting, reproduction, and kinship, or anyone interested in contemporary culture will want to read this book.

Helena Ragoné teaches anthropology at the University of Massachusetts–Boston. She is now researching her second book, *Distant Kin*, on gestational surrogacy.

Index

Printed in the United States
73916LV00004B/77